The Indigenous Paradox

PENNSYLVANIA STUDIES IN HUMAN RIGHTS

Bert B. Lockwood, Series Editor

A complete list of books in the series
is available from the publisher.

The Indigenous Paradox

Rights, Sovereignty, and Culture in the Americas

Jonas Bens

PENN

UNIVERSITY OF PENNSYLVANIA PRESS

PHILADELPHIA

Published by
University of Pennsylvania Press
Philadelphia, Pennsylvania 19104-4112
www.upenn.edu/pennpress

Printed in the United States of America on acid-free paper
1 3 5 7 9 10 8 6 4 2

A Cataloging-in-Publication record is available from the Library of Congress
ISBN 978-0-8122-5230-9

CONTENTS

ABBREVIATIONS

CERD	United Nations Committee on the Elimination of Racial Discrimination
IACHR	Inter-American Commission on Human Rights
IACtHR	Inter-American Court of Human Rights
ICCPR	International Covenant on Civil and Political Rights
ICERD	International Convention on the Elimination of All Forms of Racial Discrimination
ICESCR	International Covenant on Economic, Social, and Cultural Rights
ILO	International Labour Organization
ILO 107	International Labour Organization Convention No. 107
ILO 169	International Labour Organization Convention No. 169
INRA	Instituto National de Reforma Agraria (Nicaraguan Agrarian Reform Institute)
MADENSA	Maderas y Derivados de Nicaragua, S.A. (a Nicaraguan logging company)
MARENA	Ministerio del Ambiente y los Recursos Naturales (Nicaraguan Ministry of the Environment and Natural Resources)
NGO	nongovernmental organization
OAS	Organization of American States
RAAN	Región Autónoma del Atlántico Norte (former designation of an autonomous region on Nicaragua's Atlantic coast)
RACCN	Región Autónoma de la Costa Caribe Norte (an autonomous region in Nicaragua)
SOLCARSA	Sol del Caribe, S.A. (a Korea-based logging company)
UN	United Nations
UNO	United Nations Organization
UNDRIP	United Nations Declaration on the Rights of Indigenous Peoples

A NOTE ON TERMINOLOGY

In this book, I am aiming at outlining the term "indigenous" as a specific analytical term rather than as a default descriptor of the native inhabitants of a place, in this case the Americas. When I want to refer to those people who lived in the Americas in precolonial times, I use the adjective "native"; when referring to the European colonialists, I use the term "settlers." These perhaps overly broad terms are used to describe the colonial constellation—or, more accurately, one part of it, as the countless Africans who were forced to come to the Americas in colonial times can also be accurately described by either (or both) of the two terms. Apart from this, I try to use the terms people give themselves. The adjectives "Indian" in the U.S. context and "aboriginal" in the Canadian context are mentioned in relation to the court cases I am citing in this book.

The word I use most frequently in this book to denote collective actors is "community." I write, for instance, of native communities and indigenous communities. Writing about communities is not unproblematic. In the academic discourse, especially in the social sciences, the term has its own tradition and is often loaded with assumptions of primordial authenticity. The reader should be aware, however, that not only is indigeneity a product of sociocultural and relational processes, as I argue in this book, but that "community" itself is as well. In describing the state of the art in anthropological research, David W. Dinwoodie notes that "ethnic community in this sense is not necessarily a permanent condition, nor is it one in which all members of a population participate to the same extent. It is act- and event-based and varies in terms of how encompassing and enduring it is. In some circumstances it might become collective and enduring to the point [. . . of] being essentially permanent. In other circumstances it might dissipate almost immediately" (2010, 652). It is in this sense that I use the term "community."

I am aware that indigenous collectivities, especially in North America, place a great deal of emphasis on describing themselves as "nations," while others, especially in South America, do not. I have endeavored not to use this term indiscriminately, but rather to turn the way it is invoked into an important point of analysis in this book.

I use the descriptor "(post)colonial" to indicate that the contact and entanglement between native communities in the Americas and the legal systems of other sovereigns started with a colonial legal system and were continued and extended by a postcolonial legal system. From the perspective of the native communities, the end of formal colonial rule certainly did not mean the end of colonial power relations. But although there were some continuities in the native communities' legal relationships to the colonial states, and, later, the postcolonial states, there were also significant changes in both style and content.

CHAPTER 1

Indigeneity and the Law

At the turn of the year from 1830 to 1831, the legal representatives of the Cherokee Nation sent a bill to the U.S. Supreme Court. In doing so, the Cherokees opened a lawsuit against the state of Georgia before the highest judicial body in the United States. The document starts like this:

> To the Honourable the Chief Justice and the Associate Justices of the Supreme Court of the United States, sitting in chancery.
>
> Respectfully complaining, show unto your honours, the Cherokee nation of Indians, a foreign state, not owing allegiance to the United States, nor to any state of this union, nor to any other prince, potentate, or state, other than their own:
>
> That, from time immemorial, the Cherokee nation have composed a sovereign and independent state. . . .
>
> That, long before the first approach of the white men of Europe to the western continent, the Cherokee nation were the occupants and owners of the territory on which they now reside. . . .
>
> That on this territory they and their ancestors, composing the Cherokee nation, have ever been, and still are, the sole and exclusive masters, and governed, of right, by no other laws, usages and customs, but such as they have themselves thought proper to ordain and appoint. . . .
>
> Under these circumstances your honours cannot but see that, unless you shall interpose for their protection, these complainants have before them no alternatives but these: either to surrender their lands in exchange for others in the western wilds of this continent,

> which would be to seal, at once, the doom of their civilization, Christianity, and national existence; or to surrender their national sovereignty, their property, rights and liberties, guarantied as these now are by so many treaties, to the rapacity and injustice of the state of Georgia; or to arm themselves in defence of these sacred rights, and fall, sword in hand, on the graves of their fathers. (Peters 1831, 3, 28)

The resulting case, *Cherokee Nation v. Georgia*, would become one of the earliest indigenous rights cases in the Americas in which the claimant, an indigenous community, asserted its rights against the defendant, the (post) colonial state. At the beginning of the twenty-first century, this constellation has become a political and legal commonplace, and going to court has become an ordinary form of interaction between a state and its inhabitants. To better understand this constellation in all its complexity, however, we have to overcome our inurement and begin to appreciate how inherently odd this situation actually is. I have chosen the preceding excerpt to begin this book because it highlights what is odd about the Cherokees' petitioning the Supreme Court. Their whole claim presents a contradiction, and the claimants are very straightforward about it. On the one hand, the Cherokees present themselves in the strongest terms as a sovereign nation, an independent state even, governed by their own laws only. At the same time, they bring a case before the court of another state, the United States, and subject themselves to its foreign rule of law.

This oddity, this seemingly minor irritation, is the starting point for this book. It is my contention that indigeneity is a paradoxical formation. The paradoxical nature of indigeneity becomes apparent in the relationship between an indigenous community and the (post)colonial state, or, rather, in the relationship between an indigenous claimant and the national law. On the one hand, the indigenous community rejects the state and views the regulation of its affairs by the law of the state as a violation of its integrity. On the other hand, the indigenous community depends on the state, its courts, and its law to protect certain rights that are seen as emanating from the indigenous community itself and not from the national legal system. "We are different; we are equal," goes a Latin American indigenous rights slogan from the 1990s (Brysk 2000, 29). I call this formation, in which the indigenous must appear as both part of the state and as dissociated from it—politically as well as legally—the "indigenous paradox."

It is my argument that the phenomenon of indigeneity comes into being when native communities engage with the law of the (post)colonial state in which they find themselves. In other words, native communities *become* indigenous when they begin to occupy the paradoxical legal position I aim to describe in this book. Therefore, to understand the discourses of indigeneity, it is paramount to follow the language, the textual genres, and the doctrine of the law. In this book, I will therefore employ approaches from legal studies and anthropology to investigate the very texts that speak most explicitly to and about indigeneity: landmark indigenous rights cases in the Americas.

On Indigeneity

What does "indigenous" mean, anyway? Prior to the second half of the twentieth century, the term was mainly used in biology to refer to plants or animals native to a particular place. Since then, various rights movements have introduced the term into international legal forums such as the United Nations (UN), the International Labour Organization (ILO), and the inter-American system for the protection of human rights. In the course of this introduction into international law circles, "indigenous" has come to be used as an umbrella term that encompasses such categories as "Indian," "native," and "aboriginal"; it is now the most frequently used term inside and outside international law to signify communities whose ancestors inhabited colonized territories in precolonial times. Recent anthropological scholarship has contributed much to understanding the phenomenon of "indigeneity" as a legal category, an analytical term to signify a certain type of collective identity, and a designation used by activists to refer to themselves and their collective attachment to their communities, as well as how these various meanings of the term interact and feed back into one another (Culhane 1998; Biolsi 2001; Nesper 2002; Povinelli 2002; Niezen 2003; Kauanui 2008; French 2009; Clifford 2013; A. Simpson 2014).

One of the most cited definitions of indigeneity is the one José Martínez Cobo, then the UN special rapporteur of the Subcommission on Prevention of Discrimination and Protection of Minorities, used in his report *Study of the Problem of Discrimination Against Indigenous Populations* (the so-called Martínez Cobo Report):

> Indigenous communities, peoples and nations are those which, having a historical continuity with pre-invasion and pre-colonial societies that developed on their territories, consider themselves distinct from other sectors of the societies now prevailing in those territories, or parts of them. They form at present non-dominant sectors of society and are determined to preserve, develop and transmit to future generations their ancestral territories, and their ethnic identity, as the basis of their continued existence as peoples, in accordance with their own cultural patterns, social institutions and legal systems. (Martínez Cobo 1987 para. 379)

Although there are many other definitions of "indigeneity" and what constitutes it, Martínez Cobo mentions three aspects that are central to any description of the concept: place, time, and power. "Indigeneity" contains the idea that somebody was somewhere before somebody else came there and that now there is some form of inequality, usually manifest in the fact that those who were there first now occupy a marginalized position. These dimensions of time, place, and power can lead to different forms of indigeneity, as will be explored in the course of this book.

In the academic discourse there are a number of established ways to approach indigeneity, and in this book I will sometimes deviate from the analytical foci they advocate. One position sees indigeneity as the simple result of the fact that communities, peoples, and nations inhabited the colonized territories before the advent of colonialism. Another describes indigeneity as an identity formation that is, at least predominantly, an imposition of the colonial settler state. A third group argues that indigeneity is a result of the concepts of nation and nationalism being imported from Europe to the colonies.

The first approach is the most straightforward theory on indigeneity and underlies most commonsense understandings of the term. In this view, indigenous communities are simply the decedents of those communities that inhabited colonial territories in precolonial times. In the course of the colonial project, these communities somehow managed to preserve their coherence as a group. Colonialism introduced a sharp division between the natives and the newcomers that came to be expressed mainly in racial terms. As a result, Cherokee, Miskito, Gitksan, and Wet'suwet'en, to name but a few, refer to themselves not only by these signifiers but also as "indigenous"—and are referred to by others as such. This concept focuses on descent from precolonial groups as the basis of indigeneity. However, beyond highlighting kinship and relatedness to precolonial societies, the prior-occupation approach does not contribute much to understanding indigeneity as such. Indigeneity rather appears as just one kinship-based identity conception among others, such as nation, people, and tribe; an umbrella term for all of the native communities in the Americas.

Many scholars therefore emphasize that the phenomenon of indigeneity is largely dependent on colonial power relations, which are established by the settler society. One of the clearest statements of this approach is put forth by scholars who situate themselves in the field of settler colonial studies (Veracini 2010; Bateman and Pilkington 2011; Mikdashi 2013). Patrick Wolfe, for example, has remarked that settler colonialism is a structure rather than an event (1999, 2) and that the native–settler relationship is to a large extent determined by a colonial project of the "elimination of the native" (2006, 387). This oppressive relationship is still ongoing and largely defines the way in which indigeneity can be understood and unfolds in practice. In this view, indigeneity is a structural position that is defined by the settler colonial project and its structural determinants. This clear connection between indigeneity and the specific conditions of ongoing colonialism forms the intellectual basis of many more recent interventions of indigenous activists. Indigenous scholars, particularly those in North America, frame indigenous movements specifically as resistance against ongoing settler colonial imposition (see, e.g., T. Alfred 1999; L. B. Simpson 2017; Corntassel 2018).

A third approach shares this clear focus on the colonial endeavor to analyze indigeneity. This strand of thinking does not derive from this premise a clear activist impetus for indigenous resistance, but rather tends to be more critical of indigenous movements. In this view, indigeneity appears as a collective identity formation that largely conforms to the Euro-American idea of an ethnic community as the basis for the nation-state (see Eriksen 2002), an approach that has been critically analyzed by authors such as Benedict Anderson (1983), Eric Hobsbawm (1990), and Eric Smith (1996). Imported along with colonialism, indigenous identities as they are mobilized today are merely a variant of European nationalism. Adam Kuper (2003) is among those who have advocated the idea that indigeneity is, in effect, simply the most recent manifestation of ethnonationalism.

Scholarship based on these approaches has made important contributions to understanding indigeneity. I claim, however, that all of them, because of their chosen focus, run the risk of underestimating the degree to which indigeneity is a *relational* phenomenon. If one sees indigeneity mainly as a matter of descent from precolonial inhabitants, one is in danger of underestimating how important it is to take account of the processes of contact between native communities and settler communities. If one sees indigeneity mainly as a result of ongoing settler colonial imposition, one is in danger of underestimating how the colonial encounter has not only been shaped by the settler colonial ambition and the structures it has set up, but also by native resistance and native agency (despite the highly unequal power relations between settlers and natives). If one sees indigeneity mainly as European ethnonationalism in disguise, one is in danger of underestimating the degree to which indigenous identities are not merely European ideological impositions, but are just as much formations into which cultural features of the indigenous communities themselves are interwoven.

In this book I strive to remain aware of these analytical pitfalls by constantly foregrounding and highlighting the relational nature of indigeneity. Indigeneity as a specific form of collective identity does not emerge in and of itself, but only in relation to a colonial or postcolonial entity, a newly emerged state with which a specific legal relationship must be established. Indigeneity emerges within and through the relationship between a native community and a postcolonial state.[1] How that comes to pass and how it is inscribed into law are the topics of this book.

For this reason, it is important to heed Ronald Niezen's advice, namely, that "a rigorous definition [of indigeneity], one that in effect tried to close the intellectual borders where they were still porous, would be premature and, ultimately, futile," and that the "debates over the problem of definition are actually more interesting than any definition in and of itself" (2003, 19). In other words—and this is what I also want to highlight—the question of defining an indigenous group is not an innocent one; it is not merely a preliminary identification of who the activist in a movement or the claimant in a court proceeding is. Indigenous activists and claimants not only shape the law through their engagement in international forums and courts, but indigeneity itself takes shape through this engagement in national and international law. As Niezen explains: "Indigenous identity is thus not a simple reflection of timeless values and practices; it is based in large measure on a compendium of cultural facts and artifacts intended for consumption in a dominant national society and an international audience. Indigenous lobbying is inseparable from cultural and spiritual trends within its audiences, trends that seek some form of perfection or ancestral source of wisdom from the native, aboriginal, or indigenous 'others'" (2003, 191). The meaning of "indigenous" is linked to the meaning that indigenous claimants want it to have and the meaning that courts decide to apply to it. If one is after a definition of the term "indigenous," one must therefore follow, not least of all, legal language. When indigenous communities "play Indian" (Deloria 1999) in national and international law, it is more than a mere public relations strategy separated from the "real" identity of indigenous groups. "Playing Indian" emerges in a complicated field of indigenous self-conceptions and the expectations of nonindigenous publics.

In this context and with reference to the Négritude movement of the 1950s,[2] James Clifford speaks of the emergence of an *indigènitude*. Like negritude, *indigènitude* emerges as "a vision of liberation and cultural difference that challenges, or at least redirects, the modernizing agendas of nation-states and transnational capitalism," but it is "less a coherent ideology than a concentration of sources and projects." It is performed in conference rooms at the United Nations and the International Labour Organization, as well as through the arts and at cultural festivals, and it is "sustained through media-disseminated images, including a shared symbolic repertoire ('the sacred,' 'Mother Earth,' 'shamanism,' 'sovereignty,' the wisdom of 'elders,' stewardship of 'the land')" (2013, 16). This symbolic repertoire, these media-disseminated images, Clifford tells us, "can lapse into self-stereotyping. And they express a transformative renewal of attachments to culture and place. It is difficult to know, sometimes even for participants, how much of the performance of identity reflects deep belief, how much a tactical presentation of self" (2013, 16).

Indigeneity is a paradoxical formation that has been recognized and granted a certain status within a legal system. At a certain point in the consolidation of the settler state, the legal relationship between natives and settlers becomes characterized by an inner contradiction. Native communities are legally separate from the state; they insist on this separation and use it, sometimes to claim their sovereignty, sometimes their cultural distinctiveness, but always to assert their independence. Nevertheless, the communities are to a certain degree incorporated into the settler state's legal order and depend on the settlers' legal system to secure their independent rights. The title of this book, *The Indigenous Paradox: Rights, Sovereignty, and Culture in the Americas*, refers to this phenomenon of being legally incorporated and excluded at the same time.

The Judicialization of Politics and the History of Juridified Native–Settler Relations in the Americas

It is often assumed that today's transnational indigenous rights movements and the fact that indigenous communities increasingly bring their rights struggles before the courts can be situated in a broader phenomenon that has been called the "judicialization of politics" (Tate and Vallinder 1995; Comaroff and Comaroff 2006). This concept is based on the proposition that certain conflicts and disputes somehow get shifted from the political sphere to the judicial sphere. They are "migrating to the courts," meaning that conflicts "once joined in parliaments or by means of street protests, media campaigns, strikes, boycotts and blockades tend more and more to find their way into the judiciary" (Comaroff and Comaroff 2007, 142).

As a general trend, this observation seems intuitively to be true. The number of landmark court decisions appears to be steadily increasing, and there is much talk about the growing political power of courts. There has undoubtedly been a significant change globally in the relationship between law and politics since the emergence of human rights law in the second half of the twentieth century. The passing of the United Nations Charter in 1945 and the Universal Declaration of Human Rights in 1948 mark the beginning of this intense growth in human rights regimes. At least since the 1970s international and regional regimes of human rights protection have promoted global compliance with human rights standards. Many states have incorporated international human rights into their national legal systems, whether through the explicit incorporation of human rights legislation into national constitutions or through the consideration national courts have given the decisions of international and regional human rights bodies. It is difficult to overestimate the influence of the case law and the underlying legal ideas of the European Court of Human Rights in Strasbourg and the Inter-American Court of Human Rights in San José on the decisions of national courts in these regions. The implementation of human rights regimes and the mainstream political theory that informs them have combined to establish a global rights-based discourse that has profoundly changed the overall importance of the judiciary and led to a "global expansion of judicial power" (Tate and Vallinder 1995).[3]

Political and social actors have changed their strategies accordingly. Not only do social and political activists bring their struggles and disputes before the courts, they consciously frame their projects in legal language borrowed from rights-based and human rights-inspired discourses, often long before an actual court proceeding takes place (Kymlicka 2010, 100). Anthropologists have ethnographically investigated how human rights activism and their human rights talk shape both local political debates and the human rights ideas themselves (Wilson 1997; Riles 2001; Englund 2006; Merry 2006; Tate 2007; Speed 2008; Goodale 2009).

In Latin America the growth of human rights regimes, especially the inter-American system for the protection of human rights, has had significant impact on the relationship between law and politics (Domingo 2004; Sieder, Schjolden, and Angell 2005; Huneeus, Couso, and Sieder 2010). Partly in response to this process of negotiating political relations through legal means, partly producing and fostering it, indigenous movements in the Americas are increasingly judicializing their political struggles (Brysk 2000). And while the configurations in North America, especially in the United States, are somewhat different from Latin America, a similar form of judicialization is to be observed there.[4] The far-reaching scope that U.S. courts have for constitutional judicial review enables "a very deep involvement of the courts in politics along a number of dimensions" (Shapiro 1994, 106). Constitutional arguments therefore provide a legal discursive repertoire parallel to "human rights talk" in Latin America.[5]

While I agree that the judicialization of politics framework is a useful and effective tool for analyzing indigenous rights discourses, I remain critical of what I perceive to be a bias toward the present in these studies. My argument is that the relationship between natives and settlers becomes judicialized almost from the very beginning of the colonial endeavor. And although the rise of human rights has undoubtedly shaped and extended the legal dimension of this relationship, the idea that native–settler relations were, at some point in the past, a purely "political" matter, whatever that might mean, amounts to a misconception. When it comes to native–settler relations, I therefore see the more recent judicialization of politics through the rise of human rights only as the latest instantiation of the judicialization of these relations.

As Robert Williams (1990) has shown in his groundbreaking study on the legal discourses of colonial conquest, European colonialism in the Americas was, from the very beginning, justified and solidified by means of law. As early as the sixteenth century the Spanish and the Portuguese had set up ever more elaborate colonial administrations and developed a canon of colonial law that immediately started to compete with the native legal systems. Ethnohistorical works on native–settler relations in early colonial times have demonstrated the degree to which these relationships were judicialized very early on. Steve Stern (1993) has shown, for instance, how the so-called Toledo reforms enacted by the Spanish Crown in sixteenth-century Peru not only created an effective colonial administration and court system, but also significantly judicialized the relationship between the Spanish settlers and the native population.

Particularly with regard to British and French colonialism in North America, another important aspect of the legal relationship between settlers and natives is the history of treaty making in both the United States and Canada. From the seventeenth century onward, the British and later the United States and Canada used the form of the treaty to create a legal framework for the relationship between the settler community and the native communities (Prucha 1994; Calloway 2013; Harjo 2014; Asch 2014). To this day such treaties provide a basis for many indigenous rights claims (Borrows and Coyle 2017). The emerging international human rights regimes provide a new forum for presenting these claims, but in some cases the legal instruments on which they are based preceded the rise of human rights regimes by centuries.

My claim is, therefore, that while today's transnational indigenous rights movements can be seen in the context of the rise of human rights regimes and the current judicialization of politics, they are also a phenomenon that is deeply rooted in a historically judicialized relationship between natives and settlers that was a component of the colonial project in the Americas from its earliest days.

Contemporary Indigenous Rights Movements in the Americas

When we now focus on the contemporary transnational indigenous rights movements, many (if not most) studies locate the moment of their birth in the 1970s. Niezen points to four factors that allowed the process of international indigenism to emerge at this time: the established minority-friendly human rights system; anti-colonial legal discourses that transformed legal thinking; the undeniable failure of assimilationist policies; and an emerging "indigenous middle class." All of these factors contributed to the "rise of indigenism" from the 1970s onward (Niezen 2003, 40–42). Additionally, especially in Latin America, many indigenous groups ran into legal dead ends in their national legal systems. They therefore "turned this weakness into

Table 1. Timeline of indigenous rights achievements in international law

Year	*Event*
1923/24	Deskaheh (Levi General), spokesman for the Six Nations of the Grand River Land near Brantford, Ontario, travels to Geneva and tries—ultimately without success—to obtain a hearing before the League of Nations relating to a self-government dispute with Canada.
1957	The ILO adopts ILO Convention No. 107, "Concerning the Protection and Integration of Indigenous and Other Tribal and Semi-Tribal Populations in Independent Countries."
1977	The International NGO Conference on Discrimination Against Indigenous Populations in the Americas is held in Geneva.
1981	The International NGO Conference on Indigenous Peoples and the Land is held in Geneva.
1982	The Economic and Social Council (ECOSOC) of the United Nations establishes the Working Group on Indigenous Populations.
1989	The ILO adopts ILO Convention No. 169, "Concerning Indigenous and Tribal Peoples in Independent Countries."
2000	The ECOSOC formally approves the establishment of the United Nations Permanent Forum on Indigenous Issues (UNPFII).
2007	The United Nations General Assembly approves the United Nations Declaration on the Rights of Indigenous Peoples. Only four states vote against: the United States, Canada, Australia, and New Zealand.

strength" and pooled their limited resources internationally by targeting the less contested international legal arena, especially the International Labour Organization (ILO) and the United Nations (UN) (Brysk 1996). As the history of this engagement has been thoroughly documented in other works (Brysk 2000; Thornberry 2002; Niezen 2003; Anaya 2004a; Engle 2010), I will here confine myself to a few crucial points of orientation (see Table 1).

Indigenous rights activists have managed to broaden existing human rights treaties and adopt new legal instruments. As a result, indigenous communities in the Americas now have a number of forums available in which to bring indigenous rights cases, including those provided by the ILO, the United Nations, and the Organization of American States (OAS) (see Table 2).

Prior to this activist engagement, the human rights framework was rather ill-equipped to deal with indigenous rights. The first and second generations

Table 2. Dispute resolution bodies handling indigenous rights complaints in the Americas

Organization	*Dispute resolution body*	*Relevant legal provisions*	*Form of claim*
International Labour Organization (ILO)	ILO Governing Body and Tripartite Commission	ILO Convention No. 169 ILO Convention No. 107	Only by workers' or employers' organizations
United Nations (UN)	Human Rights Committee (HRC)	Article 27 of the International Covenant for Civil and Political Rights (ICCPR)	Individual
United Nations (UN)	Committee on the Elimination of Racial Discrimination (CERD)	International Convention on the Elimination of All Forms of Racial Discrimination (ICERD)	Individual and collective
Organization of American States (OAS)	Inter-American Commission on Human Rights	American Convention on Human Rights American Declaration of the Rights and Duties of Man	Individual and collective

of human rights, most importantly codified in the International Covenant on Civil and Political Rights (ICCPR) and the International Covenant on Economic, Social, and Cultural Rights (ICESCR), guarantee group rights generally only under narrow circumstances.[6] Indigenous communities are not mentioned specifically. However, Article 27 of the ICCPR, which guarantees individuals the right to enjoy their "own culture, to profess and practise their own religion, [and] to use their own language," is recognized as applying to indigenous individuals (although not to indigenous groups as collectives). The UN Human Rights Committee (HRC), which hears cases on alleged violations of the rights enshrined in the ICCPR, has issued a General Comment (No. 23) to Article 27, in which it explicitly sees indigenous rights, including land rights, as enshrined in that article. It has heard several indigenous rights cases before and since. The Committee on the Elimination of Racial Discrimination (CERD), which hears cases on alleged violations of the International Convention on the Elimination of All Forms of Racial Discrimination (ICERD), has also issued a General Recommendation (No. 23) stating that the ICERD does apply to indigenous groups.

The first "big break" for indigenous rights, however, was the International Labour Organization's Indigenous and Tribal Peoples Convention of 1989 (ILO 169), the first multilateral treaty codifying binding obligations for states to protect indigenous rights. ILO 169 replaced ILO Convention No. 107 from 1957, which spoke of "indigenous populations" instead of "indigenous peoples" and whose proposed measures were directed more at assimilating indigenous populations into the national state than promoting indigenous self-government.[7] Indigenous activists found ILO 107 to be largely inadequate and lobbied to have it replaced with ILO 169 (Swepston 1990; Yupsanis 2010). The American countries that have ratified ILO 169 are Argentina, Bolivia, Brazil, Chile, Colombia, Costa Rica, Dominica, Ecuador, Guatemala, Honduras, Mexico, Nicaragua, Paraguay, Peru, and Venezuela. The United States and Canada initially refused to ratify the convention but have recently changed their position.

The second "big break" came in 2007, when the General Assembly of the United Nations approved the United Nations Declaration on the Rights of Indigenous Peoples (UNDRIP). Although it represents a compromise between indigenous rights activists and the UN member states (White Face 2013), the declaration codifies a number of rights for indigenous peoples. As declarations of the UN General Assembly are considered "soft law," the declaration has no legally binding effect. Nevertheless, "soft law" plays an important role in the legal interpretation of other provisions, and the UNDRIP is an important step toward establishing binding standards of international customary law (Barelli 2009). Even before the UNDRIP was issued, visible changes in state practice regarding indigenous rights had given rise to an emerging body of international customary law providing for basic indigenous rights (Anaya 2004a, 61–96). Additionally, indigenous rights movements have since pushed for the integration of UNDRIP into national constitutions. Bolivia, for example, has already done this. Both ILO 169 and UNDRIP are regularly invoked by indigenous claimants to convince national courts of their claims (Beier 2009).

In the Americas, a fairly sophisticated jurisprudence on indigenous rights has emerged in both the Inter-American Commission on Human Rights and the Inter-American Court of Human Rights. Both bodies have determined that indigenous rights are enshrined in the American Declaration of the Rights and Duties of Man and the American Convention on Human Rights. The Organization of American States (OAS) has not yet issued an American declaration on the rights of indigenous peoples, although the commission has already approved several drafts of such a declaration.

The transnational indigenous activism that helped create the international legal framework described above was at first dominated by North American activists from the United States and Canada (although indigenous activists from Australia, New Zealand, and, to a lesser extent, northern European communities also played an important role). Indigenous rights movements from South and Central America were initially less well equipped to mobilize international legal instruments. Only from the 1990s onward has this North–South divide begun to close (Engle 2010, 71; Niezen 2003, 71). This early dominance of indigenous movements by common-law countries and former British colonies is an important aspect of the international indigenous rights discourse. This is why I have felt it necessary to devote so much attention to early indigenous rights cases from the United States—they link the more recent indigenous rights debates located in the international human rights regime back to historically earlier legal discourses and help to better contextualize and historicize recent developments.

Others have pointed out the degree to which international law is rooted in such European legal discourses as the Roman *jus gentium*, canon law, and natural law conceptions from the Middle Ages and how the colonial encounter has shaped these older European discourses into international law (Anghie 2005). Colonial legal regimes are likewise rooted in medieval and Renaissance legal thinking (Cohen 1942; Williams 1983). One way to observe how these older European discourses are translated into settler–native relationships in the Americas is to examine seminal U.S. Supreme Court decisions regarding Indian law, namely, the so-called Marshall trilogy—*Johnson v. McIntosh* (1823), *Cherokee Nation v. Georgia* (1831), and *Worcester v. Georgia* (1832) (discussed in Chapters 2–4)—named after John Marshall, the sitting chief justice of the Supreme Court, who delivered all three judgments. Although these cases are not the first court decisions in the Americas dealing with the relationship between settler colonialists and the native inhabitants (we find those from the earliest colonial times), they are the first ones to be cited internationally and therefore are the foundation of an international body of case law relating to indigenous rights. The basic principles developed in the first U.S. Supreme Court cases on federal Indian law had a great influence on the legal discourses in other common-law settler states, such as Canada, Australia, and New Zealand, and became guiding principles for the emerging body of transnational indigenous rights law.

Sovereignty and Culture

Analysis of the Marshall trilogy cases reveals that one basic principle of indigenous–settler relations in the common-law context is the unbroken sovereignty of indigenous communities after colonization. In simplified terms, from this point of view, indigenous communities are "quasi-states," similar to nation-states but somehow diminished in terms of their sovereignty. It makes sense, then, that the indigenous rights debates from the 1970s onward are directed toward the international right of self-determination. The right of self-determination is codified in Article 1(2) of the UN Charter,[8] which declares that the purpose of the United Nations is "to develop friendly relations among nations based on respect for the principle of equal rights and *self-determination of peoples*, and to take other appropriate measures to strengthen universal peace" (emphasis added). In the period of decolonization after the Second World War, the right to self-determination was the basis for acknowledging the right of former colonies to secede from colonial empires.

Following this line of argumentation, indigenous peoples, who are legal subjects of international law, should also have the right to self-determination (Cassese 1995). This reasoning presumes that indigenous peoples are in fact "nations" and can claim, if not full sovereignty and independence as states, then at least a certain degree of autonomy. The stronger version of this argument claims a right of secession for indigenous communities; weaker approaches invoke the right to self-determination in order to claim territorial and autonomy rights within the (post)colonial nation-states in which the indigenous communities reside. Niezen asserts that this legal argumentation is the basis of indigenous rights claims, and he provides ethnographic accounts of several discussions in the United Nations on the implementation of indigenous rights instruments to illustrate his point (2003, 145–192). In these cases, insistence that the word "peoples" be used in all relevant legal documents was always at the forefront of the demands of indigenous activists precisely because it then allowed them to invoke the right to self-determination.

I call this the "sovereignty approach" to indigenous rights because the rights to territory and autonomy are derived from the sovereignty vested in indigenous communities, which is, in turn, derived from the fact that they are—as nations or peoples—legal persons under international law. A sovereign entity is governed only by its own rules or by rules derived indirectly from its own sovereignty. The sovereignty approach to indigenous rights is, to be exact, not a human rights argument. Human rights are rights that protect *persons against the state*, whereas the right to self-determination protects *states*—and, it could be argued, those nations and peoples that are formally not (yet) states—*against other states*. While states are bound by the right to self-determination in relation to their peers in the international community, they are bound by human rights in relation to their own (and sometimes other states') citizens.

The sovereignty approach is not the only argumentative basis for indigenous rights movements. Beginning in the 1980s, the idea of indigenous rights as related to a human right to culture began to emerge (Sanders 1983; Engle 2010).[9] This "culture approach" is in principle detached from the concept of indigenous communities as *quasi* nation-states. In the culture approach, claims to land and self-government are derived from the idea that indigenous culture has an inherent value and that the postcolonial nation-state has to protect it from infringement. In contrast to the sovereignty approach, the culture approach is based on a human rights argument. The state has the obligation to protect the cultures of its citizens (individuals as well as collectives), including those of indigenous communities. In this view, indigenous communities are bearers of culture and can, therefore, claim state measures to have it protected, not as more or less equal partners in the international community but as a collective of citizens against "their" state.

Although they are legally different, both approaches—sovereignty and culture—aim at the same projects: recognition of land rights, a requirement of consultation, consent, and benefit sharing with regard to development projects, the right to continue performing traditional activities without interference, reparations for damages, and so forth. Both approaches invoke the legal argumentation of indigenous movements and often cannot be clearly distinguished from one another in their legal strategies. Their relative importance and dominance vary over time and also regionally in the Americas.

Delgamuukw v. British Columbia (1997), one of the landmark indigenous rights cases in Canada (discussed in Chapter 5), provides me with the opportunity to investigate how a sovereignty-related indigenous rights argument can be combined with a culture approach. I see this case as an attempt to mediate between the legal principles of the early U.S. cases, which are the basis of modern Canadian native law, and the emerging "culture approach" in international law. To better understand the "culture approach" to indigenous rights, this book presents three cases from the Inter-American Court of Human Rights: *Aloeboetoe v. Suriname* (1993), the court's first case dealing specifically with issues of indigenous rights; *Awas Tingni v. Nicaragua* (2001), generally considered *the* indigenous rights decision in Latin America with a fully developed culture argument; and *Saramaka v. Suriname* (2007), which further develops the principles of *Awas Tingni* and applies them to communities of African descent.

We will see that this characterization along the lines of sovereignty and culture is in many ways provisional, but it will help us navigate through many legal intricacies, contradictions, and inconsistencies. Of course, this book is in no way a comprehensive legal history of indigenous rights in the Americas, and certain gaps must be glossed over. The aim is rather to come to a better understanding of how an analysis of legal texts and language can make a larger systematic contribution to the field of indigenous studies in the Americas.

The Indigenous Paradox and Legal Pluralism

One of the important issues addressed in this book is how to measure the relationship between sovereignty and culture in indigenous rights doctrine. As I indicated at the beginning of this chapter, I believe both legal concepts circle around a paradox inherent in the concept of indigeneity: indigenous groups are part of the state in which they reside, and at the same time they are not. They depend on the state, but they must also—as a matter of their very existence—reject it. I argue that only an indigenous rights strategy that legally and conceptually accommodates this indigenous paradox can fulfill the task of an indigenous rights claim, namely, to invoke the rule of law in order to call for its suspension and thereby open up a space for the indigenous community's own legal system.

The whole idea of indigenous rights is practically inconceivable without a clear understanding of the concept of legal pluralism (Griffiths 1986; Benda-Beckmann 2002; Tamanaha 2008; Guevara Gil 2009; Berman 2012). The basic advice of legal pluralism scholarship is simple. Instead of conceiving of the law as a single monolithic system of rules, one should always bear in mind that "the law" represents a repertoire of different, coexisting legal orders: national and international law, official and unofficial law, state law and "traditional," "customary," or "indigenous" law, written and unwritten law, religious and secular law, and so forth. Sometimes these legal orders overlap and compete, sometimes they are more or less clearly separated from one another. For the purposes of my argument, I must differentiate at least three legal orders: indigenous law (meaning the law of the indigenous community); national law (meaning the law of the (post)colonial state); and international law (often consisting of the indigenous rights provisions of the ILO, the UN, and/or the OAS).

Indigenous rights are based on the notion that there are two legal systems competing for jurisdiction: an indigenous legal system and a (post)colonial national legal system. Sometimes international law is able to broker this relationship and sometimes it is not. Only if the two legal systems are understood as being in competition can the indigenous paradox emerge. In the case of a successful indigenous rights claim, the indigenous community can use the national legal system to call for the suspension of that very system. The result is that the indigenous legal system takes precedence, but only because the national legal system demands it. The indigenous community is therefore subject to the national law and, at the same time, to its own indigenous legal system. The aim of this book is to explore this paradox and how it shapes legal thinking entrenched in processes of identity.

Both the sovereignty approach and the culture approach give rise to some form of legal pluralism, but the legal pluralisms are different. In the sovereignty approach the legal pluralism is rooted in the legal fiction of sovereignty; in the culture approach the legal pluralism is grounded in the "extralegal fiction" of cultural difference. Both these approaches, *rooted legal pluralism* and *de facto legal pluralism*, open up legal spaces that allow the indigenous claimant to appear as both a subject of the national rule of law and independent of it. The ways in which indigeneity emerges as a paradox through the mobilization of legal pluralism is distilled from the case studies and concisely presented in Chapter 9.

Investigating Legal Texts from an Anthropological Perspective

The bulk of the material analyzed in this book comprises legal texts, mainly court decisions on indigenous rights. I investigate these texts both as a lawyer and as a legal and political anthropologist. From a theoretical perspective I conceive of these indigenous rights judgments as a mélange of ethnographic and autoethnographic accounts of indigeneity that must be analyzed with a certain sensitivity to the multiple layers that compose them.

An anthropological perspective on legal texts, as I understand it, is informed by several other approaches from neighboring disciplines. It has to be informed by the methods of legal history (see, e.g., Lobban 2004) because it treats the legal text as a source not for the development of a concrete legal argument but for the compilation of a broader description and analysis of legal argumentation. It is also similar to the study of literature, especially in the law-and-literature approach (Brooks and Gewirtz 1996; Dolin 2007), because it is interested in the legal text not as a sheet of unconnected facts but as a carefully composed story with a narrative structure. It has some affinity to psychoanalytic legal analysis (Goodrich 1995; 1997) because it goes beyond the surface meaning of the text and tries to uncover unconscious assumptions and desires coded in the text but not always openly acknowledged. But first and foremost, such an analysis is a project of anthropology. It investigates the text with the eyes of an anthropologist to discover how it uses, constructs, and argues with concepts and objects of study that are at the heart of anthropology: "the cultural," "the social," "the indigenous," and many others, including "the legal" itself.

This project of investigating legal texts can also be situated in the broader endeavor to come to terms with the confluence of language, culture, and society, as is done in the framework of semiotic anthropology (Mertz 2007). One strand of this field is based on the semiotic tradition of intertextuality (Kristeva 1986), which puts forth the idea that texts can only be understood within a cultural structure in which other texts are embedded. In legal anthropology, Brinkley Messick's (1992) work on the interaction between textual traditions, legal history, and politics is the most prominent example of this approach. In a broader sense that goes beyond the text as a written document, Elizabeth Mertz (2007, 346) has connected the project of semiotic anthropology to the discursive translation and retranslation of law into different contexts—an interest that has occupied many recent works of legal anthropology (Lazarus-Black 1994; Maurer 1997; Coutin 2003; Bowen 2003; Merry 2006).

For anthropology in general, James Clifford and George Marcus's edited volume *Writing Culture: The Poetics and Politics of Ethnography* (1986) induced a trend in anthropology to turn to written texts as objects of study and engendered a highly controversial debate (see Zenker and Kumoll 2013). The basic assumption of *Writing Culture* is relatively simple: anthropologists write narratively structured stories about "the other," and as such occupy a position of authority. Part of ethnographic research must therefore be a reflective and self-critical examination of this position of authority. My argument on the importance of the "writing culture" debate for an anthropological perspective on legal texts is equally simple. Court decisions, in our case on indigenous rights, can be read as ethnographic texts. The way in which court decisions speak about the culture of the other and its rights resembles ethnographic writing. The several layers of a judgment present different ways of conceptualizing the other, including self-conceptions or at least the self-representations of the indigenous claimants.

Following the idea of intertextuality, we can view court decisions as emerging in the context of other texts, especially those of the parties involved in the case. These, too, have an ethnographic character. Think, for example, of the statement of defense written by a state official in which the scope of an indigenous treaty right concerning land is argued. Alternatively, such texts might have an autoethnographic character, such as a brief written by an indigenous community that claims certain rights and describes its land tenure system in support of its claims. Such "autoethnographic texts" (Pratt 1991) from indigenous communities are particularly multivalent.[10] They are not "pure" autochthonous self-representations but the product of the input of indigenous communities and careful drafting in collaboration between community activists and those trained in "Western" law and serving as the communities' lawyers. In style and genre they are addressed to the nonindigenous audience, foremost the national or international court. They contain a community's own perspective on the events, the facts in question, and the legal conclusions to be drawn from these facts and often include a depiction of the long history of the indigenous community from time immemorial through the time of conquest to the present day. These legal documents are embedded in complex power relations and depend as much (and usually far more) on what nonindigenous audiences are willing and able to hear as on what indigenous peoples have to say. As I have already posited at the beginning of this chapter, indigeneity as a phenomenon itself has to be situated in these kinds of interdependencies and entanglements with the legal genre.[11]

In court decisions on indigenous rights, the indigenous peoples' bills, writs, and other documents are often not reproduced verbatim but are summarized, represented, and discussed in the judgment. The indigenous rights judgment is therefore a special form of ethnographic text, as it is a direct response to the ethnographic and autoethnographic texts of the parties, usually the indigenous community on the one hand and state officials on the other. They are a complex mélange of these different types of text. Court decisions in indigenous rights cases represent a position of authority about "the other." They become part of the discourse on indigeneity, often to a much larger degree than most ethnographic studies. It seems particularly apt, therefore, to investigate court decisions that are explicitly concerned with ethnographic issues, such as those involving indigenous rights, from an anthropological perspective.

* * * *

In the last few decades, indigenous rights movements have had a significant impact on the legal and political landscape not only in the Americas but globally as well. This *indigènitude* is deeply connected with the judicialization of politics that has come about with the emergence of international human rights regimes after the Second World War; its historical roots, however, go back to the early nineteenth century and even earlier. Indigenous rights concepts have profoundly changed national and international law and given rise to indigenous legal and political subjectivities.

The rise of indigenism is not an issue for cultural experts only; it is a phenomenon deeply embedded in legal processes. Indigenous movements have made use of opportunities for articulating their claims that the emerging human rights regimes have opened up. International organizations, dispute resolution bodies, and courts have become spaces of indigenous performances. While indigenous peoples have "played themselves" in international legal arenas, their articulations and performances get translated into law and back again into the production and reproduction of indigenous identities. The term "indigenous" itself is as much a legal term as it is a cultural one, as the legal and the cultural are not autonomous fields but are, in fact, inextricably linked.

Indigenous discourses, and therefore also indigenous rights doctrine, can be systematized along the two lines of sovereignty and culture. Indigenous communities are both part of the state and separate from it; they are dependent on the state yet cannot exist without asserting and maintaining the boundaries between themselves and the state. This paradox of indigeneity is at the center of this book. Focusing on legal texts from the Americas, this study examines the "big precedents" of indigenous rights on the continent and tracks the indigenous paradox in legal language and doctrine. To that end I try to read the law with the eyes of an anthropologist and discuss indigeneity from the perspective of a lawyer. In such a venture the boundaries between political and legal anthropology, international law, legal history, and literary studies become blurred, and the best one can hope for is to piece together a picture that is more accurate and more complete than the sum of its parts.

CHAPTER 2

The Invention of the Sovereignty Approach to Indigenous Rights

Johnson v. McIntosh

When I visited the National Museum of the American Indian in Washington, D.C., in December 2014, the museum had just started a four-year exhibition titled *Nation to Nation: Treaties Between the United States and American Indian Nations* (Harjo 2014). The immensely rich and well-researched exhibition included an introductory film in which racist quotes about American Indians were displayed. Among them were parts of a quote by John Marshall, chief justice of the United States Supreme Court, from the judgment *Johnson v. McIntosh*: "But the tribes of Indians inhabiting this country were fierce savages, whose occupation was war, and whose subsistence was drawn chiefly from the forest. To leave them in possession of their country, was to leave the country a wilderness" (590).[1] The prominent place of this quote highlights how visible and relevant this judgment still is for the political and historical debates on indigenous identity in the United States.

The quote startled me. I had just recently read *Johnson v. McIntosh* in preparation for this book and was still feeling positively impressed by its formalistic argumentation and what I had perceived as a relative lack of racist remarks in comparison to the usual rhetoric of the nineteenth century. What impressed me most was Marshall's many half-ironic comments on the reasoning of the "discovery doctrine" that he helped to establish in law. While in the book that was already beginning to take shape in my mind I had planned to use *Johnson v. McIntosh* as the starting point for indigenous rights in the Americas, I realized that in the United States the judgment is often seen as the complete opposite—as one of the chief examples of the *disregard* for indigenous rights. In the opinion of the leading U.S. scholars on indigenous rights, *Johnson v. McIntosh* "confirmed the superior rights of a European-derived nation to the lands occupied by 'infidels, heathens, and savages'" (Williams 1990, 316–17), and rules "that the natural rights of human beings to dispose of property that they held by virtue of possession did not apply to Indians of America" (G. E. White 1988, 710). And of course, these are more than fair assessments of the impact *Johnson v. McIntosh* had in the legal and political landscape of the United States in the nineteenth century. What I want to highlight in this chapter, however, is that this is not all there is to say about this case. The legal principles of *Johnson v. McIntosh* not only disenfranchised the Indian nations in the United States, they also—paradoxically—laid the foundation for a strategy of resistance against their disenfranchisement. In a way, the judgment takes away indigenous rights and grants them at the same time.

Of course, the term "indigenous" was not used at the time, but I take the liberty here of characterizing *Johnson v. McIntosh* as an indigenous rights case, because what became case law in *Johnson* is a specific form of interaction between the native communities and the emerging colonial and postcolonial nation-states: the idea that the Indian tribes are sovereign nations. As the first case of the so-called Marshall trilogy—three Supreme Court decisions in which Chief Justice Marshall laid out several of the basic principles of the United States' relationship to American Indian tribes—*Johnson v. McIntosh* is considered one of the most important precedents and cornerstones of federal Indian law, the complex of national laws in the United States that regulates relations with the Indian tribes.[2] The decision profoundly influenced the rights of indigenous peoples in other former British colonies with common-law traditions, such as Canada, Australia, and New Zealand (Watson 2010). With the "rise of indigenism" in the second half of the twentieth century, many of the principles developed in *Johnson* have also become formative for the international human rights discourses on indigenous rights, especially regarding the sovereignty approach.

What the often-cited passage in the quote above does not show is how *Johnson v. McIntosh* provides a model for the legal relations between settlers and natives that is characterized by a complex legal pluralism that indigenous communities would be able to navigate to their advantage in the future, at least to some extent. I argue in this chapter that the judgment opened up the argumentative space for the "sovereignty approach" to indigenous rights by leaving open back doors to alternative views on the underlying property conceptions that are still relevant for indigenous land rights discourses to the present day.

The Case in Context: The Indian Non-Intercourse Acts, the Royal Proclamation of 1763, and Land Speculation

In *Johnson v. McIntosh*, two white property owners were in disagreement about the ownership of certain lands formerly possessed by Illinois and Piankeshaw Indians. Thomas Johnson, the plaintiff, represented two land speculation consortiums, the Illinois Land Company and the Wabash Company, which had merged in 1779 (Robertson 2011). Their aim was to legalize massive land purchases they had made in the late eighteenth century. The Illinois Land Company, based in Philadelphia, had purchased huge tracts of land from the Illinois nation in 1773, and the Wabash Company had made an equally massive purchase from the Piankeshaw nation in 1775. William McIntosh, the defendant, had bought the same property later in 1818 from the federal government. The question was who held title: Johnson or McIntosh. The Indians themselves were not a party in the lawsuit.

The Supreme Court found in favor of McIntosh, arguing that the title Johnson had received in his transaction with the Indians could not be recognized before a court of the United States because the U.S. property system did not allow private citizens to buy Indian land. That right was solely vested in the Union.

By the time the Supreme Court ruled against Johnson, buying land directly from Indians without the consent of the federal government was already prohibited by federal law. Beginning in 1790s, the U.S. Congress had passed a series of so-called Trade and Intercourse Acts (or, in the more descriptive colloquial term, Indian Non-Intercourse Acts) regulating commerce between non-Indian U.S. citizens and Indian nations.[3] According to these Indian Non-Intercourse Acts, all land transactions with Indians tribes were contingent on the approval of the federal government.[4] Only because the transactions in question had taken place before the passing of the Non-Intercourse Acts (the sale was conducted a few years before the Declaration of Independence was adopted, thus still under British rule), the Supreme Court had to resolve the question.

Before independence, under British rule, when Johnson had bought the land from the Indians, there was a regulation similar to the Non-Intercourse

Acts prohibiting land transactions with Indians—the Royal Proclamation of 1763, issued by Britain's King George III.[5] This regulation was intended to restrict the inland advance of the British colonies and to maintain political and economic control over the fast-expanding settler community. Unregulated land sales by private individuals risked upsetting the native nations, whose role as trading partners was much more important to the Crown than their potential role as a provider of land for further settlement. In this context the respective clauses of the Royal Proclamation of 1763 were a reaction to Pontiac's War, a military conflict with several native nations formerly allied with France, which had hurt Britain significantly.[6]

The Crown's attempt to slow down the colonies' advancement in North America to a manageable pace was contrary to the economic interests of influential settlers who wished to expand the colonies faster and profit from land speculation. Thus the Royal Proclamation of 1763 became a symbol of the motherland's infringement on the settlers' rights to free enterprise and one important reason for the colonies to seek independence. In the movement for independence from Britain, legal discourses on the validity of British legislation restricting the rights of settlers were of great importance. These legal discourses highlighted the Crown legislation's incompatibility with natural law. The American radicals' legal arguments referred to Crown legislation as the "Norman yoke" on the free colonial settlers.[7] In these narratives the validity of the earlier British legislation in general was called into question (Williams 1990, 233–86).

From an economic perspective, the Royal Proclamation of 1763 was resisted because it hindered the large-scale land speculation ventures of influential settlers (Kades 2000). Among these real estate speculators were such illustrious politicians as George Washington, who would become the first president of the United States. In a letter to his associate William Crawford, dated September 21, 1767, Washington (who later as president strongly denounced illegal land purchases directly from Indians) characterized the Royal Proclamation of 1763 as "a temporary expedient to quiet the minds of the Indians" and stressed that it "must fall, of course, in a few years." He also predicted that "any person, therefore, who neglects the present opportunity of hunting out good lands, and in some measure marking and distinguishing them for his own (in order to keep others from settling them), will never regain it" (Washington 1889, 220–222).

The dispute underlying *Johnson v. McIntosh* was deeply rooted in such land speculation (Williams 1990, 285–317). Generally, it is possible to identify two groups of speculators in the first thirteen states with competing interests in the legal outcome of the case. On the one side there were land speculators, many of them in high political office in the so-called "landless states" (Pennsylvania, New Hampshire, Rhode Island, Delaware, Maryland, and New Jersey), who had invested heavily in land purchases from indigenous nations in the West. The landless states already had an established western border and did not plan to expand any farther westward. Their citizens' interests were rather directed toward privately acquiring land directly from the indigenous nations in the West. In their calculation these western lands, which were not yet part of a state or settled by non-Indians, could be acquired at bargain prices from the Indians. When the emerging nation started expanding farther westward, these lands would become much more valuable and could be sold again at great profit.

The situation of the "landed states" (New York, Virginia, Connecticut, Massachusetts, North Carolina, South Carolina, and Georgia) was different. They had no established western borders yet and wanted to expand farther themselves. A significant part of the land in question in *Johnson v. McIntosh* could be claimed by Virginia, which did not want to lose control over it and the potential profit from the sale of "preemption rights" to settlers and land speculators, a practice the landed states started during the American Revolution (Banner 2005). Land speculators bought from the state a "preemption right" to a certain parcel of land on which Indians often still resided. The holder of such a preemption right was entitled to the land in case Indians ceded the land to the federal government, usually by virtue of a treaty. Therefore, individual land purchases from Indians without government control were not in the interests of the states.

This general disagreement between the states had been settled with a compromise when the United States of America was founded and the U.S. Constitution was accepted. The deal was relatively simple. The "landless states" accepted the *status quo ante* the British had established: private land sales directly from Indians were banned. In return, the "landed states" accepted a demarcated western border. The power to regulate Indian land sales was given to the Union, which was entrusted with the authority to manage the acquisition of land in the West and establish new states where possible.

Despite this new status quo that was similar to the legal situation before independence, not everybody was happy with the way things had turned out. This was especially true of land speculators who had already purchased lands from Indians in the West, whether under British rule or in the time between independence and the establishment of the United States, and who still wanted to profit from their investment. Johnson represented such a consortium of land speculators. Chief Justice Marshall, however, would side with McIntosh, and therefore with the legal status quo. Robert Williams thus correctly concludes that "Marshall's influential discourse of conquest in *Johnson* . . . merely provided a *post hoc* legal rationalization for the Revolutionary-era political compromise on the frontier lands question" (1990, 289).

A Staged Case with Pre-Agreed Facts

Johnson v. McIntosh was a staged test case. The Illinois Land Company and the Wabash Company had clearly violated the Royal Proclamation of 1763 when they made their land purchases, but they had hoped—like many speculators at the time, George Washington among them—that the legal landscape regarding Indian land would change after the Revolution. To reach that goal they had been trying for fifty years already to legitimate their acquisitions by lobbying before legislative bodies and then decided to bring the case before the judiciary, finally filing an ejectment action before the District Court of Illinois.[8]

Thomas Johnson Jr., shareholder of the Wabash Company, was chosen as the plaintiff and the face of the case. The retired Johnson was the former governor of Maryland and had been appointed an associate justice of the first United States Supreme Court by George Washington. He died during the proceedings, but due to his prominence he was not removed from the case. Instead, his heirs represented him before the Supreme Court. The consortium approached William McIntosh, a financially ambitious former fur trader, to serve as the defendant. They needed someone from Illinois because the company had connections to a district court judge in the state from whom they expected a favorable outcome. As part of the deal, McIntosh, who was supposed to lose the case for the benefit of the merged land speculation companies, was undoubtedly offered a share in the company as compensation for his services (Robertson 2011, 35).

The collusion became apparent in the trial court proceedings when both parties issued an agreed statement of the facts in which they eliminated all potential factual objections that could have been raised against the land sales by the two companies. All they wanted the court to decide was one point, and one point only: was the Royal Proclamation of 1763 a legal impediment to a pre-Revolutionary land purchase? (Robertson 2011, 38). The argument against the validity of the Royal Proclamation of 1763 was at the heart of the case and followed the same reasoning that had already become a mainstream legal argument in Revolutionary times: while the British Parliament could have barred land purchases from Indians, the Crown could not do so by royal proclamation. Such regulation could only have been made in the form of a law passed by Parliament, not an executive action. It was further agreed that McIntosh should win the case before the District Court of Illinois in order to force the case to go before the Supreme Court. All went according to plan—the district court judge issued a pro forma decision in favor of McIntosh in 1820, and the case went before the Supreme Court.

It is highly illuminating to take a closer look at the summary of the facts agreed to by the parties before trial court, which is also represented at the beginning of the Supreme Court's judgment. In its narrative form the pre-agreed facts are a legal history of the British settlers' land acquisition in North America. They describe the Indian territory of North America as held in sovereignty by the Indian nations:

> The whole of the territory, in the letters patent described, except a small district on James River, where a settlement of Europeans had previously been made, was held, occupied, and possessed, *in full sovereignty*, by various *independent tribes or nations* of Indians, who were the *sovereigns* of their respective portions of the territory, and the *absolute owners and proprietors* of the soil; and who neither acknowledged nor owed any allegiance or obedience to any European sovereign or state whatever: and that in making settlements within this territory, and in all the other parts of North America, where settlements were made, under the authority of the English government, or by its subjects, the right of soil was previously obtained by purchase or conquest, from the particular Indian tribe or nation by which the soil was claimed and held; or the consent of such tribe or nation was secured. (545; emphasis added)

After the Europeans had purchased more land from the Indians, and during the French and Indian War (the military conflict between Britain and France over control of North America, 1754–1763), most Indian nations created alliances with either Britain or France. Nevertheless, as is stressed in the statement of facts agreed upon by the parties, the Indians never lost their sovereignty or territorial rights as a result of these alliances: "The Indian tribes or nations . . . were the allies of France in the war, but not her subjects, *never having been in any manner conquered* by her, and held the country in *absolute sovereignty, as independent nations*, both as to the right of jurisdiction and sovereignty, and the right of soil" (547; emphasis added). After the war the Indians' sovereignty remained intact until July 5, 1773, when "certain chiefs of the Illinois Indians, then jointly reprepresenting [*sic*], acting for, and being duly authorized by that tribe," sold the land to the Illinois Land Company (550). The Illinois nation received $24,000 and "freely accepted it and divided it amongst themselves" (554). The same goes for the second purchase from the Piankeshaw Indians, who received $31,000 on October 18, 1775 (555–557).

Less than a year after the purchases, however, on May 6, 1776, Virginia declared its independence from the British Crown and government. The state transformed many of the lands purchased by the companies into the "County of Illinois" and later transferred the county to the United States. The United States then sold it to William McIntosh on July 20, 1818.

The statement of facts, which was designed, as we have seen, to promote Johnson's position, laid heavy emphasis on the full international sovereignty of the Indians, which were referred to as "tribes or nations," and each tribe was alleged to have "separate and absolute ownership, in and over its own territory, both as to the right of sovereignty and jurisdiction, and the right of soil" (547).

The manner in which the history of land acquisition was told is also of relevance here. The factual statement says that the king conveyed the right to the settlers to purchase land from the Indians in North America and only to conquer it under exceptional circumstances. There was no title to North American lands per se. And indeed, historically speaking, the overwhelming majority of the United States consists of land ceded by Indian nations to the Crown and later to the Union in treaties rather than through formal conquest. The United States was, in effect, bought from the Indians, although many treaties, especially later ones, were made and revised under the implicit or explicit threat of force (Cohen 1948).

This friendly view of Indian land rights was a tactical move by the plaintiffs. The land speculators favored the idea of the territorial sovereignty of the Indians because they were only able to acquire the land if their business partners had the full right to sell it. Strong indigenous land rights were therefore in the white land speculators' interests.

Johnson's Claim and Marshall's Defense

In the trial before the Supreme Court Johnson relied almost exclusively on a single argument: because the Indians were the sovereigns of their lands, the companies could buy land from them as long as there were no legal obstacles. The only possible explicit prohibition in sight was the Royal Proclamation of 1763. Johnson contended, however, that the Royal Proclamation of 1763, if it had any legal effect at all, could not have affected the Indians' right to sell because, as they were never British subjects, they could not be bound by British law; only the settlers' right to buy could be subject to British law. Johnson further argued—in line with the political-legal rhetoric of the Revolution—that the proclamation could not legally bind the settlers because the king had superseded his authority in issuing it. Such legislation could only be passed by Parliament; it was, therefore, in the legislative and not the executive domain.

Consequently, at the time Virginia transferred the land to the United States, it was already Johnson's property, and "the legislature was not competent to take away private, vested rights, or appropriate private property to public use, under the circumstances of this case" (565). The upshot of the argument was that McIntosh could not acquire valid title to the lands Johnson had already bought.

However, McIntosh—the defendant who had set out to lose the case—told a completely different story about the Indians' legal status. He started out with a three-pronged argument. First, the Indians were "in a state of nature" and could therefore at no point in time be considered sovereign nations with territorial rights. Second, even if the Indians had been sovereign nations at one time, they had certainly lost their sovereignty and their territory to the European nations when those nations discovered North America. Third, if the Indians had been sovereign nations before discovery and did not lose their sovereignty to the European nations in the course of discovery, they must still possess it. In that third case, the plaintiffs would only possess title within an Indian legal system (if at all), and the Supreme Court could not recognize it. In other words, what McIntosh argued was that if indeed Indian sovereignty existed, then one had to conceptualize a form of legal pluralism in which a title in one system could not simply be presumed to exist in the other. Interestingly, this last alternative of competing sovereignty, which McIntosh presented as a third cascade in an "even if" argument, is relatively close to the legal principles of federal Indian law that began to take shape in the aftermath of *Johnson v. McIntosh*.

These views on Indian sovereignty, however, were only McIntosh's preliminary comments. His case rested on the Supreme Court's acceptance of versions one or two of his arguments: that the Indians were not (at least not any more) sovereign nations. Therefore, "the extent of their right of alienation [i.e., the right to sell their land] must depend upon the laws of the dominion under which they live" (568), which was, in this case, the United States. Under these circumstances it was not necessary to show that the Indians were not U.S. citizens (Indians were not conferred U.S. citizenship until 1924).[9] Instead, McIntosh argued that the Indians had the legal status of neither citizen nor alien: "They are of that class who are said by jurists not to be citizens, but perpetual inhabitants with diminutive rights. The statutes of Virginia, and of all the other colonies, and of the United States, treat them as an inferior race of people, without the privileges of citizens, and under the perpetual protection and pupilage of the government" (569).

McIntosh then invoked a natural law argument that was relatively popular at the time to determine the land rights of Indians, asserting that, "by the law of nature, they had not acquired a fixed property capable of being transferred" (569). This argument is important because it allowed McIntosh to speak against the common-law rule that physical occupancy can be a source of property in law, whereby Indians could have property rights simply by virtue of their physical occupation of the lands at the time of discovery. Without mentioning this potentially dangerous argument explicitly, McIntosh nevertheless made a remarkable counterargument against it. Citing Grotius, Pufendorf, and, most important, Locke, he presented a rule on how property could be acquired by occupancy: "the measure of property acquired by occupancy is determined, according to the law of nature, by the extent of men's wants, and their capacity of using it to supply them" (569). This argument connects to a theory, very popular at the time, that posits that the emergence of property is not established merely by the occupation of a thing, but by its use. Land therefore is "appropriated by a people of cultivators" (579). Land that the Indians do not use for agriculture cannot not belong to them: "Upon this principle the North American Indians could have acquired no proprietary interest in the vast tracts of territory which they wandered over; and their right to the lands on which they hunted, could not be considered as superior to that which is acquired to the sea by fishing in it. The use in the one case, as well as the other, is not exclusive" (569–570).

The Lockean property theory McIntosh presented was seen by many as a legal instrument to conceptualize the dispossession of those Indians subsisting on hunting and gathering. McIntosh concluded that the British Crown passed to the settlers "absolute grants of the soil" in North America and that purchasing land from the Indians was legally unnecessary. "It is true," he argued, "that, in some cases, purchases were made by the colonies from the Indians; but this was merely a measure of policy to prevent hostilities" (570). The Royal Proclamation of 1763, McIntosh argued, was valid and prohibited land sales (he did not, however, speak to the arguments of the king's alleged lack of authority to pass such legislation). In other words, Johnson's pre-independence purchases of land from the Illinois and Piankeshaw nations were, according to McIntosh, invalid.

Marshall's Judgment

Marshall could have chosen the easy way out. He would simply have had to find that the Royal Proclamation of 1763 was valid, and the case would have been dead. Johnson would have been prohibited from buying the land at the time of the purchase and would hold no valid title to it. And that was indeed what Marshall found, but with a twist.

The plaintiffs had contended that the proclamation was invalid because the king had transcended his authority in issuing it. Invoking the precedent set in the *Campbell v. Hall*, a case decided by the Court of King's Bench in 1774, Marshall found that the king had indeed superseded his authority by imposing taxes without Parliament's consent, but not by issuing the Royal Proclamation, which was concerned with land questions. Marshall argued that it was not the Royal Proclamation that prohibited private land purchases from Indians, but a more general common-law rule he called the "discovery doctrine." He interpreted the Royal Proclamation as the written manifestation of this customary legal rule.[10] Marshall then devoted the bulk of the judgment to general elaborations on indigenous land rights and indulged in a complex historical analysis that culminated in a model of legal pluralism that allowed him to conceptualize and incorporate Indian land rights in the United States.

In his very first sentence Marshall defined what he saw as the real legal issue underlying this case. According to the chief justice, the case was not about the validity of Johnson's title; rather, "the question is, whether this title can be recognised in the Courts of the United States" (572). And he explained where he intended to go with this refined question. The stated facts had already established that the Indians were "in rightful possession of the land they sold." Moreover, "the authority of the chiefs who executed the conveyance" was not in question. "The inquiry, therefore, is, in a great measure, confined to the power of Indians to give, and of private individuals to receive, a title which can be sustained in the Courts of this country" (572).

These introductory remarks already illustrate Marshall's sensitivity to the legal pluralism and the competing sovereignties involved. The question is not whether the title is "valid," but whether it "can be sustained in the Court of *this country*," simultaneously implying that he cannot speak to other countries' courts. That these "other countries" are the indigenous nations runs like a thread through all three cases of the Marshall trilogy. Marshall's guideline for his decision was the property law of the United States.

Marshall went on to clarify: "As the right of society, to prescribe those rules by which property may be acquired and preserved is not, and cannot be drawn into question; as the title to lands, especially, is and must be admitted to depend entirely on the law of the nation in which they lie" (572). With this statement Marshall implicitly acknowledged two competing property systems: a U.S. property system and an Indian property system. But only the former was relevant for him to decide the case, even if it was not in accord with natural law. Marshall continued: "It will be necessary, in pursuing this inquiry, to examine, not singly those principles of abstract justice, which the Creator of all things has impressed on the mind of his creature man and which are admitted to regulate, in a great degree, the rights of civilized nations, whose perfect independence is acknowledged; but those principles also which our own government has adopted in the particular case, and given us as the rule for our decision" (572). Steven Newcomb notes that in this passage Marshall in effect admitted "that the Court had reached a decision in *Johnson* on the basis of *injustice*, or *unjust* concepts, so far as the rights of the Indians were concerned" (2008, 75; emphasis in original). And Marshall indeed indicates throughout the judgment that he does not consider his ruling to be particularly just for the Indians (in terms of natural law). But I believe that this passage contains something else that, albeit more subtle, is just as important. It has to do not with the perspective of "just" and "unjust" but with a perspective regarding "principles of natural law" (which is in all the legal opinions Marshall cited—such as *Vattel*—the source of the principles of international law) and the "principles of our own government" (by which he means the national law of the United States). Marshall conceded that the case touched aspects of international law, but eventually had to be decided by national law. He also indicated that the case may have been decided differently before an international court, which the Supreme Court is not.

Marshall's argumentation is thus admittedly positivist, meaning that his guideline was positive law, not abstract justice derived from natural law. His argumentation refers to the nature of property rights as they are determined by each independent state for itself. He explained that "the right of society, to prescribe those rules by which property may be acquired and preserved . . . must be admitted to depend entirely on the law of the nation in which they lie" (572). Consequently, Marshall confined himself mostly to an inquiry into the property system of the United States and what it says about the Indians' property rights to land; in other words, Marshall's decision was guided exclusively by the U.S. property system. Because the U.S. legal system has developed historically out of the British system, Marshall engages in telling a story of the legal history of the Americas—from the perspective of the law as it has developed among the European nations:

> On the discovery of this immense continent, the great nations of Europe were eager to appropriate to themselves so much of it as they could respectively acquire. . . .[11] But, as they were all in pursuit of nearly the same object, it was necessary, in order to avoid conflicting settlements, and consequent war with each other, to establish a principle, which all should acknowledge as the law by which the right of acquisition, which they all asserted, should be regulated as between themselves. This principle was, that discovery gave title to the government by whose subjects, or by whose authority, it was made, against all other European governments, which title might be consummated by possession. (572–573)

What Marshall describes here is what would go down in legal history as the "discovery doctrine": that discovery by European nations conveys territory. Marshall emphasized that the discovery doctrine was the law between European states only and did not touch directly on the relationship between the European and the native nations. Generally, international law emerges through consent between international actors, and those states not consenting to a rule are not bound by it. The logical conclusion to be drawn from Marshall's view is that the European nations made treaties with the Indian nations for the acquisition of land precisely because the land was not already theirs in the first place. The discovery doctrine did not convey full real property from the Indians per se but was primarily directed toward preventing other European nations from claiming it. Marshall added, "Those relations which were to exist between the discoverer and the natives, were to be regulated by themselves" (573).

If the discovery doctrine only binds European nations, what effect does it have for the Indians? Marshall's answer is simple: none. The question for him is not whether the Indians lost rights as legal subjects of *international law*, but which rights were recognized in the *national law* of the European nations, legal systems in which the indigenous nations had no say. The answer to this second question again could have been "none," bolstered by some kind of *terra nullius* assumption. But that is not the answer Marshall gave. In his historical analysis, the European legal systems did indeed recognize indigenous land rights:[12]

> In the establishment of these relations, the rights of the original inhabitants were, in no instance, entirely disregarded; but were necessarily, to a considerable extent, impaired. They were admitted to be the rightful occupants of the soil, with a legal as well as just claim to retain possession of it, and to use it according to their own discretion; but their rights to complete sovereignty, as independent nations, were necessarily diminished, and their power to dispose of the soil at their own will, to whomsoever they pleased, was denied by the original fundamental principle, that discovery gave exclusive title to those who made it. (574)

Marshall clarified that Indians had not lost their rights from an international perspective, but the full extent of their sovereign rights was "disregarded" by the European legal systems. The Europeans saw the Indians as having a right of occupancy to the soil they live on,[13] a right Marshall called "Indian title." Land the native nations held in Indian title was restricted in the sense that they could not sell it "to whomsoever they pleased"; they could sell it only to the European state holding the title of discovery. This restriction was first and foremost directed toward preventing other European nations from purchasing Indian land that another European nation had discovered:

> Conquest gives a title which the Courts of the conqueror cannot deny, whatever the private and speculative opinions of individuals may be, respecting the original justice of the claim which has been

> successfully asserted. The British government, which was then our government, and whose rights have passed to the United States, asserted a title to all the lands occupied by Indians, within the chartered limits of the British colonies. It asserted also a limited sovereignty over them, and the exclusive right of extinguishing the title which occupancy gave to them. These claims have been maintained and established as far west as the river Mississippi, by the sword. The title to a vast portion of the lands we now hold, originates in them. It is not for the Courts of this country to question the validity of this title, or to sustain one which is incompatible with it. (588–589)

This paragraph shows very clearly Marshall's complex model of Indian land rights. First of all, Marshall again clarified that his ruling was grounded in a positivist view of U.S. law, which had an inherent and open bias against the Indians. He described the Supreme Court as a "court of the conqueror" and a "court of this country" (not an international court) that has to decide on the basis of what "*this* country" considers the law of the land. As customary law inherited from its European predecessors, the discovery doctrine had become the law of the United States, "whatever the private and speculative opinions of individuals may be, respecting the original justice of the claim." Marshall indicated that he himself may be one of these private individuals, but that he was acting not as a private person but as a judge in a "court of the conqueror."

Marshall equated the title of the United States to North America to the title a conqueror acquires to the territory of a conquered nation, which, of course, also entails sovereignty over the conquered people.[14] He stated that "most usually, they are incorporated with the victorious nation, and become subjects or citizens of the government with which they are connected. The new and old members of the society mingle with each other; the distinction between them is gradually lost, and they make one people" (589). In that case the rights of the conquered people to their private property remain unimpaired. Marshall argued that this solution was not practicable in the case of the American Indians. Marshall's justification for this comes in one of the judgment's most cited passages:

> But the tribes of Indians inhabiting this country were fierce savages, whose occupation was war, and whose subsistence was drawn chiefly from the forest. To leave them in possession of their country, was to leave the country a wilderness; to govern them as a distinct people,

> was impossible, because they were as brave and as high spirited as they were fierce, and were ready to repel by arms every attempt on their independence.
>
> What was the inevitable consequence of this state of things? The Europeans were under the necessity either of abandoning the country, and relinquishing their pompous claims to it, or of enforcing those claims by the sword, and by the adoption of principles adapted to the condition of a people with whom it was impossible to mix, and who could not be governed as a distinct society, or of remaining in their neighbourhood, and exposing themselves and their families to the perpetual hazard of being massacred. . . .
>
> That law which regulates, and ought to regulate in general, the relations between the conqueror and conquered, was incapable of application to a people under such circumstances. The resort to some new and different rule, better adapted to the actual state of things, was unavoidable. Every rule which can be suggested will be found to be attended with great difficulty. (590–591)

What Marshall argues here is that the savagery of the Indians demanded a different solution from "usual" conquest. The solution the European nations and later the United States' legal system found was that Indians had no fee simple property to their land but something less: Indian title, a property right conveying a right of occupancy but limited in its alienability in that the land could not be bought by anyone other than the government or a private person authorized by the government.

Nevertheless, I would argue that the often-cited passage above ("Indians were fierce savages . . .") is, standing on its own, not representative of Marshall's general line of argumentation in *Johnson v. McIntosh.* At heart Marshall's argument is positivistic and exhibits a certain distance from the legal reasoning of European colonialism regarding Indian rights. So it is not surprising that after this brief excursion into the reasons why the status quo may be not only legal but also reasonable (in terms of natural law), Marshall directly comes back to the "real" topic:

> However extravagant the pretension of converting the discovery of an inhabited country into conquest may appear; if the principle has been asserted in the first instance, and afterwards sustained; if a country has been acquired and held under it; if the property of the

> great mass of the community originates in it, it becomes the law of the land, and cannot be questioned. So, too, with respect to the concomitant principle that the Indian inhabitants are to be considered merely as occupants, to be protected, indeed, while in peace, in the possession of their lands, but to be deemed incapable of transferring the absolute title to others. However this restriction may be opposed to natural right, and to the usages of civilized nations, yet, if it be indispensable to that system under which the country has been settled, and be adapted to the actual condition of the two people, it may, perhaps, be supported by reason, and certainly cannot be rejected by Courts of justice. (591–592)

I believe this passage is far more representative of Marshall's style of argumentation. In short, he is arguing that title by discovery disregards Indian territorial sovereignty to a large extent, but it is the law that he as a judge in the "court of the conqueror" must apply. If Marshall had to apply natural law (meaning international law), he indicates, the decision could be different.

Apart from this positivist argumentation there is a dollop of open pragmatism. Title by discovery is not only customary law, but it is the very basis of the United States as a settler nation—in Marshall's words, "indispensable to that system under which the country has been settled." For Marshall that is another argument why he—as a judge in a U.S. court responsible not for natural justice but foremost for the good of the United States—cannot decide differently. After all, so the core argument goes, the native nations have lost the battle and are now a conquered people. Marshall openly acknowledges the anti-Indian bias that is built into U.S. law, as the whole colonial enterprise must disregard the rights of the original inhabitants to a certain degree. But Marshall bases his decision not on praise for the colonial endeavor or the justice and reasonableness of the principles of title by discovery and racist devaluation of non-European peoples but on this kind of positivistic argument.

What is even more important for the conception of indigenous rights is that this positivist argument, which presupposes a plurality of legal systems, includes some room for the indigenous nations' continuing sovereignty. We see this in a second excursion in his argumentation:

> If an individual might extinguish the Indian title for his own benefit, or, in other words, might purchase it, still he could acquire only that title. Admitting their power to change their laws or usages, so far

> as to allow an individual to separate a portion of their lands from the common stock, and hold it in severalty, still it is a part of their territory, and is held under them, by a title *dependent on their laws.* The grant derives its efficacy from their will; and, if they choose to resume it, and make a different disposition of the land, the Courts of the United States *cannot interpose for the protection of the title. The person who purchases lands from the Indians,* within their territory, incorporates himself with them, so far as respects the property purchased; *holds their title under their protection,* and subject to their laws. If they annul the grant, we know of no tribunal which can revise and set aside the proceeding. (593; emphasis added)

Although this passage is not often cited, I believe it contains a key to understanding Marshall's legal pluralism.[15] On the one hand, Marshall acknowledges in this passage a legal pluralism that recognizes the coexistence of U.S. private law and Indian private law. As John Borrows and Leonard Rotman (1997, 14) put it, "In observing that non-native people could hold title to land under Indian law the court recognized the continued existence of Indian law." This legal pluralism of private law systems emerges from the fact that Indians had been independent nations before conquest. The legal persons of international law are sovereign entities (usually states) who deal with each other on an equal footing. The United States cannot unilaterally decide that another nation has ceased to exist; it can only decide what rights it wants to give the Indians within the framework of the U.S. legal system and to what extent the U.S. legal system recognizes the Indians' ongoing sovereignty.

This has important consequences for a nonindigenous American citizen dealing with an indigenous nation. If the individual were to buy land from the indigenous nation, a dispute concerning that purchase could not come before a U.S. court because U.S. law prohibits private land purchases from Indians. The result would not necessarily be that the private individual had gained nothing because, as the quotation above makes clear, the Indians could still honor the agreement with regard to their law. But that would not concern the U.S. legal system.

When Marshall ruled that Indians have a right of occupancy to their land, alienable only to the federal government (Indian title), we can interpret this as the legal translation of Indian territorial sovereignty into the U.S. legal system. The model of Indian title represents the amount of recognition the U.S. legal system (the system of the conqueror) was willing to grant regarding the territory of a sovereign nation it has conquered. Marshall carefully avoids overstepping his authority and ruling on Indian tribes' international sovereignty (recall that McIntosh's central argument was that Indian tribes were not sovereign nations).

Because of this model, I contend, several legal doors opened up for American Indians. With *Johnson v. McIntosh* and the following two cases I discuss later in the book, the U.S. legal system acknowledged that it would accommodate at least some of the Indians' international sovereignty. This kept the door open to ongoing discussions about how far this sovereignty goes in the U.S. legal system.

Legal Pluralism and Ongoing Indigenous Sovereignty

I have tried to establish that Marshall's model of title by discovery and Indian title emerges out of a complex model of legal pluralism. The plurality is twofold: on the one hand there is international law and national law; on the other there is U.S. law and indigenous law. These spheres (national/international; U.S./indigenous) are separate in principle.

In his seminal article "Original Indian Title," Felix Cohen offers the important advice that "the decisions on Indian title can hardly be understood unless it is recognized that dealings between the Federal Government and the Indian tribes have regularly been handled as part of our international relations" (1947, 43). As such it is important first to systematize the pluralism of national and international legal categories, as they are the basis of Marshall's argumentation.

Nations are the legal persons in international law, and these nations are also usually states in that they are recognized as independent and fully sovereign persons of international law. Nations and states deal with each other on an equal footing. Internally, nations regulate their own affairs by setting up national legal systems. Corresponding to this distinction between national law and international law is the distinction between "property" and "territory." To understand the case, and land rights questions in general, it is paramount to have a clear understanding of these two notions. *Territory* is held by nations. It is a right to land that states or nations claim against other states or nations. *Property*, on the other hand, is a right within the national legal frame. Citizens claim private property vis-à-vis other citizens or the nation-states within which they reside. Alternatively, the nation-state may claim public property in relation to its citizens. *Property* is a category of national law, *territory* a category of international law.

The use of the term "title" obscures this distinction. "Title by discovery" refers to the principle that that the discovering (European) nation receives title (or better, "dominion") over *territory* in North America. "Title by discovery" is therefore a principle of international law: one state holds that title in relation to other states. The fact that a nation-state holds territory says nothing about whether the land also belongs to the state as full public property, because that would be a question of national law. The state parcels out its territory to persons according to its national property system. "Indian title" is, similar to fee simple, a property right to land. It exists within the national logic of the United States' legal system (and other national common-law-influenced legal systems).

With these categories in the back of our mind, what is now—according to Marshall, that is—the legal status of Indians in relation to their land? First of all, from the perspective of international law, the Indian tribes are "states or nations": they have sovereignty over their territory. In this Marshall clearly draws on an established legal argumentation derived from early writings in public international law (Anaya 2004a, 168). From the perspective of U.S. national law, however, the United States can claim "title by discovery" for Indian lands. So according to the United States' legal logic, a large extent of the Indians' territory belongs to the United States. The Europeans and their successors, the United States, have imposed that rule "by the sword." The result is that Indians continue holding their land as territory, but the United States claims it as well. In other words, we have competing territorial claims.

The second result is that Marshall implicitly recognizes not only competing territorial claims (of which only one—namely, the claim of the United States—gains acceptance in U.S. courts) but also competing private law systems. There is the U.S. system, which he represents, and there are the indigenous nations' legal systems, where he has no authority. We have seen above that in one of his argumentative excursions he clearly indicates that Indian tribes can have their own property systems as well as their own court systems in which the rules of their property systems can be enforced. In Marshall's view, the U.S. courts have no business interfering with Indian tribes' legal proceedings.

Marshall's argumentation entails an understanding of himself occupying a certain perspective within the field of tension that exists between national law, international law, U.S. law, and indigenous law. In interpreting *Johnson v.*

McIntosh it is important to understand the basic logic of the four perspectives and situate Marshall's view in this field. He represents, as he clearly admits, the perspective of the national law of the United States.

What is this national perspective of U.S. law? The United States sees Indian country as its territory (that this may not "actually" be the case is a question of international law, and Marshall, as a U.S. judge, is not concerned with that). But does the United States hold the territory on which the Indians still reside in public property as well? Marshall's answer is, "Yes, but . . ." He constructs the following model: the individual states (not the federal government) hold the land in fee simple but are burdened with Indian title. In other words, indigenous lands are the property of the individual states, but that does not help them much because Indian title prevents the state from even entering them. And the right to "extinguish Indian title" (usually through purchase or, in rare cases, by other means) lies with the Union, not the individual states.[16]

What are the differences, then, between regular real estate owners and indigenous nations who hold land in Indian title? In the case of regular real estate owners, the owner holds the land in fee simple, while the states only hold the land as territory. If the state (or the Union) wishes to transform this private property into public property, it must either purchase the land from the private owner or expropriate the land from him or her, with expropriation usually triggering an obligation to pay compensation to the owner. In the case of the indigenous nations, the tribe holds the land in Indian title while the states claim it as their territory *and* hold the land in fee simple. When the state (or the Union) wants to transform indigenous lands in full public property, Indian title must first be extinguished[17] either by purchase or by other means similar to expropriation but with—as we will see in later jurisprudence—fewer obligations to pay compensation.[18]

This puts indigenous nations at a legal disadvantage in relation to other real estate holders, but Indian title as a legal construct is still a relatively effective property interest. The assertion that the states, not the Indians, hold the land in fee simple, although powerful in principle, was still far from *terra nullius*. Indian title was, because of the exclusive power of the federal government to extinguish it, even more effective against the states than regular fee simple. If we take a look at more recent cases that are celebrated as indigenous rights breakthroughs in other common-law countries (one of which, *Delgamuukw v. British Columbia* in Canada, we will investigate later), they all operate on the legal basis of Indian title with explicit reference to *Johnson v. McIntosh*. The large settlements between Maori and New Zealand concerning fishing rights and between Alaska Natives and the United States concerning land recognition are also based on the model of Indian title.

One other disadvantage of Indian title when compared to fee simple is its inalienability (i.e., the inherent prohibition against selling) to anyone but the Union. Considering the centuries-long struggle of American Indians to protect their lands and hold them together, however, the prohibition against selling is—to this day—not the most pressing problem for indigenous movements. That is why the claim to free alienability of indigenous lands by indigenous movements in the international arena is far from front and center. Many argue that when it comes to alienability, nothing should change at all (Engle 2010, 177–181).[19]

Only if one understands Marshall's legal pluralism of national law, international law, U.S. law, and indigenous law is it possible to grasp the opportunities for future indigenous movements to argue on the basis of the sovereignty approach. They were now able to depict themselves as being on the side of international law and Indian law, whereas the United States was on the side of national U.S. law. Future indigenous movements would be able to argue on the basis of *Johnson v. McIntosh* to claim a similarly valid legal position.

Marshall's Explicit Eurocentrism as a Door Opener for Indigenous Rights

Johnson v. McIntosh is heavily concerned with property conceptions. John Locke's major work *Second Treatise on Government* ([1764] 1772) had a great influence on legal debates in the emerging United States. For American radicals like John Adams and Thomas Jefferson, "Locke's famous discussion of natural law and property was regarded as a canonical text" (Williams 1990, 246).

For reasons of space I cannot delve too deeply into Lockean property theory, so some brief remarks on a few of Locke's general ideas will have to suffice. Like all contractualist political philosophers, Locke conceptualizes the political order as based on a fictive social contract. All members of a political order have entered into this social contract, thereby bringing to an end the "state of nature" humans had found themselves in before. In the state of nature there is no established legal system to secure private property, which Locke sees as the very basis of society and political order. Consequently, in the state of nature no private property exists: "The earth, and all that is therein, is given to men for the support and comfort of their being. And though all the fruits it naturally produces, and beasts it feeds, belong to mankind in common, as they are produced by the spontaneous hand of nature; and no body has originally a private dominion" ([1764] 1772, 195). Locke's postulate that every man has property in his own person leads him to the conclusion that everything that man creates from the work of his hands belongs to him as private property:

> Though the earth, and all inferior creatures, be common to all men, yet every man has a *property* in his own *person*: this no body has any right to but himself. The *labour* of his body, and the *work* of his hands, we may say, are properly his. Whatsoever he then removes out of the state that nature hath provided, and left it in, he hath mixed his *labour* with, and joined to it something that is his own, and thereby makes it his *property*. . . . For this *labour* being the unquestionable property of the labourer, no man but he can have a right to what that is once joined to at least where there is enough, and as good, left in common for others. ([1764] 1772, 196; emphasis in original)

In Locke's view property emerges when humans properly use that which originally belongs to all in common. Property emerges not by mere possession or occupation, but by using human labor to transform what nature provides into private property. Humans enter into the social contract precisely because they see it as advantageous to establish a private property system that legally secures this originally produced property.

But in contrast to contemporary contractualists, for Locke the state of nature was not a theoretical fiction. His famous dictum "in the beginning all the world was America" ([1764] 1772, 214) indicates that the native inhabitants of the American continent themselves lived in a prelegal state of nature where no notion of property existed.

In the view of the American radicals (following Lockean principles), the Declaration of Independence is the original social contract for the American continent. This philosophical view renders all social, cultural, and political orders of North American natives invisible, or at least locates them in a nonpolitical "before" of civilization in which notions of private property do not yet exist. This discourse was intended to depict Indians as "before" civilization and society, in a state where they had not yet entered into a social contract. The consequence was that the native nations had no place in the family of independent and civilized nations. The project of the United States of America, then, is presented as British Americans constructing "a society out of a hostile wilderness" (Williams 1990, 247).

Locke's concept of original property emerging through human labor also entails the idea that where there are more than enough common goods available, and their appropriation by private individuals is a right guaranteed by natural law: "On the vast, unenclosed expanses of the American frontier, where the state of nature was experienced as a reality and not as an assumption in service to a theory, denial of this self-preserving right to acquire the Indians' waste lands therefore not only contradicted 'common sense' but natural law" (Williams 1990, 247–248).

Stuart Banner (2005) has highlighted the centrality of discourses of wandering Indians who were not engaging in cultivating the land they lived on. The idea of the Indians still being in a state of nature "Lockean style" was often invoked (2005, 158). Banner highlights "the common perception of the Indian gradually transformed from farmer to hunter, and that had the effect of weakening support among educated Americans for recognizing Indian property rights" (2005, 160). These discourses described by Banner ignored the fact that many native societies were engaged in agriculture at the time of conquest and in colonial times, though often supplementary to hunting and gathering practices. Their agriculture was rendered invisible, while their primary subsistence activities—hunting, fishing, and gathering—were deemed, with reference to a property theory of which John Locke's work was a manifestation, insufficient to establish property on the lands they inhabited: "The more the Indians were perceived as hunters instead of farmers, the less Anglo-Americans would recognize them as owners of the land beneath them" (Banner 2005, 157). Banner argues that this is one important ideological basis for shifting indigenous land rights from fee simple to Indian title, a mere right of occupancy. This shift, which Banner calls "from ownership to occupancy," had taken place since the American Revolution and found its jurisprudential expression in *Johnson v. McIntosh*.[20]

While Marshall's judgment completes this shift "from ownership to occupancy," it is important to note that his argumentation is not based on the idea of the "Lockean savage," despite the fact that it was a discourse he easily could have tapped into. Rather, with reference to customary law and legal pluralism, Marshall argues that the Indians lacked the ability or at least the use practices to hold territory in property. The Indian land rights model in *Johnson v. McIntosh* is far more complex than just denying Indians' land rights. It is about who recognizes whose sovereignty and under what circumstances.

Newcomb (2008) interprets the key argument of *Johnson v. McIntosh* in quite a different light than I have done thus far:

> The injustice that the Court applied to Indian nations had to do with the way that the Court categorized nations: "civilized nations" and "uncivilized nations." . . . European nations were deemed by the Court to possess "perfect independence" and "perfect sovereignty." Indian nations, on the other hand, were deemed by the Court to not be civilized. Since only Christian European "civilized nations" were deemed to possess "perfect independence," this meant that Indian nations considered to be uncivilized were also considered to possess an imperfect independence, or to not be independent. (2008, 75–76)

I do not think that this assessment, which may be representative of how *Johnson v. McIntosh* is usually interpreted, accurately represents Marshall's argument. I would go so far as to contend that Marshall says the exact opposite. Even if the Indian tribes are not as civilized as the European nations and the United States (and some parts of the judgment, though not too many, indicate that Marshall believes this to be the case), this is not the reason for the existence of "title by discovery." From an international legal perspective (Marshall speaks of "abstract justice"), Indian tribes had been completely sovereign nations with unimpaired rights to their territory before conquest. Marshall does not follow McIntosh's argument that Indians—being savages, after all—could never have been international legal persons. Otherwise, Marshall's whole model of deriving the principle of title by discovery from customary law would have been unnecessary. Marshall's argument is not that Indians lost their territory to the United States because of their *legal* inability to retain it (being uncivilized), but because of their *factual* inability. U.S. law derives title by discovery from that part of international law where only European nations had made the rules. The rule of title by discovery is nothing but the legal fiction that "discovering" America was legally the same as "conquering" it. This built-in bias in U.S. law declares that Indian country is U.S. territory. The Indians' purportedly uncivilized state had nothing to do with it, at least not at the heart of the legal argumentation.

From several possible alternative legal discourses Marshall chose one that, pejorative constructions of indigenous savagery notwithstanding, introduces some ideas of relative equality between Indians and Europeans. Both can be nations, form territory, and establish property systems. The relationship between Indians and their land is not fundamentally different from the relationship between Europeans and their land. The legal discrimination against indigenous nations developed in *Johnson v. McIntosh* is, I contend, not based on a radical essentialist discourse of alterity regarding Indians, but on the assumption that the Supreme Court is on the side of the victors of conquest who make the rules in their own property system: "Conquest gives a title which the Courts of the conqueror cannot deny" (588).

I call this line of argumentation "explicit Eurocentrism." Marshall is consciously aware of the inherent bias in the European-derived international legal rule of discovery. It is precisely this open acknowledgment of the Eurocentric bias and the fact that he identifies it, not Indian savagery, as the legal cornerstone of the Indian land regime that opens up strategic opportunities for indigenous nations in U.S. courts. Some kind of *terra nullius* doctrine based on the legal inability of indigenous nations to retain territory would have foreclosed any such opportunities. Now new questions arise: If the Indian tribes had been sovereign states or nations before conquest, how much of this sovereignty have they retained on land they have never ceded? How similar to fee simple is "Indian title"? Must its extinguishment be compensated and, if so, under what circumstances? After all, as Marshall said, "It has never been contended, that the Indian title amounted to nothing" (603). So, if Indian title does amount to more than nothing, what is its scope and content? One effect the legal argumentation in *Johnson v. McIntosh* had, and which is often underestimated in the literature and commentary on the ruling, is that it was the first judicial expression (however incomplete by today's standards) that American Indians could gain something with a legal strategy directed toward the "sovereignty argument."

There is no doubt that the way the discovery doctrine is conceptualized systematically disenfranchises American Indians in the U.S. legal system, and it is still loosely associated with interpretative frames of racial inferiority. But I have tried to argue that in this case Marshall appears to be more of a white pragmatist than a white supremacist. Lindsay Robertson has shown that, for Marshall, the outcome had specific political reasons that had to do with contemporaneous politics (2011, 53–54). But to reach the desired outcome—the stabilization of the status quo—Marshall chose from the possible legal models before him one that was relatively sympathetic toward the indigenous nations. There is no need to praise the chief justice for his philanthropy. As Banner has said, "Marshall may have sympathized with the Indians, but he probably sympathized even more with the settlers and speculators who had been granted parcels of unsold Indian land, a group that included himself, his family, and his friends" (2005, 186).

As a white pragmatist rather than a white supremacist, Marshall developed a legal argument that is akin to a "tough luck" attitude. The United States has decided, in the tradition of European colonialist nations, that it will treat the indigenous nations as conquered. The indigenous nations' territorial sovereignty may be not completely disregarded, but only a shadow of it gets translated into the U.S. legal system. That the indigenous nations are stuck with this is due to the fact that they are now confronted with a legal system they did not give to themselves but which European settlers had established without their consent: that is the Indians' "tough luck."

As cynical as this "explicit Eurocentrism" is from today's perspective, it nevertheless manages to circumvent much fiercer discourses of alterity that we find elsewhere, for example in the arguments of the defense. The "advantage," if one can call it that, of this kind of argumentation is that it leaves open an unspoken alternative history. If things had gone differently on military grounds, Indians would not have to deal with a legal system that Marshall clearly describes as biased; rightfully biased, in his opinion, not primarily because Indians are racially inferior, but primarily because the European settlers had won the war and now consider Indian territory U.S. territory. This cynical "tough luck" attitude contains the seeds of hope for "better luck next time." And indigenous activists would go on to tap into this hope in the form of the "sovereignty approach" to indigenous rights.

* * * *

Johnson v. McIntosh is the first major indigenous rights case in the Americas not only because it laid the groundwork for the principles of U.S. federal Indian law and served as a template for common-law settler states, such as Canada, Australia, and New Zealand, but also, and perhaps more important, because it is the first expression of the "sovereignty argument" for indigenous rights. Marshall's complex legal pluralism of national law, international law, U.S. law, and indigenous law not only justified the legal dispossession of American Indians but also planted the seed for legal resistance against it. Although there was an available legal theory of systematic devaluation of the humanity of indigenous peoples that called into question their ability to institutionalize legal orders—the "Lockean savage" argument—Chief Justice Marshall chose not to put it at the center of his argumentation. Instead he concentrated on a complex positivistic argumentation based on "explicit Eurocentrism," an acknowledged bias within the U.S. court system as the "court of the conqueror." This argument allowed doors to strategies of indigenous rights movements based on the "sovereignty argument" to remain open, most notably the idea that Indian tribes as former persons of international law are still sovereign nations.

CHAPTER 3

"Domestic Dependent Nations" and Indigenous Identity

Cherokee Nation v. Georgia

Cherokee Nation v. Georgia resembles in many aspects contemporary indigenous rights cases.[1] Here the classic constellation emerges: a native community, even referring to itself as a "nation," brings a case against the postcolonial state in whose territory it is located. The Cherokees asked the Supreme Court to prevent the state of Georgia from interfering in their internal affairs and to stop intrusions into their territory. It was the first time an Indian nation brought a case before the Supreme Court; it can serve, therefore, as a precedent-setting example of how the phenomenon of indigeneity took shape and continues to take shape in legal spaces and is tightly bound up with legal doctrine.

But the case would not be decided on the merits. The material legal questions would be addressed later in *Worcester v. Georgia*—at heart the same case but brought by a different claimant against a criminal conviction by a Georgia state court. The Supreme Court decided that it could not adjudicate *Cherokee Nation v. Georgia* because, under article 3 of the U.S. Constitution, the Cherokees could only bring the case if they qualified as a "foreign state." The Supreme Court decided that the Cherokees did not qualify as such, but only after considerable controversy. The fact that three justices issued separate opinions—a practice that, while common today, was still relatively rare in the early decades of the court—indicates just how contested the decision was.

The Case in Context: Indian Sovereignty, States' Rights, and the Abolition of Slavery

For most of the nineteenth century, the federal government dealt with Indian tribes in the form of treaty making, as had Britain, Spain, and France before independence, until Congress decided to end the practice in 1871. In choosing the legal instrument of the treaty, the United States implicitly and often explicitly recognized Indian tribes as sovereign entities of international law with which they could only establish a legal framework based on consensual treaty relations.[2]

As already indicated in the context of *Johnson v. McIntosh* in Chapter 2, the question of land purchases from Indians and more generally the status of Indian tribes had been paramount in the constitutional debates among the thirteen states. As a result of a compromise, the so-called commerce clause of the U.S. Constitution (article 1, section 8, clause 3) transferred all authority to deal with Indian tribes to the federal level. The clause establishes that all authority "to regulate commerce with foreign Nations, and among the several States, and with Indian Tribes" lies with the Union. The commerce clause not only enables the federal government to deal with Indian tribes but also precludes the states from doing so. Naturally, the constitutional debates on Indian issues were seen as embedded in questions of federal and state sovereignty in general, and thus the distribution of power between the federal and the state level. Those different views on state sovereignty and authority and the power struggles connected to it—not least over the issue of who has the authority to abolish or maintain the practice of slavery—would ultimately lead to a civil war in the United States.

The southern states advocated the preeminence of state sovereignty in most, if not all, cases where there was a conflict between federal and state authority.[3] Consequently, the southern states did not welcome federal action to enforce Indian treaty rights against them, especially as the federal government had negotiated the respective treaties without the states' consent. The southern states dismissed what they felt was an illegal intrusion into their sovereignty. These discussions then triggered fear of the growing movement to abolish slavery in the northern states that had begun to dominate Congress. Many people in the South viewed these Indian issues as a "rehearsal for abolition" (Strickland 2011, 63).

The Cherokees on Their Way to Court: From a Political to a Legal Strategy

The conflict between the Cherokee Nation and the state of Georgia was a prime example of a situation that revolved around the question of states' rights. The Cherokees had signed their first treaty with the United States, the Treaty with the Cherokee (also known as the Treaty of Hopewell), in 1785.[4] In this treaty the Union recognized the Cherokees' homeland located inside the territory of Georgia. At that time, the population of the Cherokee nation numbered approximately 16,000 (Fogelson 2004, 341). The state of Georgia was unhappy with the enclave because it had no jurisdiction over Cherokee country, therefore was not allowed to tax the land and its residents nor to permit its citizens to settle in the area. Georgia was, therefore, determined to abolish the special status of Cherokee territory within its borders.

To that end, the state negotiated the so-called Georgia Compact with the federal government in 1803–1804, in which the Union promised to remove all Indians from within Georgia "as soon as it can be done peaceably and upon reasonable terms." This agreement, which ran counter to the Union's treaty obligations to the Cherokees, was a concession granted to Georgia in the course of a compromise: Georgia recognized a western border and thus no longer claimed all lands extending to the Pacific Ocean; in return, the state received the prospect of Cherokee removal. For the next decades, however, the Union did not make good on its promise.

In the late 1820s the conflict between Georgia and the Cherokee nation began to escalate. Illegal settling in Cherokee country by whites intensified when gold was found in the region. In reaction to this intrusion, the Cherokee nation underwent a series of legal reforms that included the passing of a constitution similar to that of the United States and the establishment of a court system including the creation of a Supreme Court for the Cherokee nation. These reforms were intended to underline Cherokee sovereignty over their territory.

Georgia, however, argued that the federal-level Treaty of Hopewell was not binding on the state because of the state's distinct sovereignty and because Cherokee country was a part of Georgia. In 1828 and 1829 the state reacted to the Cherokee legal reforms by passing several laws claiming jurisdiction over Cherokee lands, allowing its citizens to settle there, declaring all Cherokee laws established within the territory of Georgia null and void, and implementing other measures such as barring Cherokee individuals from testifying as witnesses before state courts.[5]

The presidential election of 1828 brought into office Andrew Jackson, who would later become infamous for his brutal anti-Indian policies (Rogin 1975; Satz 1975; Remini 2001). On his initiative, Congress passed the Indian Removal Act one year later. The act, motivated not least by powerful economic interests (Carlson and Roberts 2006), authorized the federal government to set aside lands west of the Mississippi for Indian settlement and funds to cover the costs of resettling large numbers of Indians westward. Going far beyond the measures authorized in the Indian Removal Act, Jackson would later expel Indian nations from their homelands by military force (Cave 2003). One of those communities faced with forced deportation was the Cherokee nation, which had to endure what has come to be known as the "Trail of Tears" (Perdue and Green 1995).

Before the late 1820s the Cherokees had deployed an intergovernmental approach in their dealings with the United States. The Cherokees had always emphasized that they, as a sovereign nation, stood legally on an equal footing with the United States: treaties were made between sovereign governments. After Jackson came into office, he effectively refused to abide by the treaties made by the Union and to enforce the Cherokees' treaty rights against Georgia. In fact, federal officials and military personnel even supported Georgia in enforcing its new laws.

This forced the Cherokees to change their political strategy. It seemed insufficient to deal with the United States merely "from the outside," government to government, as a foreign nation would do; rather, they had to become engaged in the internal political processes of the Union. Thus they began to address the houses of Congress and lobbied against the Indian Removal Act in an effort to avoid removal westward and to stop the dangerous political trend on the federal level. This strategy failed when Congress passed the Indian Removal Act, despite the Cherokees' lobbying efforts.

As a last resort, the Cherokees focused on the U.S. Supreme Court to enforce their treaty rights against Georgia. Part of their legal strategy was to hire as their attorney the highly respected William Wirt, who had been attorney general of the United States in the Monroe and Adams administrations. Wirt's participation and a formidable public relations campaign by Cherokee officials transformed both this trial and the following one, *Worcester v. Georgia*, into highly publicized media events (Strickland 2011, 71). Wirt's strategy was to address the Supreme Court directly about the enforcement of treaty rights, which meant preventing Georgia from imposing legal regulations on Cherokee territory. He therefore filed with the Supreme Court "an injunction, to restrain the State of Georgia . . . from executing and enforcing the laws of Georgia . . . within the Cherokee territory, as designated by treaty between the United States and the Cherokee nation" (2).[6]

To that end Wirt first had to establish the jurisdiction of the Supreme Court. Article 3, section 2 of the U.S. Constitution enumerates the kinds of disputes that can be adjudicated by the Supreme Court. They extend to "controversies . . . between a state or the citizens thereof, and foreign states, citizens or subjects." The controversy was between the state of Georgia and the Cherokee nation. To be under the jurisdiction of the Supreme Court, the Cherokees had to establish that their nation qualified as a "foreign state" in the sense of the provision. And that was exactly how the Cherokees presented themselves when they filed the injunction as "the Cherokee nation of Indians, a foreign state, not owing allegiance to the United States, nor to any state of this union, nor to any prince, potentate, or state, other than their own" (3).

On the surface the outcome of the case was a disappointment. The Supreme Court found the Cherokee nation not to be a foreign state and therefore decided that it could not adjudicate the case. But the decision, which was delivered by six justices at the time, was a two–two–two split. Two justices found the Cherokee nation not to be a state at all, and therefore denied the jurisdiction altogether. On the other side of the spectrum, two justices found that the Cherokee nation qualified as a foreign state in the full sense of the word and wanted to adjudicate the case. Two justices, including Chief Justice Marshall, took the middle road. They found that the Cherokee nation qualified as a state, but was not a foreign state in the sense of article 3, section 2 of the Constitution. The Cherokees' sovereignty had been impaired and they were, from the perspective of U.S. law, something between a foreign state and an entity completely incorporated into the U.S. legal system. The term Marshall found for this was "domestic dependent nation."

In the course of the conflict with Georgia and the federal government the Cherokees' political strategy had been transformed from an intergovernmental approach to an ever closer engagement in the internal affairs of the United States, first by lobbying Congress and finally by becoming a complainant before the U.S. Supreme Court. As the Cherokees lost power as a sovereign political subject, they pushed for becoming a subject of U.S. law—first by receiving favorable legislation from Congress and finally by winning a fair judgment from the Supreme Court. But while seeking the help of a "foreign" legal system, they also portrayed themselves as being subject to no law but their own.

The Cherokees' Autoethnography

In the first chapter I have discussed how the judgments of indigenous rights cases can be seen as ethnographic texts and how they produce a mélange out of the other ethnographic and autoethnographic texts that the parties have brought to the attention of the court. In the case of *Johnson v. McIntosh*, these autoethnographic aspects brought in by the Cherokees are of interest because they shed light on a legal and discursive strategy that is typical of interactions that occur in the "contact zone."

Mary Louise Pratt's notion of the contact zone as "social spaces where cultures meet, clash, and grapple with each other, often in contexts of highly asymmetrical relations of power such as colonialism, slavery, or their aftermaths as they are lived out in many parts of the world today" (1991, 34) can easily characterize the courtroom in *Cherokee Nation v. Georgia*. In my view, the most important aspect of the contact zone is not the "contact," but the "asymmetrical power relations." The Cherokees were under severe pressure from federal and state intrusions; their contact with the U.S. court system was clearly not on an equal footing.

The Cherokees set forth their claim in a "bill" (that is, their written motion) to the Supreme Court. In it, the Cherokees complain about the acts the Georgia legislature had enacted on their territory. In their view Georgia lacks the authority to enact such regulation, and the enforcement of these laws would infringe on the Cherokees' rights as a sovereign nation. They speak directly to the most controversial legal issue, their own legal status. The Cherokees characterize themselves as follows:

> The Cherokee nation of Indians, *a foreign state*, not owing allegiance to the United States, nor to any state of this union, nor to any other prince, potentate, or state, other than their own:
>
> That, from time immemorial, the Cherokee nation have composed *a sovereign and independent state*, and in this character have been repeatedly recognized, and still stand recognized by the United States, in the various treaties subsisting between their nation and the United States.

> That, long before the first approach of the white men of Europe to the western continent, the Cherokee nation were the occupants and owners of the territory on which they now reside; deriving their title from the Great Spirit, who is the common father of the human family, and to whom the earth belongs.
>
> That on this territory they and their ancestors, composing the Cherokee nation, have ever been, and still are, *the sole and exclusive masters, and governed, of right, by no other laws, usages and customs, but such as they have themselves thought proper to ordain and appoint.* (3; emphasis added)

After this self-description, which includes contentions regarding their territorial sovereignty, the Cherokees unfold a history of land acquisition by white colonists. The story had been told in the framework of the U.S. Supreme Court before, most famously in the case *Johnson v. McIntosh* (see Chapter 2), but the difference this time is that the history of colonial land acquisition is told from the perspective of a native nation. The way the Cherokees present their claim can be seen as an indigenous articulation: they "play themselves" for the nonindigenous audience and engage in an "indigenous performance." We will see that these indigenous articulations and performances, although in many points deviating from mainstream legal discourse, are deeply dependent on what the nonindigenous audience is willing and able to accept. Nonindigenous expectations are as important as indigenous discourses for the way indigeneity is articulated and performed.

The story begins with a grant in 1732 by King George II, whom the Cherokees describe as a "monarch of several islands on the eastern coast of the Atlantic ocean [i.e., Britain]" (3). At the time of the royal grant the land between the Savannah and Altamaha rivers was "occupied and owned by several distinct, sovereign, and independent nations of Indians, and, among others by the Cherokee nation." The basis of this royal grant, from which the United States derives its territorial title to the region, is the right of discovery, to which, the Cherokees point out, "the Indian proprietors have never given their assent; and which they deny to be a principle of the natural law of nations, or obligatory on them" (4). The Cherokees describe this "discovery": "A ship manned by [. . . the King's] subjects had, about two centuries and a half before, sailed along the coast of the western hemisphere, from the fifty-sixth to the thirty-eighth degree of north latitude, and looked upon the face of that coast without even landing on any part of it" (3–4). From such "discovery," they argue, there could have arisen no legal effect for the Cherokee nation. But if the court should find that the right of discovery existed, such a right for the European nations meant only "that the first European discoverer has the prior and exclusive right to purchase these lands from the Indian proprietors," and nothing approaching a property title for the discoverer per se: "It never was alleged by George II. the king of Great Britain and Ireland . . . any right to disturb or to question the exclusive right of possession by the Indians, or to interfere in any manner with their own self government within their respective dominions. That, on the contrary, the first adventurers . . . entered into a treaty with . . . the Indians . . . and received from them a voluntary cession of a part of those lands for a valuable consideration; . . . no pretension having been then, or at any subsequent time, set up that the charter conferred . . . any authority to introduce the system of British laws into the country owned by the Indians" (4). The Cherokees argue that both the state of Georgia and the Union (like the British before them) had always acknowledged Cherokee sovereignty by making several treaties with them, among them the Treaty of Hopewell of 1785, the Treaty of Holston of 1791, and, most recently, the Treaty of Washington of 1819, "in all of which the said Cherokee nation, and other nations have been recognized as sovereign and independent states" (4). Consequently, the Cherokees still possess "both the exclusive right to their territory, and the exclusive right of self government within that territory" (4).

According to the Cherokees, all the treaties show "an anxious desire" by the United States "to lead the Cherokees to a greater degree of civilization, and to induce them to become *herdsmen* and *cultivators*, instead of remaining in their original *hunter* state" (9). In this desire the United States had engaged in a policy that linked removal of the Cherokees to the presumed lack of development of Cherokee society and civilization. The understanding was that if the Cherokees could lift up their level of civilization, then they could remain on their territory. In this passage we encounter the same discourse discussed in Chapter 2. Mainstream Anglo-American property theory as manifested in Locke's political philosophy equates civilization with certain forms of appropriating nature: while agriculture is a form of land use that creates private property for the agriculturalists, hunting and gathering do not represent the same degree of effort and labor and therefore do not establish the bond of property to the land.

The implicit agreement underpinning the various treaties is to tolerate the Cherokees' territorial enclave inside Georgia if they use the land properly. If the Cherokees "only" used the land for hunting and gathering, their ties to the land would remain "loose," leaving "the country in a wilderness," to use Marshall's words from *Johnson v. McIntosh*, and the land would not be considered their "property." Consequently, it would be a violation of natural law (as Locke and most U.S. lawyers would interpret it) to keep perfectly good lands from settlers willing to use it properly by cultivating it. The settlers' natural law right to economic enterprise would then far outweigh the Indians' right to hunt and gather on land that cannot be considered their property. According to this legal opinion, the United States argued that hunting and gathering in the unappropriated wilderness could be done just as well west of the Mississippi, which was not (yet) part of the Union.

As an indigenous articulation, it is remarkable that the Cherokee bill did not argue against this theory of law or this way of conceptualizing civilization. On the contrary, the Cherokees took the United States at its word and directed attention to the progress that the Cherokee nation had already made to civilize itself. In other words, if "civilization" is what it was going to take to be recognized as a sovereign nation, then that was what the Cherokees were willing to implement. They therefore listed the measures they had taken to fulfill their part of the bargain:

> They have established a constitution and form of government; the leading features of which they have borrowed from that of the United States; dividing their government into three separate departments, legislative, executive and judicial. In conformity with this constitution, these departments have all been organized: they have formed a code of laws, civil and criminal, adapted to their situation; have erected courts to expound and apply those laws, and organized an executive to carry them into effect. They have established schools for the education of their children, and churches in which the Christian religion is taught; they have abandoned the hunter state and become agriculturists, mechanics, and herdsmen; and, under provocations long continued and hard to be borne, they have observed, with fidelity, all their engagements by treaty with the United States. (11)

It is interesting here to note how the bill highlights the Cherokee legal system, with its features so similar to the U.S. legal system. The Cherokees were aiming to establish their legal personhood as a sovereign state under international law. To that end they had to prove that they were "civilized" in a Euro-American fashion.

For them to argue against Lockean inspired property theory and the concept of civilization connected with it surely would have been pointless. Virtually the entire national project of the United States was—and to a great extent still is—founded on the idea that every regulation restricting the economic enterprise of private individuals against natural law was illegitimate. This economic enterprise was based first and foremost on appropriating land still in its natural state and transforming it into original property through the work of one's own hands, usually by cultivating it. As we have seen in the Chapter 2, the Royal Proclamation of 1763 was resisted so fiercely because it represented just such an illegitimate regulation issued by an illegitimate government.

The Cherokees could argue in terms of territory and property—these were notions Anglo-Americans understood. But they could not argue that they chose *not* to use their lands with due and industrious agricultural activity but only to the degree they needed for a comfortable life, when others wanted to make their fortune too. The indigeneity discourse the Cherokees promoted was therefore clearly intended to show that they were equal to the white settlers in terms of civilization, a point they made quite explicitly:

> Under the promised "*patronage, aid* and *good neighbourhood*" of the United States, they have become *civilized, Christians*, and *agriculturists*; and have no more land than is sufficient for their subsistence and that of their posterity. . . . In all these respects they are willing that a comparison shall be instituted between them and their white brethren around them . . . If practicing justice, and the doing to others as we would have them do unto us, be the tests of civilization and Christianity, and the proportion of the cultivators of the soil to the whole number of the population be the test of the agricultural character of a nation, with reference to the theory in question, they apprehend that they have at least as little reason as their white brethren around them to shrink from such tests. (12)

After establishing their progress in reaching the necessary level of civilization, the Cherokees came back to the legal heart of the case: the question of federal and state jurisdiction. They argued that the treaties they made with the United States are the "supreme law of the land," and the individual states, Georgia included, must abide by them. Most important, with the creation of the United States all power to negotiate treaties and regulate commerce with

Indian tribes had been transferred to the Union. The Constitution declares that Indian affairs are under the authority of the federal government, "and consequently forbids all interference by any one of the states" (7). The state of Georgia had no business meddling in Indian affairs.

The Cherokees argued that the land cessions they had made had all been voluntary and were an expression of their national sovereignty. In other words, if they had not held their land legitimately, the federal government would not have had to negotiate with the Cherokees for its cession. "The Cherokee nation went on amicably to meet the wishes of the United States and of the state of Georgia, by ceding, from time to time, as much of their lands as they could spare, until, by the cession of 1819, they had reduced their territory into as small a compass as their own convenience would bear; and they then accordingly resolved to cede no more" (16). Here mainstream property theory appears again. The Cherokees implicitly argued that they ceded as much land as they were willing to give to the United States for others to use properly. The rest, which they kept for themselves, was their core territory, which they have already begun to use properly and in a civilized manner, through agriculture. From this rest of their former territory they would cede nothing more and—by extension—nobody could demand it from them under arguments of natural law.

The Cherokees then brought up the Indian Removal Act, which had been passed by Congress in 1830. According to the Cherokees, the act only applied to those Indians who chose freely to leave their territory in exchange for lands west of the Mississippi, and "nothing therein contained shall be construed as authorising or directing the violation of any existing treaty between the United States and any of the Indian tribes" (18). They again clearly stated that they have ultimately decided not to move westward.

Finally the Cherokees come to the salient question of Supreme Court jurisdiction. Arguing that they are a "foreign state" in the sense of the Constitution, they described their desperate situation. The state of Georgia intrudes into their vested treaty rights and their courts provide no judicial forum. The United States refuses to provide any help against Georgia. In fact, its troops would even co-operate with the civil officers of Georgia in enforcing state law upon them. The violation of their rights is unbearable. The Supreme Court is—apart from military force, which they do not want to resort to—their last hope. In their own words: "these complainants are wholly without remedy of any kind, except by the interposition of this honourable court, they have as little hesitation in averring" (28).

Inventing the "Domestic Dependent Nation"

It is again Chief Justice Marshall who writes the majority opinion in *Cherokee Nation v. Georgia.* In his very first sentences he indicates his sympathy with the Cherokees' claim:

> If courts were permitted to indulge their sympathies, a case better calculated to excite them could scarcely be imagined. A people once numerous, powerful, and truly independent, found by our ancestors in the quiet and uncontrolled possession of an ample domain, gradually sinking beneath our superior policy, our arts and our arms, have yielded their lands by successive treaties, each of which contains a solemn guarantee of the residue, until they retain no more of their formerly extensive territory than is deemed necessary for their comfortable subsistence. To preserve this remnant, the present application is made. (159)

It is remarkable that Marshall begins which such conciliatory, albeit paternalistic, language. From a legal standpoint, the depiction of the Cherokees as a completely independent nation before conquest is quite remarkable. The adjectives Marshall uses—"numerous, powerful, and truly independent" and in "quiet and uncontrolled possession" of their territory—are notable because they represent the style of Marshall's depiction of Indianness. He uses attributes that neither convey the image of a particularly "civilized" society nor evoke the usual images of savagery. These are words one could attribute to any nation, but only to "nations" in the true sense of the word: independent legal persons as understood in international law. Without especially valuing Cherokee culture, he also shows a certain reluctance to evoke the "Lockean savage."[7]

After these preliminary remarks Marshall immediately comes to the key question of the case: jurisdiction. He explains that according to article 3, section 2 of the Constitution, a "foreign state" may bring a case before the Supreme Court against one of the states of the Union. Georgia, as one of the states of the United States, can therefore be sued. The question is whether the Cherokee nation can bring a suit before the Supreme Court. To do so, the Cherokee nation would have to qualify as a "foreign state." Marshall begins with the determination that the complainant's argument, as much as it was "intended to prove the character of the Cherokees as a state, as a distinct political society, separated from others, capable of managing its own affairs and governing itself, has, in the opinion of a majority of the judges, been completely successful" (160). Marshall also concurs with the Cherokees' argument that the United States had always accepted Cherokee sovereignty by regularly making (international) treaties with them.

Marshall then elaborated on a question that the Cherokees had only addressed in passing. The Constitution demands that the complainant be a "foreign state." The "state" part had been settled for Marshall, but what about the "foreign" part? Marshall argued that, while it was to be granted that the Cherokees are a sovereign state, they were not foreign to the United States. To establish this contention he first repeats the Cherokees' central argument: "The counsel have shown conclusively that they are not a state of the union, and have insisted that individually they are aliens, not owing allegiance to the United States. An aggregate of aliens composing a state must, they say, be a foreign state. Each individual being foreign, the whole must be foreign" (160). Marshall rebuffs this logic by arguing that the relationship between the United States and the Indian tribes would be significantly different from those of the United States and other foreign states: "The condition of the Indians in relation to the United States is perhaps unlike that of any other people in existence. . . . The relation of the Indians to the United States is marked by peculiar and cardinal distinctions which exist no where else" (160).

Marshall explains these peculiarities: "The Indian territory is admitted to compose a part of the United States" (161), as had already been established in *Johnson v. McIntosh*. The British had gained this territory by discovery, and the United States legally succeeded the British in that respect. Consequently the indigenous nations "are considered as within the jurisdictional limits of the United States, subject to many of those restraints which are imposed upon our own citizens" (161).

The Cherokees themselves had accepted this fact in the same treaties they quote to validate their contention that the United States had recognized their sovereignty: "They acknowledge themselves in their treaties to be under the protection of the United States; they admit that the United States shall have the sole and exclusive right of regulating the trade with them, and managing all their affairs as they think proper" (161). Accordingly, the Cherokees had been allowed in the Treaty of Hopewell to send a deputy to Congress, which indicates that they acknowledged that important decisions regarding them were now made in Washington (161).[8] Marshall then concludes with the most frequently cited passage of the judgment:

> Though the Indians are acknowledged to have an unquestionable, and, heretofore, unquestioned right to the lands they occupy, until that right shall be extinguished by a voluntary cession to our government; yet it may well be doubted whether those tribes which reside within the acknowledged boundaries of the United States can, with strict accuracy, be denominated foreign nations. They may, more correctly, perhaps, be denominated *domestic dependent nations*. They occupy a territory to which we assert a title independent of their will, which must take effect in point of possession when their right of possession ceases. Meanwhile they are in a state of pupilage. *Their relation to the United States resembles that of a ward to his guardian.* (161; emphasis added)

This remarkable phrase "domestic dependent nation" encapsulates a number of concepts that need to be unpacked. First, it acknowledges the sovereign character of the Indians with the word "nation." In certain ways the indigenous nations are "dependent" on the sovereignty of the United States. But they are "domestic," a term that signals that they are not foreign in the sense of the constitutional provision in question. This term "domestic dependent nation" grammatically embodies what I have called "the indigenous paradox": the Cherokees are foreign *and* domestic at the same time.

Marshall summarizes that "the court has bestowed its best attention on this question, and, after mature deliberation, the majority is of opinion that an Indian tribe or nation within the United States is not a foreign state in the sense of the constitution, and cannot maintain an action in the courts of the United States" (164).

The Idea of "Domestic Dependent Nation" and the Indigenous Paradox

Two justices, William Johnson and Henry Baldwin, agreed with the majority judgment, but only regarding the result, namely that the Cherokees' case could not be entertained by the Supreme Court. Contrary to the majority opinion written by Marshall, they did not think of the Cherokees as a domestic dependent nation; in fact, they refused to recognize the Cherokees as any kind of state at all. But with their votes the majority of four to two was secured.

Justices Smith Thompson and Joseph Story, however, both disagreed with the judgment. They believed that the Cherokee nation was a foreign state in the sense of the Constitution. The dissenting opinion, written by Thompson, asserts that sovereign states do not lose their sovereignty through conquest, a then well-established principle of international law:

> We ought therefore to reckon in the number of sovereigns those states that have bound themselves to another more powerful, although by an unequal alliance. The conditions of these unequal alliances may be infinitely varied; but whatever they are, provided the inferior ally reserves to itself the sovereignty or the right to govern its own body, it ought to be considered an independent state. . . . Tributary and feudatory states do not thereby cease to be sovereign and independent states, so long as self government, and sovereign and independent authority is left in the administration of the state. (197)

Measured on this scale, according to Thompson, "it is not perceived how it is possible to escape the conclusion, that they [the Cherokees] form a sovereign state" (197). Thompson also maintains, contrary to the majority, that the Cherokees are a *foreign* state. In his view, for a sovereign entity to become something other than foreign to the United States, it must have lost its sovereignty at some point:

> And if the Cherokees were then a foreign nation; when or how have they lost that character, and ceased to be a distinct people, and become incorporated with any other community?
>
> They have never been, by conquest, reduced to the situation of subjects to any conqueror, and thereby lost their separate national existence, and the rights of self government, and become subject to the laws of the conqueror. (198)

Thompson's argument that Indian tribes are foreign states is rooted in the original character of "Indian title" that the Supreme Court had established in *Johnson v. McIntosh*. Indians have a right of occupancy to their former territory, which has its roots not in a grant by the United States but in a reservation of sovereignty, "accompanied with the right of self government, according to their own usages and customs; and with the competency to act in a national capacity, although placed under the protection of the whites, and owing a qualified subjection so far as is requisite for public safety. But the principle is universally admitted, that this occupancy belongs to them as a matter of right, and not by mere indulgence (199)." Thompson makes an important point in this passage: *Johnson v. McIntosh* had established that "Indian title"—the Indians' right of occupancy to their land—is the legal translation of their former full territorial sovereignty into the U.S. legal system. The United States recognizes and accommodates the full sovereignty of Indians only in a diminished form, but the right itself has its origins not *inside* but *outside* the U.S. legal system. "Indian title" is therefore not a mere "indulgence" of the U.S. legal system. For Thompson this indicates that the Indians are not incorporated into the United States and they are not fully subject to U.S. law in the way a conquered people would be. The Cherokees still have sovereign rights, but in Thompson's opinion this argument is not valid for all Indians. In his argumentation he refers

> only to such as live together as a distinct community, under their own laws, usages and customs; and not to the mere remnant of tribes which are to be found in many parts of our country, who have become mixed with the general population of the country: their national character extinguished; and their usages and customs in a great measure abandoned; self government surrendered; and who have voluntarily, or by the force of circumstances which surrounded them, gradually become subject to the laws of the states within which they are situated. (204)

This argument raises an issue that is crucial to every indigenous rights case: if an indigenous nation once had sovereignty, it can lose it by abandoning the ties that bind its members together as an entity. Those communities indistinguishable from the rest of society with no remnants of the original bond created in pre-European times—whether it be political or cultural—cannot be called sovereign nations. This aspect of distinctiveness is ineluctable for indigenous rights claims because they require a rights holder who is able to enforce rights stemming from within a distinct legal system.

This insistence on distinctiveness, without which every indigenous rights claim must fail, is only one half of the indigenous paradox. The indigenous community also needs the (post)colonial state to protect "their" rights. Although indigenous rights must be seen as originating outside the (post) colonial state, the indigenous community has to be within the (post)colonial state just enough to claim the protection of its legal system. So would being a "foreign state" in the sense of the U.S. Constitution actually help the Cherokees' cause, as the two dissenting judges seem to think? On this question we find elaboration where we would least expect it—in the separate opinion of Justice Johnson, the denier of Cherokee sovereignty.

Johnson sees no room for Indian sovereignty after colonial discovery and the rights it conferred on the European nations: "When the eastern coast of this continent, and especially the part we inhabit, was discovered, finding it occupied by a race of hunters, connected in society by scarcely a semblance of organic government; the right was extended to the absolute appropriation of territory, the annexation of it to the domain of the discoverer" (166). Analyzing the language of treaties between the United States and Indian nations, especially the highly relevant Treaty of Hopewell, Johnson concludes: "This is certainly the language of sovereigns and conquerors, and not the address of equals to equals. . . . Certainly this is the language of concession on our part, not theirs" (167).

But Johnson does not stop there. He subsequently asks the highly interesting question of what would happen if the court found that the Cherokees were indeed a "foreign state." Even in this case, he argues, the Supreme Court would be unable to assume jurisdiction over the Cherokees' claim: "I cannot entertain a doubt that it [the Cherokees' claim] is one of a political character altogether, and wholly unfit for the cognizance of a judicial tribunal. There is no possible view of the subject, that I can perceive, in which a court of justice can make jurisdiction of the questions made in the bill" (172). What Johnson addresses here is the so-called political question doctrine, a legal rule that permits the Supreme Court to recuse itself in cases that involve political issues more appropriately resolved by the political branches of government (Green 2005, 723).[9] Johnson argues that if the Cherokees see themselves as a foreign state and Georgia imposes its laws upon them and enforces its regulations with violence, this situation would effectively characterize a state of war. The questions arising would be highly political and not for the judiciary to decide. As Johnson puts it, "Either the Cherokee nation are a foreign state, or they are not. If they are not, then they cannot come here [to the Supreme Court]; and if they are then how can we extend our jurisdiction into their country? . . . But suppose that Georgia should claim to be put in possession of the whole Indian country; and we should decide in her favor; how is that decree to be carried into effect?" (173–174).

Johnson's opinion is highly relevant for the model of the indigenous paradox I have introduced at the beginning. At many points in the cases presented here we come to the point where the indigenous claimants have to signal their difference from mainstream society and the national legal system. But the paradoxical nature of indigeneity demands that the indigenous claimant must be similar *and* dissimilar. It is my contention that being recognized as a "foreign state" by the national courts would exactly lead to the consequences Johnson describes: the native nation's claim could not be entertained by the Supreme Court because it would be outside the scope of the laws of the (post)colonial state.

As we have seen, *Cherokee Nation v. Georgia* was not a unanimous decision. Three different legal opinions emerged in the Supreme Court, of which one—Marshall's—served as a compromise. The first opinion we already know from *Johnson v. McIntosh*. It follows the line of thought the defendant McIntosh had advocated: Indians are uncivilized savages, in a state of nature, incapable of sovereignty or property rights. Therefore they are not even states, let alone "foreign states" in the sense of the Constitution. This extreme argumentation never became the basis of federal Indian law.

The two other opinions are of interest to us: either the Cherokee nation is a foreign state or it is neither a foreign state nor part of the United States but something in between—a domestic dependent nation. I believe this neologism of Marshall's describes very well what I call the indigenous paradox. The sovereignty argument that the Cherokees mobilized in *Cherokee Nation v. Georgia* exemplifies this paradox: on the one hand the Cherokees assert territorial sovereignty and see the treaties made with the United States as treaties between sovereign states; on the other hand they bring a case before a court of the United States, which implies a degree of subjection to the United States.

International sovereigns usually do not interact in this manner. If two sovereigns have a dispute, they have basically three options: negotiation; joint subjugation to an international body to settle the dispute (say, an international court); or violence in its several forms. In the case of the Cherokees, negotiations had failed, an international court was not available, and violence was not an option for reasons of clear military inferiority.

Mobilizing the counterpart's own court system to enforce international treaty rights is more of a theoretical option. If a national court were to entertain such a case, it would have to encroach far into a domain—international relations—that is clearly under the authority of the executive branch. If a foreign state wants to bring a case before a national court, it is usually only disputes related to private law that can be entertained, not those of public law. In other words, to bring a case before the Supreme Court as a sovereign foreign state has a certain whiff of the paradoxical about it because the very act contradicts the allegedly purely international character of the relationship between the native nation and the United States. That was an articulation of indigeneity in the sense I am putting forward in this book.

* * * *

Cherokee Nation v. Georgia is often referred to only as a prelude to *Worcester v. Georgia* and for providing the phrase "domestic dependent nation." I have argued in this chapter that *Cherokee Nation* is the first indigenous rights case in the Americas in the sense that it strongly resembles contemporary cases in which an indigenous community sues the state it resides in. Consequently, the judgment entails an autoethnographic account of the Cherokees that can be read as revealing the strategy of an indigenous nation in the contact zone. Indigenous identity emerges as unequally dependent not only on what indigenous communities want to say but even more on what the nonindigenous audience is willing to hear. This strategy also reveals the indigenous paradox of being sovereign *and* dependent at the same time, a paradox rooted in the everyday reality of indigenous peoples. Marshall's neologism of "domestic dependent nation" is the legal expression of the paradoxical nature of indigeneity: an inevitable phenomenon every indigenous rights approach must accommodate through a conceptual model of legal pluralism.

CHAPTER 4

How to Win with the Sovereignty Approach

Worcester v. Georgia

What *Cherokee Nation v. Georgia* had left for the Cherokees was "an open invitation, encouraging them to find another case, and even hinting at the possibility of a positive outcome" (Strickland 2011, 72). Chief Justice Marshall had said that "the mere question of right might perhaps be decided by this court in a proper case with proper parties" (Peters 1831, 164). The Cherokees' legal representative William Wirt took it upon himself to find a proper party, which he did in the person of missionary and translator Samuel A. Worcester.[1]

Worcester v. Georgia put the general principles of federal Indian law to the test.[2] Were those indigenous rights that had been acknowledged by the Supreme Court—namely, "Indian title," "tribal sovereignty," and the federal government's exclusive authority to engage in Indian affairs—able to effectively repel Georgia's incursions into Cherokee territory? The case was a success in the courtroom but in the end did not prevent the Cherokees' Trail of Tears. Nevertheless, *Worcester v. Georgia* is a landmark case for indigenous rights because it established the basic outlines of the "sovereignty approach" to indigenous rights in the United States and beyond.

Finding Another Plaintiff Against Georgia

Samuel A. Worcester lived and worked as a missionary on the Cherokee territory and openly supported their sovereignty and treaty rights. As a protest against Georgia's legal intrusions, he intentionally did not comply with Georgia's regulation obliging all whites to obtain a license if they wanted to reside on Cherokee territory.[3] In March 1831 the Georgia State Guard arrested Worcester and other missionaries and eventually tried them before the Superior Court of the County of Gwinnett.[4] Worcester and the other defendants claimed in their defense that the Gwinnett County court had no jurisdiction in Cherokee land and that the laws that were the basis of their indictment were null and void for three reasons: (1) they ran counter to the treaties the United States had made with the Cherokees, and the U.S. Constitution declares all such treaties to be the supreme law of the land;[5] (2) any legal interference by the state of Georgia on Indian territory contradicts the federal government's constitutionally established exclusive authority over Indian affairs; and (3) Georgia's law was in direct violation of the Indian Non-Intercourse Acts. The court dismissed this defense and convicted Worcester and his fellow missionaries, sentencing them to four years of hard labor in September 1831. Worcester and his associates decided to bring the case before the Supreme Court. Worcester was an ideal plaintiff, as Strickland describes: "He was as articulate as he was determined and the press took to his cause, which came to symbolize the power of a giant state oppressing an individual standing on moral principle in defense of the wronged. Worcester's long letters from the Milledgeville jail were reprinted in *The Cherokee Phoenix* and received wider circulation in other papers and missionary circles as well" (2011, 73).[6]

William Wirt, who had represented the Cherokees in *Cherokee Nation v. Georgia,* served also as the attorney for Worcester and his fellow missionaries. Together they brought the case before the Supreme Court. There the plaintiffs contended that the laws Georgia had enacted and under which Worcester and his companions had been indicted and convicted were unconstitutional for all the reasons Worcester and his fellow defendants had already pointed out in the criminal proceedings before the Superior Court in Gwinnett County. As in *Cherokee Nation v. Georgia*, the state of Georgia refused to take part in the proceedings, contending that the federal Supreme Court had no jurisdiction to review state court criminal proceedings.

This time the Supreme Court ruled on the merits. The opinion of the court, delivered again by Chief Justice Marshall, was that the state court's criminal conviction against Worcester was unconstitutional. The federal government's authority to engage in Indian affairs precluded the state of Georgia from interfering. The judgment was a political bomb. President Andrew Jackson, who was a strong proponent of Indian removal and sympathized with Georgia's anti-Cherokee policies, was furious with Marshall's decision. Referring to the outcome of the case, Jackson is reported to have said, "Marshall has made his law, now let him enforce it," thus clearly asserting that federal troops would not intervene in Georgia on behalf of the Cherokees.[7] Tragically, the provocative Supreme Court decision even accelerated Jackson's removal policy. Georgia stepped up pressure for the Cherokees to be removed westward. The state had given up land claims in the West to join the Union, but had negotiated with the federal government that, in return, the state would have full control over all state territory. Cherokee country was in the way. Strickland summarizes the situation as follows: "Marshall had the law, Jackson had the troops" (2011, 76).[8]

After Jackson was elected for his second term in 1834, a majority of the Cherokees, faced with the threat of military force, agreed to be removed. In the wake of this majority decision, the Cherokees were plunged into a civil war between those who were willing to give in to removal and those who hoped that the Supreme Court decision would still have its effect in the future (Perdue 1989). The first faction resettled to Oklahoma in 1836–1837, the second faction, consisting of 16,000 Cherokees, was driven out of their homeland by federal troops in 1838–1839 in what has come to be known as the "Trail of Tears." More than 4,000 did not survive the forced deportation. The civil war among the Cherokees continued in Oklahoma, and many tribal leaders lost their lives even after removal.[9]

While the Supreme Court decision and its acknowledgment of the principle of tribal sovereignty was not able to prevent these tragic events in Cherokee history, the doctrine of federal Indian law had changed substantially. For nearly fifty years the idea of federally guaranteed Indian territorial sovereignty held up. In general, states could not exert jurisdiction over Indian country. This principle started to get watered down, but not before the end of the nineteenth century.[10]

Winning with the Sovereignty Approach

Marshall first dipped into the question of the Supreme Court's jurisdiction over the matter, not least because of the heated debates over conflicting jurisdiction that dominated the legal discourse at that time. In his view there were no legal difficulties (536–541). Worcester was a citizen of Vermont, not of Georgia. Article 3, section 2, clause 1 of the U.S. Constitution, which granted the Supreme Court jurisdiction in "Controversies . . . between a State and Citizens of another State," and the Judicial Act, which operationalized this constitutional provision, clearly provided a legal basis for his suit against Georgia. The Supreme Court summarized that it was "too clear for controversy, that the act of congress, by which this court is constituted, has given it the power, and of course imposed on it the duty, of exercising jurisdiction in this case. This duty, however unpleasant, cannot be avoided" (541). In his elaboration on the merits of the case, Marshall seized the opportunity to lay out further the legal construction of the basis of federal Indian law and its underlying principle: the discovery doctrine.

He first described the legal situation on the American continent before the arrival of the Europeans: "America, separated from Europe by a wide ocean, was inhabited by a distinct people, divided into separate nations, independent of each other and of the rest of the world, having institutions of their own, and governing themselves by their own laws" (542–543). With that description Marshall underlines his view that the indigenous nations indeed had been sovereign nations before discovery and conquest by the Europeans. This was under debate at the time. In *Johnson v. McIntosh* the plaintiffs had asserted the view that Indians did not have the necessary level of cultural development or sophistication to conceive of property rights or the rule of law, and therefore could not be considered sovereign entities. Marshall had already rebuffed this argument in *Johnson v. McIntosh* and reiterates this idea even more forcefully in this case: "It is difficult to comprehend the proposition, that the inhabitants of either quarter of the globe could have rightful original claims of dominion over the inhabitants of the other, or over the lands they occupied; or that the discovery of either by the other should give the discoverer rights in the country discovered, which annulled the pre-existing rights of its ancient possessors" (543). Subsequently he poses a series of questions about what the Europeans might have thought when they first arrived on the American coast about "a people who had made small progress in agriculture or manufactures, and whose general employment was war, hunting, and fishing" (543). Could it really be possible that landing on the American coast and establishing small settlements could give them a rightful dominion over the American continent? Could it have been that "nature, or the great Creator of all things, conferred these rights over hunters and fishermen, on agriculturists and manufacturers" (543)?

He does not answer his own questions—not because they were rhetorical questions the answers to which were so obvious that they do not need to be answered, but because they are philosophical questions that *cannot* be answered easily, if at all. Marshall implies that, as a judge who is only entitled to address questions that the law is able to answer, he is not competent to answer philosophical questions. He therefore simply stops asking and hints—in a typical Marshall-like move—at the normative power of the factual: "But power, war, conquest, give rights, which, after possession, are conceded by the world; and which can never be controverted by those on whom they descend. We proceed, then, to the actual state of things, having glanced at their origin; because holding it in our recollection might shed some light on existing pretensions" (543). Marshall here reiterates the same principle he had already laid out in *Johnson v. McIntosh*. There he had indicated that the principle of discovery, which gives title to the discoverer, may be "extravagant" but has nonetheless become a customary legal rule that has been followed by the European nations and, subsequently, by the United States ever since its establishment. It was a rule of European nations for European nations and never took into account the legal status of Indians: "To avoid bloody conflicts, which might terminate disastrously to all, it was necessary for the *nations of Europe* to establish some principle which all would acknowledge, and which should decide *their* respective rights as *between themselves*" (543; emphasis added).

Marshall admits that the discovery doctrine, in its disregard for the natural law rights of Indians, builds a bias into international law; as he puts it, "the rule was acknowledged by all Europeans, because it was the interest of all to acknowledge it" (544). As regrettable as this may be, the United States did incorporate this bias into its legal system when it became the legal successor to the British Crown after independence. This bias, which now so blatantly privileges the United States over the native nations, was born out of the fact that the process of rulemaking only included the European states. But it also stands to reason that because the Indians were not included in this rulemaking, the discovery doctrine could not impair their sovereignty. The doctrine could only impair those rights they can assert before an American court. In Marshall's words, "It was an exclusive principle which shut out the right of competition among those who had agreed to it; not one which could annul the previous rights of those who had not agreed to it. It regulated the right given by discovery among the European discoverers; but could not affect the rights of those already in possession, either as aboriginal occupants, or as occupants by virtue of a discovery made before the memory of man" (544). The legal conclusion Marshall draws from this is important: the discovery doctrine "gave the exclusive right to purchase [to the United States], but did not found that right on a denial of the right of the possessor [the Indian tribes] to sell" (544). This again shows the degree to which Marshall's reasoning is based on a legal pluralism model, as was discussed in Chapter 2 with regard to *Johnson v. McIntosh*. The discovery doctrine had been established by a legal order—international customary law between European nations—in which the indigenous nations had no part. The Europeans consequently could only decide which rights of the indigenous nations they would *recognize*; they could not determine, bestow, or revoke the rights themselves. Indigenous sovereignty had, therefore, not been diminished. It was merely the degree of recognition that was decided by the legal system of the emerging colonial state, which would later become the United States of America.

What the discovery doctrine created for the United States was (public law) dominion over large parts of the North American continent and, in addition, an exclusive (private law) purchase right to acquire property from the Indians and thereby extinguish Indian title. Whether the Indians wanted to sell or not remained their business. In Marshall's words:

> The extravagant and absurd idea, that the feeble settlements made on the sea coast, or the companies under whom they were made, acquired legitimate power by them to govern the people, or occupy the lands from sea to sea, did not enter the mind of any man. They were well understood to convey the title which, according to the common law of European sovereigns respecting America, they might rightfully convey, and no more. This was the exclusive right of purchasing such lands as the natives were willing to sell. The crown could not be understood to grant what the crown did not affect to claim; nor was it so understood. (544–545)

Interestingly, Marshall here seems to shift his argumentation away from the position he took in *Johnson v. McIntosh*. There he had introduced the idea that complete private law title had been transferred to the discovering nation during discovery, but that this private law title was burdened with "Indian title." In *Worcester v. Georgia* it sounds like the discovering nation gained only dominion, not property. But the practical consequences of this distinction for Indians, at least legally, are minimal: in either case the Crown had to purchase the land to extinguish Indian title. To substantiate his opinion Marshall analyzes the wording of the several charters the Crown had given to the settlers in early colonial times. In those he does not find anything indicating that the settlers' colonial endeavor had provided them with full sovereignty and property over the whole continent: "These motives for planting the new colony are incompatible with the lofty ideas of granting the soil, and all its inhabitants from sea to sea. They demonstrate the truth, that these grants asserted a title against Europeans only, and were considered as blank paper so far as the rights of the natives were concerned. The power of war is given only for defence, not for conquest" (546).

Analyzing the charters further, Marshall concludes that the stated objectives, such as the civilization and Christianization of the Indians, presupposed peaceful behavior toward the inhabitants of the continent. "Instead of rousing their resentments, by asserting claims to their lands, or to dominion over their persons, their alliance was sought by flattering professions, and purchased by rich presents" (546). The question of rights to the continent was then directed not at the Indians but at the other European nations who were competing for the right to establish important trade relations with the Indians. According to Marshall, the issue of complete dominion over and property rights to the whole continent was simply unimaginable at that time, given the historical circumstances. The decision of the Indians to enter into these treaties had to be interpreted in light of the same historical circumstances: "Not well acquainted with the exact meaning of words, nor supposing it to be material whether they were called the subjects, or the children of their father in Europe; lavish in professions of duty and affection, in return for the rich presents they received; so long as their actual independence was untouched, and their right to self government acknowledged, they were willing to profess dependence on the power which furnished supplies of which they were in absolute need, and restrained dangerous intruders from entering their country" (546–547). The perspective of the native nations is important: if they could not lose their rights simply through the discovery doctrine, they could very well lose them by treaty. Treaties, however, must be interpreted, and Marshall provides a guideline for these interpretations. His line of reasoning remains to this day in the legal principle that treaties with Indian tribes have to be interpreted in a way that is favorable to the Indians. In particular, certain words indicating a transfer of rights to the United States must not be interpreted too widely.[11]

Marshall narrowly interprets the Royal Proclamation of 1763 as the legal manifestation of the Crown's principle that settler intrusions into Indian country be prohibited—with the explicit goal of not endangering important trade relations. In his view, this policy clearly contradicts any efforts to claim complete and exclusive dominion and property over Indian lands. Marshall summarizes the Crown's legal position on the Indians as follows: "[Great

Britain] considered them as nations capable of maintaining the relations of peace and war; of governing themselves, under her protection; and she made treaties with them, the obligation of which she acknowledged" (548–549). This analysis of the British legal view is important because the United States is the legal successor of the British Crown. In the peace treaty between the Crown and the new republic, the Crown ceded all rights it held to its former colonies in North America. But, as Marshall rightly notes, "the king of Great Britain, at the treaty of peace, could cede only what belonged to his crown" (560). As the Crown had never claimed all the lands of the Indians, the United States could not have acquired such a right from the Crown.

Marshall goes on to analyze the early policies of the United States vis-à-vis the Indians during and shortly after the War of Independence in order to find out if the emerging nation was in some way "advancing a claim to [Indian] lands, or asserting any right of dominion over them" (549). He finds no such indications. On the contrary, Congress had reiterated that it was the policy of the nation to secure and preserve friendship with the Indians. And the first treaty the United States made with a native nation, the Delaware in 1778, "in its language, and in its provisions, is formed, as near as may be, on the model of treaties between the crowned heads of Europe" (550).

When Marshall analyzes the Treaty of Hopewell, he finds in it this same "language of equality." The treaty's preamble states that the United States would offer peace to the Cherokees and accept them under the protection of the Union under the conditions spelled out in the treaty. Marshall rebuffs the contention that such language indicates that the Cherokees had surrendered their sovereignty. He asks rhetorically: "When the United States gave peace, did they not also receive it? Were not both parties desirous of it? If we consult the history of the day, does it not inform us that the United States were at least as anxious to obtain it as the Cherokees? We may ask, further: did the Cherokees come to the seat of the American government to solicit peace; or, did the American commissioners go to them to obtain it? The treaty was made at Hopewell, not at New York. The word 'give,' then, has no real importance attached to it" (551).

The passage in the Treaty of Hopewell that stated that the Cherokees were now under the protection of the United States is, in Marshall's view, a common provision in Indian treaties. Its main purpose was to seal an exclusive relationship to one European nation and exclude all others: "The Indians perceived in this protection only what was beneficial to themselves—an engagement to punish aggressions on them. It involved, practically, no claim to their lands, no dominion over their persons. It merely bound the nation to the British crown, as a dependent ally, claiming the protection of a powerful friend and neighbour, and receiving the advantages of that protection, without involving a surrender of their national character" (552).

With similar arguments he disagrees with the contention that the treaty provisions granting the United States the power to "manage all affairs" of the Indians mean that the Cherokees had surrendered all sovereign rights. He concludes that "to construe the expression 'managing all their affairs,' into a surrender of self-government, would be, we think, a perversion of their necessary meaning, and a departure from the construction which has been uniformly put on them" (553–554). The provision's positioning in the text of the treaty clearly indicates that this wording applies to trade relations and not to the Cherokees' internal affairs, "the most important of these, are the cession of their lands, and security against intruders on them" (554).

In his analysis of the subsequent Treaty of Holston (1791), which was renewed frequently over the following decades, Marshall arrived at the same conclusion. Marshall acknowledged that the language of the treaties did not presume equal power relations, but the relationship between the parties was nevertheless "that of a nation claiming and receiving the protection of one more powerful: not that of individuals abandoning their national character, and submitting as subjects to the laws of a master" (555). To support this contention, Marshall refers to international law: "The settled doctrine of the law of nations is, that a weaker power does not surrender its independence, its right to self government, by associating with a stronger, and taking its protection. . . . 'Tributary and feudatory states,' says [the international law theorist] Vattel, 'do not thereby cease to be sovereign and independent states, so long as self government and sovereign and independent authority are left in the administration of the state'" (560–561).

Marshall then revisits several legal manifestations of the Union's Indian policies, beginning with the Trade and Intercourse Act, all of which implicitly and explicitly recognized the Indian tribes as distinct political communities. He further states that during the unsettled times of early independence, Congress, thus the federal power, exercised the same authority that had been vested in the Crown, including the exclusive right to engage in foreign and Indian affairs. This provisional state of affairs was solidified when the Articles of the Confederation, the United States' first constitution (in force from 1781 to 1789), was enacted. The Articles explicitly vested in the Union "the sole and exclusive right and power of . . . regulating the trade and managing all affairs with the Indians, not members of any of the States; provided that the legislative right of any State, within its own limits, be not infringed or violated" (article 9, section 4). This ambiguous language led to legal debates in which Georgia and North Carolina contended that they, and not Congress, had full authority over Indian affairs within their own state borders. As a result of these discussions, it was agreed that this more ambiguous language, which seemingly restricted federal authority over Indian affairs, was ultimately not included in the U.S. Constitution. The commerce clause—still in force—asserts that the U.S. Congress has the authority "to regulate trade with Indian tribes" without any restriction. In Marshall's opinion this meant that "the shackles imposed on this power, in the confederation, are discarded" (559). In other words, Indian affairs are entrusted to Congress and Congress alone.

Marshall concludes his analysis of the legal status of Indian tribes from the perspective of U.S. law with a summary of his findings: "The Indian nations had always been considered as distinct, independent political communities, retaining their original natural rights, as the undisputed possessors of the soil, from time immemorial, with the single exception of that imposed by irresistible power, which excluded them from intercourse with any other European potentate than the first discoverer of the coast of the particular region claimed: and this was a restriction which those European potentates imposed on themselves, as well as on the Indians" (559). What, then, is the legal status of Indian tribes in Marshall's construction? Indian tribes are fully sovereign states and members of the international community. The sole impairment of this sovereignty (factually, not legally) was imposed on them by the Europeans, who demanded of the Indians and of themselves exclusivity in trade relations. The discovery doctrine prevented all European citizens—including the Crown's own citizens—from buying land from the Indians. That did not legally impair the Indians from the perspective of international law. They did not lose sovereignty as a result of discovery. What they factually lost were trading partners, because no European legal order would recognize a sale to anyone but the conquering nation.

What had been the British Crown had now become the federal government of the United States, but the legal situation had not changed. The U.S. courts did not recognize Indian land sales to anyone but the federal government, and because no other courts were around to hear the case, the legal rule that was only accepted among Europeans now factually impaired the indigenous nations. Legally speaking, the discovery doctrine did not erase the Indians' right to sell their land to whomever they wished; it just hindered the recognition of that right in the "courts of the conqueror" (*Johnson v. McIntosh*, 591). Marshall contends that Georgia had generally accepted and complied with both of these statements—that the Indians are distinct nations and that the exclusive right to conduct Indian affairs is vested in the Union—until the state began to enact its overreaching legislation into Cherokee territory in 1828. Marshall concludes his opinion with the most cited passage of the judgment: "The Cherokee nation, then, is a distinct community occupying its own territory, with boundaries accurately described, in which the laws of Georgia can have no force, and which the citizens of Georgia have no right to enter, but with the assent of the Cherokees themselves, or in conformity with treaties and with the acts of congress. The whole intercourse between the United States and this nation, is, by our constitution and laws, vested in the government of the United States" (561). Accordingly, the laws Georgia had enacted were declared unconstitutional and thus void, and the criminal conviction of Samuel A. Worcester and his fellow missionaries was nullified.

Marshall closes with a short explanation of why this judgment, coming from a federal court, is able to nullify the criminal conviction handed down by a state court. Marshall's reasoning for this emphasizes the grave unconstitutionality of the unusually strong interference of the state in matters under the authority of the Union.

Legal Positivism, Legal Pluralism, and the Possibility of Equality

Worcester v. Georgia completes the Marshall trilogy of federal Indian law cases in reiterating the systematic principles developed in *Johnson v. McIntosh* and *Cherokee Nation v. Georgia*. The discovery doctrine, developed out of customary law, acknowledged the exclusive right of the discovering European nation to engage in negotiations with the Indians. The native nations, international sovereigns at the time of discovery, retain their sovereignty over unceded territory, which they hold in "Indian title." With the establishment of the United States, the sole authority to extinguish Indian title via treaty or purchase passed on to the federal government of the United States. Private land acquisition from Indians and intervention in Indian affairs by the individual states are prohibited.

These principles are developed by way of a positivist methodology and in a framework of legal pluralism—both features already apparent in *Johnson v. McIntosh* and *Worcester v. Georgia*. These features open up, I contend, the possibility of asserting equality between the United States and the Indian nations and provide the conceptual basis for the sovereignty approach to indigenous rights.

The importance of this combination of legal pluralism and legal positivism in Marshall's argumentation cannot be overstated. For Marshall the U.S. legal system is derived not from a monistic natural law but from a plurality of international and national law. The U.S. law on the rights and privileges of the native inhabitants comes from international customary law agreed upon among the European nations and incorporated into the legal order of the emerging settler state.

The concept of natural law with its universalistic approach could not serve as the basis for such an argument. Marshall's legal positivism could be paraphrased as follows: It is the law because it has been agreed upon and has never been changed since. This line of argumentation has an element of inevitability to it. Even if Marshall wanted to grant more rights to the Indians, he would not have been able to do so. If Marshall had referred to natural law, granting full property rights to the Indians, he would have removed precisely this inevitability from his argumentation and would have brought an element of instability into his legal reasoning.

Marshall's choice of method of interpretation—positivism—is consistent with his conservative attitude on the topic. As Dieter Grimm (1987) explains, the choice of interpretive method in law depends to a large extent on the desired outcome. In his analysis, interpretation methods are "power bases." But his analysis deviates from the classical conception that the antagonism between positivist interpretation and realist interpretation (in U.S. legal debates often referred to as "formalism" versus "realism") is practically identical with the political antagonism between the political right and the political left ("positivism = right wing" and "realism = left wing"). Grimm argues for the configuration "positivism = conservative" and "realism = progressive," whereby "conservative" is not necessarily "right wing" and "progressive" is not necessarily "left wing." For example, if a left-leaning lawyer wants to maintain the status quo in order to conserve existing social rights, he or she will choose a positivist and therefore conservative interpretive method. If, on the other hand, a right-leaning lawyer's desired outcome is to change the status quo of the existing legal landscape in order to restrict certain social or civil rights, he or she will choose a realist and therefore progressive interpretive method. Maintaining or changing the legal status quo is, politically speaking, neither leftist nor rightist. The political position depends on what the status quo is.

Marshall is a good example of this. His positivist argumentation was intended to maintain the status quo: acknowledgment of the principle of title by discovery (to stabilize the legal foundation of the national project of the United States), indigenous land rights in the form of a right of occupation (to save the market for preemption rights, but not to completely disenfranchise Indians), prohibition of private land sales from Indians (to save the legal status quo and not to endanger established land tenure systems), and the twin pillars of tribal sovereignty and exclusive federal authority to engage in Indian affairs (to stabilize the constitutional structure of a strong union and to keep the states out of Indian affairs). This positivist style is, as a by-product, also advantageous for indigenous rights. As we can gather from an overview of the United States' Indian policies in the nineteenth and the beginning of the twentieth century, the situation for indigenous communities would become much more difficult from the 1830s onward. Marshall's conservative jurisprudence would help solidify some principles that were—as we have seen from our reading of the judgments—already heavily disputed at the time: indigenous communities do have sovereignty over unceded lands and retain at least in principle property rights to their territory. In addition, while the strengthening of federal authority did not protect the indigenous communities from violent policies when the political climate changed at the federal level, the Union was still more likely to slow the pace of disenfranchisement of indigenous communities than the land-hungry states, whose profit interests were much more direct than those of the Union. Indigenous sovereignty and the idea that—in principle, at least—Indian affairs were governed by international law survived and were then available to be applied as established principles to indigenous issues the world over in the late twentieth century.

This principle of sovereignty, which was the fruit of the early indigenous rights jurisprudence in the United States and the way it was conceptualized (on the basis of customary international law), is still an important feature of the concept of indigenous rights in general. We have seen that Marshall's reluctance to base indigenous sovereignty on natural law was fortunate for indigenous rights because a natural law solution (the way natural law was interpreted by U.S. legal scholars at the time) would have referred to the indigenous communities' legal incapacity to hold sovereignty and property rights. We have already described how the prevalent discourses of Lockean property theory lead to that conclusion.

The reference to sovereignty as a principle of international law had the (perhaps unintended) consequence of shifting the obvious inequality between the United States and the indigenous communities from a legal to a factual level. The idea of U.S.–Indian relations as something at least partially governed by international law put both parties in a situation of legal parity. The principle that sovereign actors of international law are *pares inter parem* has found a codified expression in the principle of the sovereign equality of states in UN Charter Article 2, paragraph 2. Hans Kelsen, himself a passionate proponent of legal positivism, discussed the principle of sovereign equality in the debates on the establishment of the United Nations. He explained that this legal equality is separate from factual inequalities of power, an argument very much in line with Marshall's view: "For if 'power' does not refer to the realm of norms or values, but to the realm of reality determined by laws of causality, and means capability of producing an effect, it is then easy to demonstrate that sovereignty as a supreme power in this sense cannot be a characteristic of States as legal entities. For States differ very much from each other with respect to their actual power" (1944, 208).

Indian rights in U.S. law are not a question of the sovereign rights of indigenous communities but rather a question of their recognition in the U.S. legal system. The legal disenfranchisement of indigenous communities in the U.S. legal system is caused by its habitual unwillingness to fully recognize sovereign indigenous rights and translate them into national rights of property and autonomy. This is not caused by some legal incapacity (Lockean style) on the side of the natives. The indigenous communities' dependence on the U.S. legal system to settle disputes is a factual problem for the Indians—a question of power, not of law.

I have already argued that precisely this "explicit Eurocentrism"—more than its possible alternative, the Lockean savage—empowered indigenous rights movements by providing them with the sovereignty approach to indigenous rights. The Supreme Court had, in effect, said: You may be sovereign, but we decide for ourselves what rights we recognize in our legal system. That meant two things: first, sovereignty was retained on unceded land, at least as long as it was not taken by Congress; and, more important, the question of the degree of indigenous autonomy was still in play because there were competing legal systems and competing sovereignty—a plurality of legal systems rooted in sovereignty. This opened up room for negotiation over the degree to which the United States would recognize indigenous rights. This negotiation of sovereignty, this politics of recognition, continues to the present day.

* * * *

Worcester v. Georgia put the principles developed in *Johnson v. McIntosh* and *Cherokee Nation v. Georgia* to the test against state interference in Indian affairs. It recognized that "Indian title" as a translation of the territorial sovereignty of indigenous nations into the U.S. legal system meant that indigenous nations still had sovereignty on unceded territory. The constitutional framework, which had transferred all authority for extinguishing Indian title to the Union, prevented the states from interfering. Marshall's discovery doctrine worked under premises and argumentative styles of legal pluralism and legal positivism. The derived principles, while discriminating against indigenous communities in the U.S. legal system, nevertheless opened up legal opportunities for indigenous movements to operate with the sovereignty approach to indigenous rights. The general principle of indigenous sovereignty survived even the darkest chapters of U.S. Indian policies and was available in the mid-twentieth century to be used as the basis of an argumentative framework supporting the "rise of indigenism."

CHAPTER 5

"Rooted Legal Pluralism" and Its Culturalized Boundaries

Delgamuukw v. British Columbia

The "sovereignty approach" to indigenous rights, born in nineteenth-century U.S. case law, still governs indigenous rights doctrine in the United States and other common-law jurisdictions such as Canada. In 1997 the Canadian Supreme Court decided a land rights case that was brought by Gitksan and Wet'suwet'en communities. The aboriginal communities had started the proceeding thirteen years earlier, in 1984. Their strategy was in accord with the sovereignty approach to indigenous rights, but culture also played an important role in their legal argumentation. To prove their claim of sovereignty over their territory, they presented as evidence oral history and material culture instead of written documents. They asked the court to accept a type of evidence that was generally not admissible in its common-law tradition, and in doing so the Gitksan and Wet'suwet'en were demanding respect for their cultural and legal traditions. While the trial court had dismissed their claims and the appeals court had only partially found in their favor, the Supreme Court not only decided to deviate from common-law traditions by agreeing to evaluate the evidence but also took the opportunity to elaborate on the nature and scope of indigenous rights. These elaborations are the focus of this chapter.

Although the claim in *Delgamuukw v. British Columbia* is based on the sovereignty approach to indigenous rights, cultural arguments reverberate throughout the judgment in two dimensions: as proof of and as constraint on aboriginal rights. Indigenous rights, especially "aboriginal title" (the parallel term to "Indian title" in the United States), are conceptualized as *sui generis*—following the reasoning that these rights are rooted in the precolonial sovereignty of the indigenous communities. It is possible to read this judgment—much like *Aloeboetoe v. Suriname*, which we will discuss in Chapter 6—as a case that falls in between arguments. Are indigenous claims based on precolonial international sovereignty or on ongoing cultural difference? But while *Aloeboetoe v. Suriname* dismissed the sovereignty approach and provided the basis for the culture argument, *Delgamuukw v. British Columbia* keeps the sovereignty approach intact and incorporates cultural arguments, resulting in, among other consequences, restrictions on the scope of aboriginal title.

Although the situations of indigenous communities in Canada and the United States are similar, especially when compared to Latin American legal systems, there are notable differences that should be briefly examined. Before analyzing the argumentative structure of the judgment, I will discuss how the case came about and provide an overview of the trial court and appeals court decisions preceding the Supreme Court decision in the *Delgamuukw* case.

The Case in Context: Canadian Aboriginal Law and U.S. Federal Indian Law

Delgamuukw v. British Columbia can be seen as the Canadian equivalent of the Marshall trilogy—the foundational U.S. federal Indian law cases discussed in the previous chapters (R. T. Anderson 2011, 592). In contrast to U.S. case law, the doctrinal basis of "Indian title" was not clearly established in the Canadian legal system until the second half of the twentieth century.

In 1763, after the French and Indian War, Britain's King George III issued the Royal Proclamation of 1763, in which private land acquisitions directly from Indian tribes without the Crown's consent were prohibited.[1] As we have seen in *Johnson v. McIntosh*, the U.S. Supreme Court saw in this proclamation one of many manifestations of the discovery doctrine, which established not only the exclusive right of the federal government to acquire lands from Indian tribes but, as its flip side, the existence of "Indian title." "Indian title," or "aboriginal title," as it is called in Canadian jurisprudence, is less than a full property right; it is described as a right of occupancy for aboriginal communities to their ancestral lands.[2]

The discovery doctrine, which was derived from international customary law, stated that the legal right of Indians to their land was not created by the U.S. legal system but preceded it. Indian title was the concept used to translate what little remained of the Indians' former full territorial sovereignty into the U.S. legal system. What the United States had gained with discovery was the territory, but not the full property rights to Indian lands. To own the land in a private law sense, the United States had to acquire it from the Indians first—in the terminology of federal Indian law, they had to "extinguish Indian title."

The legal situation in Canada was different because its courts did not apply the specific construction of Indian title through the discovery doctrine. "Aboriginal title" was recognized first in *St. Catherine's Milling and Lumber Co. v. The Queen* (1888), in which it was seen as originating not in the former territorial sovereignty of the Indians but directly in the Royal Proclamation of 1763. In Canada the Royal Proclamation was seen as the *source* of aboriginal title and not as a *manifestation* of a customary legal doctrine that granted aboriginal title, as it was in the United States. It was not until the 1973 case *Calder v. Attorney General of British Columbia* that the Canadian Supreme Court indicated that the Royal Proclamation of 1763 was not the sole source of aboriginal land rights.

The landmark *Calder* case, which generally recognized aboriginal rights, fueled the demand to incorporate indigenous rights into the constitution. The process of constitutional reform was initiated in 1978 because the francophone province of Quebec, home to powerful separatist and nationalist movements, pushed for extended regional autonomy. The Canadian government's willingness to accommodate Quebec's urge for constitutional reform also opened up an opportunity for indigenous rights movements to put the question of aboriginal rights on the table.[3] The outcome of the *Calder* case, which was sympathetic to indigenous movements, came in handy as it could be argued that the courts had already taken the first steps down the road toward expanding the recognition of aboriginal rights (Slattery 2007, 111). The constitutional compromise of 1982 eventually included the introduction of an aboriginal rights clause into the Canadian constitution (Slattery 1982; Pentney 1988; Isaac 1991). The first sentence of section 35 reads: "The existing aboriginal and treaty rights of the aboriginal peoples in Canada are hereby recognized and affirmed." From a legal history standpoint, the clause also defused the problems connected to the foggy doctrinal basis for aboriginal title because the wording ("recognized" and "affirmed") acknowledges that aboriginal rights are not created by the constitution, but originate outside of it. "In a way, then, Canadian law now recognizes . . . that the governments of the Aboriginal nations were independent entities, and formed relations with the settlers through treaties" (Imai 1999, 7).

But the constitutional discussions on aboriginal issues were not over with the creation of the aboriginal rights clause in 1982. The indigenous movements had not reached their goal of incorporating a self-government clause into the constitution, mainly because such constitutional changes for aboriginal communities would open up another "can of worms": Quebecois separatism. The failure to implement further constitutional change led to widespread discontent among the aboriginal nations, culminating in a violent confrontation between a group of Mohawks and the community of Oka in Quebec in 1990, in the course of which major streets and bridges were blockaded for weeks and a Quebecois policeman was killed (G. R. Alfred 1995). In the aftermath, the federal government appointed the Royal Commission on Aboriginal Peoples, which issued a report in 1996 with several recommendations to institutionalize legal change in Canada within the current constitutional framework. This report was very influential for the ensuing court decisions (Imai 1999, 14–18).

It can be said that the court cases after 1982, and even more so after 1996 when the reports of the Royal Commission on Aboriginal Peoples became available, changed Canada's indigenous rights policies significantly and brought the legal framework regarding the rights of Canada's aboriginal peoples closer to the standards of U.S. federal Indian law.[4]

The Gitksan's and Wet'suwet'en's Long Way to Court

The case concerned the Gitksan and Wet'suwet'en of north-central British Columbia.[5] Neither group had ever made a treaty with the British or later with Canada. After initial contact with Europeans in 1823, the native nations resisted white settlement on their land, resulting in a river blockade in the 1870s and long-standing negotiations until the early 1900s.

In 1871 the province of British Columbia entered the Canadian Confederation. The authority to deal with indigenous communities was entrusted to the federal government—a construction similar to that of the U.S. context. The Gitksan and Wet'suwet'en were declared "bands" under the Indian Act, and reserves were established for each such "band," which included the villages and the area immediately surrounding the villages.[6] These reserves covered only a small portion of the land traditionally regarded as Gitksan and Wet'suwet'en territory, but included a few burial sites and other lands important for subsistence activities. Indian agents appointed by the federal government administered the "bands" and their reserves: "The reserve allocations were unilaterally imposed by the provincial and federal governments. All the Tsimshian[7] groups [among them the Gitksan and Wet'suwet'en] protested the attempt at usurpation and have continued to assert title to their entire aboriginal territories" (Inglis et al. 1990, 285).

In 1977 the Canadian government indicated that it would enter into comprehensive negotiations for land recognition but would not negotiate without the province of British Columbia at the table. The province, however, refused to recognize the principle of aboriginal title or any land rights whatsoever for the indigenous nations in British Columbia and blocked all land rights negotiations between the parties. When the province did not modify its position even after the constitutional reform in 1982 and permitted companies to commence intensive, large-scale logging operations on Gitksan and Wet'suwet'en territory, the nations decided to bring the case to court in 1984. The aim was to force the province to the negotiating table by asking the court to recognize that they held their territory in unextinguished aboriginal title. At that time the Crown was beginning to help with the initiation of several test cases on indigenous land rights to determine a jurisprudential framework for aboriginal title. *Delgamuukw v. British Columbia* was then counted among those test cases.

The plaintiffs comprised thirty-eight Gitksan house leaders and twelve Wet'suwet'en house leaders.[8] These house leaders claimed individually and for their house members separate portions of a large tract of land in northern British Columbia. Delgamuukw, the head chief of one of the Gitksan houses, served as the spokesperson for the plaintiffs. Their legal position was clear: because they never had a treaty with the Crown and therefore had never ceded any land, their aboriginal title had never been extinguished. This situation is typical of British Columbia. In the province there had never been any treaties or cessions by indigenous peoples to the Crown, and the province never formally extinguished aboriginal title through other means. The consequence from the viewpoint of the Gitksan and Wet'suwet'en plaintiffs was that practically the whole of British Columbia comprised territory held in aboriginal title, and almost no land was held by the Crown.[9] While British Columbia refused to acknowledge indigenous land rights in the *Delgamuukw* case, the plaintiffs' goal was to obtain a judgment legally recognizing their exclusive land rights.

Delgamuukw Before Allan McEachern: The Worst Possible Outcome

The trial court for *Delgamuukw v. British Columbia* was the Supreme Court of British Columbia.[10] Chief Justice Allan McEachern[11] led the proceedings and delivered the opinion of the court.[12] Delgamuukw (or Earl Muldoe, his anglicized name)[13] and the other plaintiffs alleged "ownership" of and "jurisdiction" over a tract of land of 22,000 square miles in northern British Columbia. The villages themselves and the area immediately surrounding them had already been declared reserve lands by the Indian Act. Thus the majority of the claim regarded lands in the wider area outside the reserve lands.

In choosing to frame their claim as one of "ownership" and "jurisdiction," they followed the classic sovereignty argument. Their position was that, because they never gave up their territory to the Canadian state, they had retained their territory in full sovereignty. They explicitly did not claim recognition of "aboriginal title" to their land; they claimed ownership and jurisdiction and therefore indicated that they asserted full control as sovereigns of the land under international law.[14] In their opening statement to the Supreme Court of British Columbia, Delgamuukw and Gisday Wa, one of the Wet'suwet'en chiefs, explained their reasons for claiming ownership and jurisdiction instead of aboriginal title:

> If the Canadian legal system has not recognized our ownership and jurisdiction, but at the same time not extinguished it, what has been done with it? Judges and legislators have taken the reality of aboriginal title as we know it and tried to wrap it in something called aboriginal rights. An aboriginal rights package can be put on the shelf to be forgotten or to be endlessly debated at constitutional conferences. We are not interested in asserting aboriginal rights; we are here to discuss territory and authority. When this case ends and the package has been unwrapped, it will have to be our ownership and our jurisdiction *under our law* that is on the table. . . . The purpose of this case then, is to find a process to place Gitksan and Wet'suwet'en ownership and jurisdiction within the context of Canada. We do not seek a decision as to whether our system might continue or not. It will continue. (cited in Monet and Skanu'u 1992, 22–23; emphasis added)

The defendant, the province of British Columbia, wanted the court to declare that the claimants had no right to or interest in the land. If the court should find that the plaintiffs did indeed have a claim, then it should be directed to the Canadian government in the form of a claim for compensation.

For their land rights to be acknowledged by the court, the plaintiffs had to prove their occupation of the claimed lands in pre-European times. This is one of the important features of the sovereignty approach that had not yet emerged in the earlier indigenous rights cases in the United States. For indigenous sovereignty to be recognized by the (post)colonial state, indigenous communities had to prove that the land in question had been theirs before the arrival of the Europeans and that there was—at least in principle—an unbroken chain of sovereignty to the present day. To prove their claim, the plaintiffs concentrated on their own oral history accounts. In their opening statement they explain why this approach is appropriate:

> Never before has a Canadian court been given the opportunity to hear Indian witnesses describe *within their own structure* the history and nature of their societies. The evidence will show that the Gitksan and Wet'suwet'en are and have always been properly counted among the civilized nations of the world; that their ownership of their territory and their authority over it has always existed; and that they have shaped a distinctive form of confederation between House and Clan. The challenge for this court is to hear this evidence, in all its complexity, in all its elaboration, as the articulation of a way of looking at the world which pre-dates the Canadian Constitution by many thousands of years. (cited in Monet and Skanu'u 1992, 24; emphasis in original)

Delgamuukw and the other house leaders presented to the court several bodies of evidence to prove their claim to historic use and ownership of their land. First and foremost, they entered their collections of oral history accounts into evidence. In the case of the Gitksan, they presented the *adaawk*, a body of sacred oral tradition about their ancestors, histories, and territories. In the case of the Wet'suwet'en, they brought into evidence the *kungax*, a spiritual song and dance in the course of whose performance their connection to the land is manifested. Additionally they presented, as a piece of evidence of material culture, a feast hall. This space is used for gatherings in which the house members meet, tell and retell their stories, identify their territory, and remind each other of the sacred connection they have to their land. The ceremonial feast has a ritual character and is also a moment when deliberations and decision-making take place.[15] The plaintiffs also presented nonindigenous expert witnesses on topics of genealogy, linguistics, archaeology, anthropology, and geography.

This resulted in an extensive hearing of evidence during which indigenous witnesses and anthropologists testified to the Gitksan's and Wet'suwet'en's use and occupancy of the land and the cultural, social, and political links they maintain with their territory. Chief Justice McEachern enumerates the evidence in the trial court judgment:

> A total of 61 witnesses gave evidence at trial, many using translators from their native Gitksan or Wet'suwet'en language; "word spellers" to assist the official reporters were required for many witnesses; a further 15 witnesses gave their evidence on commission; 53 territorial affidavits were filed; 30 deponents were cross-examined out of court; there are 23,503 pages of transcript evidence at trial; 5,898 pages of transcript of argument; 3,039 pages of commission evidence and 2,553 pages of cross-examination on affidavits (all evidence and oral arguments are conveniently preserved in hard copy and on diskettes); about 9,200 exhibits were filed at trial comprising, I estimate, well over 50,000 pages; the plaintiffs' draft outline of argument comprises 3,250 pages, the province's 1,975 pages, and Canada's over 1,000 pages; there are 5,977 pages of transcript of argument in hard copy and on diskettes. All parties filed some excerpts from the exhibits they referred to in argument. The province alone submitted 28 huge binders of such documents. At least 15 binders of reply argument were left with me during that stage of the trial. (trial court, para. 56)[16]

The trial court dismissed the claim of the Gitksan and Wet'suwet'en. McEachern generally did not accept oral history accounts of the indigenous witnesses as statements of fact, saying that they blurred the boundary between fact and belief. McEachern likewise refused to accept the accounts of the two anthropological experts. He found them to be too close to the plaintiffs and too uncritical of their oral history.[17]

In the judgment McEachern examined the claim of land "ownership" and "jurisdiction," and then addressed the claim to "aboriginal rights," although the plaintiffs had not made that claim.

Concerning "ownership" of the land, McEachern found—especially because he evaluated most of the oral evidence of the plaintiffs and much of the expert testimony as unreliable—that the Gitksan and Wet'suwet'en houses could not prove conclusively that they owned more than the land of the villages and their immediate surroundings—lands that were already part of the reserves.

Interpreting "jurisdiction" as the right to "govern the territory free of provincial control in all matters where their aboriginal laws conflict with the general law," which would be tantamount to sovereignty (para. 16), McEachern rejected the plaintiffs' claim to jurisdiction primarily for two reasons. First, he stated that after British Columbia had become a province of Canada in 1871, sovereignty over all land was divided between the Crown and the province. This left no room for the sovereignty of the Gitksan and Wet'suwet'en. Recognition of the indigenous groups' sovereignty would furthermore presuppose that they had and still have gubernatorial and legal control over the lands. McEachern was (again because he found the evidence unreliable) not convinced that the Gitksan and Wet'suwet'en exerted gubernatorial control beyond the village sites. He described the customary rule system governing Gitksan and Wet'suwet'en affairs as a "most uncertain and highly flexible set of customs which are frequently not followed by the Indians themselves." He concluded: "In my judgment, these rules are so flexible and uncertain that they cannot be classified as laws" (para. 20). This alone would preclude the possibility of Gitksan and Wet'suwet'en asserting legal control over their territory.

On the question of "aboriginal rights," the trial court took the position that these had been generally extinguished—despite the absence of land cession or military conquest: "The reality of Crown ownership of the soil of all the lands of the province is not open to question and actual dominion for such a long period is far more pervasive than the outcome of a battle or a war could ever be. The law recognizes Crown ownership of the territory in a federal state now known as Canada pursuant to its Constitution and laws" (trial court, para. 567).

Needless to say, McEachern's judgment was less than satisfying for the plaintiffs. The trial court had not only dismissed their claim, but denied the possibility of any aboriginal rights for the Gitksan and Wet'suwet'en by promoting a theory of general extinguishment of aboriginal rights, which would leave the plaintiffs with no land rights whatsoever outside their small reserve lands. The plaintiffs decided to appeal the judgment and go before the British Columbia Court of Appeal.

The Court of Appeal Steps In

The rather extreme theory of general pre-provincial extinguishment of aboriginal title that McEachern asserted in his judgment did not have much support even at the time (R. T. Anderson 2011, 611). When the case came before the Court of Appeal, the provincial government, which was now headed by the New Democratic Party whose policies were more conciliatory regarding indigenous issues, agreed not to argue general extinguishment of aboriginal rights. Before the appellate court the plaintiffs objected to the trial courts' rejection of their oral history accounts. The Court of Appeal took a more sympathetic approach to the indigenous communities' claim.

Alan Macfarlane, who delivered the opinion of the court, first developed the content of aboriginal title out of Canadian case law and also with reference to the *Mabo v. Queensland* case, which had been argued before the Australian High Court in 1992. In the judgment he described five features of aboriginal title: "First, such rights arise from historic occupation and possession of the aboriginal peoples' tribal lands. Second, they arise by operation of law and do not depend on a grant from the Crown. Third, they are not absolute, but they are subject to regulation and extinguishment. Fourth, they are *sui generis* communal rights. Fifth, they cannot be alienated other than to the Crown. Finally, they are related to aboriginal activities which formed an integral part of traditional Indian life prior to sovereignty" (para. 31).

Macfarlane agreed with McEachern that the claim of "ownership" over the land in question could not be proven. "Ownership" would indicate an exclusive right to the land, and an "aboriginal interest" would, as the Supreme Court had held in *Guerin v. The Queen*, not amount to full ownership. Although Macfarlane expressed some concern over McEachern's approach on the evidence presented, he took the position that it would be improper for the appeals court to interfere with the trial court's decision on the evidence and impose its own opinion. The appeals court, after all, was unable to hold a hearing on the evidence itself.[18] Concerning "jurisdiction" over the land, Macfarlane again essentially agreed with McEachern: "When the Crown imposed English law on all the inhabitants of the colony and when British Columbia entered the Confederation, the aboriginal people became subject to Canadian (and provincial) legislative authority" (para. 34).

On the question of aboriginal title, however, Macfarlane took a different position. While he conceded that aboriginal title could have been extinguished prior to 1982 without consent of the indigenous nations,[19] he asserted that aboriginal title could only be extinguished when the Crown had "clear and plain intent" to do so. Macfarlane disagreed with McEachern's suggestion that the Crown had proven that it had acted with "clear and plain intent" in the case of the Gitksan and Wet'suwet'en lands. Consequently, Macfarlane rebuffed the assumption that there had been blanket extinguishment of aboriginal title before the establishment of the province in 1871. "After 1871, the exclusive power to legislate in relation to 'Indians, and Lands reserved for the Indians' was given to the federal government by virtue of s. 91(24) of the Constitution Act, 1867" (para. 37). Macfarlane therefore found that the plaintiffs did have certain aboriginal rights, whose extent would have to be established in a new trial.

The majority opinion by the Court of Appeal was shared by all of the judges. Three justices—Wallace, Lambert, and Hutcheon—issued separate opinions that are of interest because all three map out the relationship between the concepts "ownership" and "aboriginal title" differently.

Justice Wallace did not accept the strong distinction McEachern and McFarlane had drawn between "ownership" and "aboriginal title." In his view, aboriginal interests "may resemble a proprietary title, not unlike those in western proprietary law systems, or they may be restricted to certain uses of the land" (para. 42). In other words, Wallace did not share the opinion that aboriginal title is conceptually different from a common-law proprietary interest as "ownership." But he did think that the protected uses of the land should be restricted to the pre-European uses and patterns of occupation. The result would be that the Gitksan and Wet'suwet'en could very well claim exclusive ownership of the land in question, but only if they could prove that they had exclusive ownership of the land in pre-European times. Like McEachern, Wallace believed that the plaintiffs had not met this burden of proof. If the claimants were to claim "aboriginal rights" instead of ownership, the result would not be any different. The test would be the same: the rights must be connected to pre-European use and occupation.

Justice Lambert, in agreement with Macfarlane and against Wallace, took the position that aboriginal title and aboriginal rights were indeed legal concepts *sui generis* and "not easily explicable in terms of ordinary western jurisprudential analysis or common law concepts" (para. 48). But in contrast to Wallace he believed that aboriginal rights were "not frozen at the time of contact," but that "they must be permitted to maintain contemporary relevance in relation to the needs of the holders of the rights as those needs change along with the changes in overall society" (para. 49). Contrary to the trial court's decision, he believed that the plaintiffs had proven use and occupation of the territory far beyond their villages and their immediate surroundings. He furthermore felt that the plaintiffs had proven that they had governed themselves free of outside intervention and therefore had a right to self-government—albeit perhaps in a diminished form because of the establishment of Canadian and provincial sovereignty.

Justice Hutcheon took yet a different position on the relationship between "ownership" and "aboriginal title." Instead of stating that aboriginal title was a form of ownership, as Wallace claimed, or that it is inherently different from common-law ownership (a *sui generis* right), like Macfarlane and Lambert, he found it sufficient to state that aboriginal rights can "'compete on an equal footing' with proprietary interests" (para. 68). He also believed, like Lambert, that the plaintiffs had proven use and occupation beyond the villages and the immediate surroundings and that the Gitksan and Wet'suwet'en had exercised self-government at the time of the integration of their land into Canada.

Delgamuukw Before the Supreme Court

When the case went before the Supreme Court of Canada, the province of British Columbia changed its legal strategy and focused more on the argument that there was a difference between "aboriginal title" and "aboriginal rights." The province expressed the view that British Columbia held "underlying title" to all lands in the province that it had not explicitly granted to third parties. These lands could under certain circumstances be subject to "aboriginal rights" and in some cases to "aboriginal title," but it did not belong to the First Nations simply by virtue of the fact that the Crown had not extinguished title. Rather, "aboriginal title" could only be claimed when there was "an important link to the land."

Over the long course of the legal action the Gitksan and Wet'suwet'en also had changed their strategy. After first claiming ownership of and jurisdiction over their lands (for each house separately), it had become clear that the only promising legal avenue would be to claim aboriginal title. The trial court had already de facto transformed the claim into an aboriginal title claim—one for each indigenous nation—and the plaintiffs went along with it. If their land could not be recognized as their sovereign territory, then they would claim recognition of certain occupation and use rights to their land. In addition, they claimed damages for extracted or otherwise compromised natural resources.

The Supreme Court heard the case of the Gitksan and Wet'suwet'en in 1997. It ruled that the trial court's rejection of the oral history testimony of the plaintiffs had been motivated by an ethnocentric bias and had led to serious mistakes in the evaluation of the evidence. The Supreme Court stated that "aboriginal title" was less than full ownership in fee simple, as the plaintiffs had claimed, but more than just a use right to engage in certain activities on the land, as British Columbia had claimed. Aboriginal title was indeed a right in land and more than a mere use right, but it was limited in its scope. Because aboriginal title had its source in the precontact uses of the land by the indigenous communities, its scope was limited to the traditional practices carried out on the land in pre-European times.

Chief Justice Antonio Lamer, who delivered the Supreme Court's majority opinion, first elaborated on the problem of how the Supreme Court could interfere with the findings of fact by the trial court. According to Lamer, the Supreme Court should, generally speaking, be very reluctant to interfere with the findings of fact by a trial court, especially when the findings are grounded in the assessment of the testimony of witnesses and their credibility, because the trial judge is in direct contact with the evidence presented and the witnesses heard and is in a much better position to evaluate their credibility. The Supreme Court can only evaluate such testimony on paper. The Supreme Court should, therefore, only interfere on the level of findings of fact when it can be established that a trial court had made a "palpable and overriding error"[20] in the assessment of the facts (para. 78).

In aboriginal rights cases the Supreme Court had already ruled in *R. v. Van der Peet* that such a "palpable and overriding error" is made when courts "undervalue the evidence presented by aboriginal claimants simply because that evidence does not conform precisely with the evidentiary standards that would be applied in, for example, a private law torts case" (*Van der Peet*, para. 68). Aboriginal rights cases in general were intended to reconcile the fact that, when the Crown had assumed sovereignty over the territory that is now Canada, aboriginal peoples already lived there. To do so it would be necessary to bridge "aboriginal and non-aboriginal cultures" (*Van der Peet*, para. 42). Courts therefore have to take into account not only the common-law perspective but the perspective of the aboriginal nations' laws as well. The doctrine of aboriginal rights (hence their recognition through common law) is a common-law doctrine, while the content of the aboriginal rights is *sui generis*. This fact "demand[s] a unique approach to the treatment of evidence which accords due weight to the perspective of aboriginal peoples" (para. 82).

In *R. v. Van der Peet*, Lamer had developed these principles especially to allow aboriginal peoples to prove precontact cultural practices. Because there are no written records from precontact times, the modified standard of evidence allows indigenous nations to present evidence of *post-contact* practices in order to establish that they had already existed in *precontact* times. Lamer explains further: "In practical terms, this requires the courts to come to terms with the oral histories of aboriginal societies, which, for many aboriginal nations, are the only record of their past" (para. 84).

In citing the already mentioned *Report of the Royal Commission on Aboriginal Peoples* (1996), Lamer points to the stylistic differences between Western and aboriginal historical accounting. The oral history tradition was focused less on the establishment of historic truth because the teller of the story was part of the story. It would be seen as arrogant for him or her to try to fix the content of the story for all times. Aboriginal oral history accounts are more than a mere vessel for historical record keeping; they serve a number of purposes, including "to educate the listener, to communicate aspects of culture, to socialize people into a cultural tradition, or to validate the claims of a particular family to authority of prestige" (para. 85). In contrast to written history in Western tradition, aboriginal oral history is not a "detached recounting of factual events," but rather "many histories, each characterized in part by how a people see themselves, how they define their identity in relation to their environment, and how they express their uniqueness as a people" (para. 85).[21]

Lamer then summarizes what the challenges of this form of evidence are in relation to established common law principles of evidence: "The difficulty with these features of oral histories is that they are tangential to the ultimate purpose of the fact-finding process at trial—the determination of the historical truth. Another feature of oral histories which creates difficulty is that they largely consist of out-of-court statements, passed on through an unbroken chain across the generations of a particular aboriginal nation to the present-day. These out-of-court statements are admitted for their truth and therefore conflict with the general rule against the admissibility of hearsay" (para. 86).[22] Despite these challenges Lamer emphasizes that "this type of evidence can be accommodated and placed on an equal footing with the types of historical evidence that courts are familiar with, which largely consists of historical documents" (para. 87).

This conceptualization of "aboriginal evidence" is based on recognition of a form of legal pluralism. An aboriginal legal system, following its own evidentiary standards and parameters, exists independently of the common-law legal system. Common law has to recognize—at least in part—aboriginal law, but this legal translation must allow for a complex balancing of different legal standards. To disregard this and simply apply the evidentiary standards usual in common law would be to disregard this challenge of legal translation.

In Lamer's view the trial court, or more specifically, Justice McEachern, had failed precisely in this point of legal translation. The plaintiffs had brought their oral history accounts to court in the form of the Gitksan *adaawk*, the Wet'suwet'en *kungax*, and their material manifestation as totem poles, crests, and blankets.[23] The *adaawk* was presented by the Gitksan as proof of historical use and occupation of their territory; the *kungax* served for the Wet'suwet'en as a means to prove the significance the land has for their culture and society. McEachern had not declared the *adaawk* and the *kungax* inadmissible according to the hearsay rule, but declared that an exception would be necessary because there was no other way to prove the history of the Gitksan and Wet'suwet'en. After declaring the oral history accounts admissible in general, however, McEachern did not give them any significant evidentiary value. Lamer quotes a series of remarks from McEachern's judgment that suggest that the trial court judge did not really value those accounts:

> Although he had earlier recognized, when making his ruling on admissibility, that it was impossible to make an easy distinction between the mythological and "real" aspects of these oral histories, he discounted the *adaawk* and *kungax* because they were not "literally true," confounded "what is fact and what is belief," "included some material which might be classified as mythology," and projected a "romantic view" of the history of the appellants. . . . Finally, he questioned (at p. 181) the utility of the *adaawk* and *kungax* to demonstrate use and occupation because they were "seriously lacking in detail about the specific lands to which they are said to relate." (para. 97)

Lamer claims that McEachern had declared the *adaawk* and the *kungax* admissible only for the sake of appearances, when in reality he did not think they had any evidentiary value whatsoever. This conclusion was founded on an ethnocentric bias:

> Although he framed his ruling on weight [of the evidence] in terms of the specific oral histories before him, in my respectful opinion, the trial judge *in reality based his decision on some general concerns*

> *with the use of oral histories as evidence* in aboriginal rights cases. In summary, the trial judge gave no independent weight to these special oral histories because they did not accurately convey historical truth, because knowledge about those oral histories was confined to the communities whose histories they were and because those oral histories were insufficiently detailed. . . . *The implication of the trial judge's reasoning is that oral histories should never be given any independent weight* and are only useful as confirmatory evidence in aboriginal rights litigation. I fear that if this reasoning were followed, the oral histories of aboriginal peoples would be *consistently and systematically undervalued by the Canadian legal system*, in contradiction of the express instruction to the contrary in *Van der Peet* that trial courts interpret the evidence of aboriginal peoples in light of the difficulties inherent in adjudicating aboriginal claims. (para. 98; emphasis added)

In the same manner McEachern had undervalued the personal statements of the indigenous witnesses concerning their family histories (which were not part of the *adaawk* or the *kungax*) and a number of territorial affidavits in which the plaintiffs had testified to land ownership.[24] Lamer summarized:

> The trial judge's treatment of the various kinds of oral histories did not satisfy the principles I laid down in *Van der Peet*. These errors are particularly worrisome because oral histories were of critical importance to the appellants' case. They used those histories in an attempt to establish their occupation and use of the disputed territory, an essential requirement for aboriginal title. The trial judge, after refusing to admit, or giving no independent weight to these oral histories, reached the conclusion that the appellants had not demonstrated the requisite degree of occupation for "ownership." Had the trial judge assessed the oral histories correctly, his conclusions on these issues of fact might have been very different. (para. 107)

To correct these errors it would be necessary to assess the evidence again in a new trial.

The chief justice of the Supreme Court did not stop there; he took the opportunity to elaborate more generally on the nature of aboriginal title and the relationship between aboriginal title and other common-law property conceptions. Lamer therefore explains the notion of aboriginal title *sui generis*, which is based on a conception of legal pluralism and indigenous sovereignty. Lamer states that "all of the parties have characterized the content of aboriginal title incorrectly" and that "the content of aboriginal title, in fact, lies somewhere between these positions" (para. 110–111).

In Lamer's view aboriginal title is, on the one hand, not just a right to engage in specific activities, but a right to land. The activities aboriginal peoples conduct on their land "are parasitic on the underlying title." On the other hand, aboriginal title differs from fee simple in that it has an "inherent limit." The "range of uses is subject to the limitation that they must not be irreconcilable with the nature of the attachment to the land which forms the basis of the particular group's aboriginal title" (para. 111). This inherent limitation, which distinguishes aboriginal title from fee simple, makes aboriginal title, in Lamer's words, a right *sui generis*: "Aboriginal title has been described as *sui generis* in order to distinguish it from 'normal' proprietary interests, such as fee simple. However, as I will now develop, it is also *sui generis* in the sense that its characteristics cannot be completely explained by reference either to the common law rules of real property or to the rules of property found in aboriginal legal systems. As with other aboriginal rights, it must be understood by reference to both common law and aboriginal perspectives" (para. 112).

Lamer gives an elaborate explanation of why aboriginal title is a *sui generis* right, stressing that "various dimensions" distinguish it from fee simple. The first dimension of aboriginal title is its inalienability—lands held in aboriginal title cannot be sold to anyone but the Crown. Lamer stresses that this inalienability does not mean that aboriginal title is a mere "license to use and occupy" (para. 113). The second dimension of aboriginal title is its source, which is not to be found in the Royal Proclamation of 1763. Lamer explains that "it is now clear that although aboriginal title was recognized by the Proclamation, it arises from the prior occupation of Canada by aboriginal peoples" (para. 114). The common-law rule that physical occupation is proof of possession in law is the source of this title.[25] "What makes aboriginal title *sui generis* is that it arises from possession before the assertion of British sovereignty, whereas normal estates, like fee simple, arise afterward" (para. 114). "What this suggests is a second source for aboriginal title—the relationship between common law and pre-existing systems of aboriginal law" (para. 114). The third dimension that renders aboriginal title a *sui generis* right "is the fact that it is held communally. Aboriginal title cannot be held by individual aboriginal persons; it is a collective right to land held by all members of an aboriginal nation" (para. 115).

Aboriginal peoples' land has, according to Lamer, "an important non-economic component," which means that the land "has an inherent and unique value in itself." This also means that "the community cannot put the land to uses which would destroy that value" (para. 129). The consequence is that "if aboriginal peoples wish to use their lands in a way that aboriginal title does not permit, then they must surrender those lands and convert them into non-title lands to do so" (para. 131): "This is not, I must emphasize, a limitation that restricts the use of the land to those activities that have traditionally been carried out on it. That would amount to a legal straitjacket on aboriginal peoples who have a legitimate legal claim to the land. The approach I have outlined above allows for a full range of uses of the land, subject only to an overarching limit, defined by the special nature of the aboriginal title in that land" (para. 132).

Lamer subsequently comes to the question of how to prove the existence of aboriginal title. Aboriginal title is a right to land; other activities that are protected as aboriginal rights are parasitic on the underlying title. Lamer lays out the necessary criteria to prove aboriginal title. The community must prove that the land was occupied prior to sovereignty. By "sovereignty" in this context he means the establishment of the Crown's sovereignty, not that of the indigenous community, which, in the case of British Columbia, was 1846.[26] At the time the Crown asserted sovereignty over the indigenous territory, the indigenous occupation must have been exclusive. Occupation of the land at the time of the establishment of the Crown's sovereignty is often difficult to prove.[27] What aboriginal claimants can conclusively establish is usually only their present-day occupation of the land. If claimants, then, prove continuity between present-day occupation and occupation at the time of the establishment of British sovereignty, Lamer sees that as sufficient: "Conclusive evidence of pre-sovereignty occupation may be difficult to come by. Instead, an aboriginal community may provide evidence of present occupation as proof of pre-sovereignty occupation in support of a claim to aboriginal title. What is required, in addition, is a continuity between present and pre-sovereignty occupation" (para. 152).

In reference to the test of "substantial maintenance of the connection" developed in the Australian landmark case *Mabo v. Queensland*, Lamer clarifies that to prove an unbroken chain of continuity in occupation is not necessary: "The occupation and use of lands may have been disrupted for a time, perhaps as a result of the unwillingness of European colonizers to recognize aboriginal title" (para. 153). Land occupation patterns can change over time without precluding claimants from proving aboriginal title, but one must always bear in mind that the flexible boundary of cultural development may not be overstretched in that process: "I would like to make it clear that the fact that the nature of occupation has changed would not ordinarily preclude a claim for aboriginal title, as long as a substantial connection between the people and the land is maintained. The only limitation on this principle might be the internal limits on uses which land that is subject to aboriginal title may be put, i.e., uses which are inconsistent with continued use by future generations of aboriginals" (para. 154).

After some further deliberations on the requirement to prove exclusive occupation at the time of the establishment of the Crown's sovereignty and the circumstances under which the federal government is justified to infringe on aboriginal title, Lamer concludes the judgment by encouraging the opposing parties to negotiate: "This litigation has been both long and expensive, not only in economic but in human terms as well. By ordering a new trial, I do not necessarily encourage the parties to proceed to litigation and to settle their dispute through the courts. . . . Subsequent negotiations . . . should also include other aboriginal nations which have a stake in the territory claimed. Moreover, the Crown is under a moral, if not a legal, duty to enter into and conduct those negotiations in good faith" (para. 186).

Following the favorable outcome for the plaintiffs in *Delgamuukw*, the province of British Columbia engaged in long-standing negotiations with the indigenous nations to come to a settlement concerning land rights.

Rights *Sui Generis*: Rooted Legal Pluralism

Two aspects of *Delgamuukw v. British Columbia* are of special interest with regard to the paradoxical structure of indigenous rights. The first aspect concerns the way in which the judgment elaborates on the nature and scope of indigenous rights in Canada. At the center of the concept of "aboriginal title" is its *sui generis* nature. In the context of *Delgamuukw*, the term *sui generis* is used as inextricably linked to the conceptualization of aboriginal nations as sovereign entities. It is important to carve out the specifics, because, as we will discuss in Chapter 6, the Inter-American Court of Human Rights also insists on the idea of the specificity of indigenous property rights, but with an emphasis on cultural difference rather than on difference in sovereignty.

In explaining the nature and scope of aboriginal title, Chief Justice Lamer points out that aboriginal title is *sui generis*. *Black's Law Dictionary* tells us the Latin term means "of its own kind or class; unique or peculiar" (Garner 2011, 729). *Sui generis* is a nonclassification; it provides a category for legal instruments that one is hesitant to categorize. Legal formations *sui generis* are similar to certain other legal formations, but not similar enough to be subsumed under an existing category.

In that sense one can draw a line from the term *sui generis* to the formation I have called the indigenous paradox. Indigeneity demands the fragile incorporation of contradictory requirements: the indigenous person must be similar to other legal persons inside the jurisdiction of a court but also different enough not to be subsumed under one of the established categories. "Indigenous" must signify "the same, but different." It needs the rule of law in general, but must also reject it in the individual case. Indigenous claimants themselves could be called "claimants *sui generis*."

"Categorizing" a right as *sui generis* is a gesture of awkwardness, and it bears a moment of indeterminateness and undecidability. This perfectly fits the context of the indigenous paradox, which itself benefits from the status of undecidability and must try to freeze or keep in a suspended state this liminal stage of indecision. At the moment indigenous claimants are categorized fully as *the same* or *different*, the case is lost. It is, therefore, unsurprising that some specialists sympathetic to indigenous rights in Canada fully support the idea of the *sui generis* nature of aboriginal rights and caution the courts not to lose sight of just how *sui generis* aboriginal rights really are. Otherwise, the courts would be in danger of losing the indigenous perspective completely (Borrows and Rotman 1997; McKay 2005).

As a *sui generis* right, aboriginal title resembles a "regular" property interest like fee simple. The question is, what makes it different enough not to be a property interest? Lamer gives us the three dimensions differentiating aboriginal title from regular property that we have already investigated thoroughly: aboriginal title is *inalienable* (to anybody other than the Crown); it is held *communally*; and it *originates outside common law*—namely, in the indigenous land tenure systems before the establishment of colonial sovereignty.

Let us now investigate these three dimensions of the *sui generis* nature of indigenous land rights. The first aspect, inalienability to anybody but the government, we have already explored in *Johnson v. McIntosh*. Marshall developed the feature of inalienability out of international customary law and saw a clear manifestation of that rule in the Royal Proclamation of 1763. Generally, alienability is a defining feature of real property, but common law also recognizes the concept of restricted property rights. It is possible to conceptualize aboriginal title simply as a form of fee simple that is restricted in its alienability. However, inalienability in and of itself does not make aboriginal title a *sui generis* right.

The second aspect, communality, is obviously not an exclusive feature of aboriginal title. Common law recognizes communal forms of property, with public property being the most prominent type. Chief Justice Marshall himself described the kind of property the colonial state gains through discovery with the words: "They acquire a title in common. The title of the whole land is in the whole society. It is to be divided and parcelled out according to the will of the society, expressed by the whole body, or by that organ which is authorized by the whole to express it" (*Johnson v. McIntosh*, 595). Communal property is not at all alien to "Western law." Communal land does not belong to *nobody*; it belongs to a collective person—a state, an indigenous nation, a corporation, or a cooperative. How or if the collective person makes use of its collective property internally is usually its business.

The third feature differs from the first two in the sense that it indeed hinders the easy categorization of aboriginal title as restricted collective property: the source of aboriginal title outside of common law. Aboriginal title is marked as *sui generis* because it differs from other property rights in common law in the way that it is *guaranteed by* common law but does not *originate in* common law. The reason for this is rooted in the concept of competing sovereignties in common law regarding indigenous rights—an argumentative structure we have already investigated with regard to the Marshall trilogy cases of the U.S. Supreme Court: indigenous communities had full sovereignty over their territory at the time of discovery, and common law respected this by recognizing the aboriginal title rights of the original inhabitants. While aboriginal title is a common-law right, the reason for it to exist lies outside common law, in another's sovereignty.

This situation of legal pluralism can be called "rooted legal pluralism." As I have mentioned, every indigenous rights strategy must accommodate the indigenous paradox, which describes the situation whereby an indigenous claimant must count as a legal person within the national legal system to be able to bring a case, but must also be outside the national legal system to be able to claim special group rights. The sovereignty approach, which we can observe in *Delgamuukw*, accommodates the indigenous paradox through a right—aboriginal title—that incorporates this paradox: it is part of the national legal system by way of accommodating another's territorial sovereignty originating outside the legal system. The Canadian courts reflect this paradoxical nature of aboriginal title by applying the nonclassification term *sui generis* to it. I call the type of legal pluralism that underpins the construction of the *sui generis* right of aboriginal title "rooted" because it is conceptualized as being based in two distinct sovereignties: the Crown's and the aboriginal nation's. Clearly, it is not possible for both of these competing sovereignties to exert their legal force to the full extent over the same territory. Which of the two sovereigns is able legitimately to exert which powers is a question of negotiation and recognition, but within a context of unequal power relations.

We can therefore summarize at this point the prevalent features of the sovereignty approach to indigenous rights. The sovereignty approach accommodates the indigenous paradox by providing an argumentative basis for a rooted legal pluralism of national law and indigenous law. This legal pluralism is rooted in the competing sovereignties of the postcolonial state and the indigenous community.

The relevance of the debate over the *sui generis* nature of aboriginal title becomes clearer in light of the fact that several judges in the *Delgamuukw* case advanced differing opinions on the matter. For instance, in the appeals court Justice Hutcheon refused to answer the question of whether aboriginal title was *sui generis* or a "regular" property interest; he found it sufficient to note that aboriginal title and real estate property interests compete "on an equal footing." In light of the distinction I have indicated in Chapter 1 between "rooted legal pluralism" and "de facto legal pluralism," such an argument amounts to the recognition of a "de facto legal pluralism"—a concept that relates more to the "culture" approach to indigenous rights that we will begin to explore in Chapter 6. We can see that the sovereignty approach and the culture approach, which seem to be bound to their specific legal systems in North America and Latin American respectively, are indeed interacting and cross-fertilizing independently of their origins.

A different opinion was expressed in the appeals court by Judge Wallace, who argued that aboriginal title is not *sui generis*, but a more or less "regular" property interest, albeit more restricted in scope than full real estate property. Such an approach is "dangerous" from the perspective of an indigenous rights claimant because it is based on a monistic legalism instead of a legal pluralism model and therefore does not accommodate the indigenous paradox. As we have seen, indigenous claimants profit from the recognition of legal pluralism because it allows them to claim rights in the national legal system while still shielding themselves from the regulation of the national legal system by claiming legal autonomy. A monistic model does not provide such room for maneuver—they either have land rights in the national legal system or they do not, but the possibility of special group rights outside of what the state is willing to provide is foreclosed.

From Sovereignty to Culture: Culture as Proof and Constraint

The second aspect I would like to highlight is the way "culture" appears in the *Delgamuukw* judgment. Although not the basis of the sovereignty approach, it plays two important roles in the argumentation of the Canadian Supreme Court: first as proof of the existence of aboriginal title and second as a constraint on the scope of aboriginal title. Although culture does not replace sovereignty as the basis of indigenous rights—as happens in the more recent judgments before the Inter-American Court of Human Rights that we shall look at later—we can observe in *Delgamuukw v. British Columbia* how the court incorporates the argument of "difference in culture" to both enable and restrict aboriginal rights claims.

We have learned of one limitation of aboriginal title that does not exist with fee simple: its alienability only to the Crown. This limitation was already incorporated in the earliest Marshall trilogy cases in the United States. In the Canadian Supreme Court's conception of aboriginal title, a second limitation emerges that we have not discussed in the previous cases: an inherent limitation on the use of lands held in aboriginal title.

The idea is simple: at the time of conquest the emerging common-law nation that eventually became Canada accommodated aboriginal sovereignty by establishing the common-law principle "aboriginal title." But aboriginal title was granted to accommodate sovereignty as it materialized at the time. What the Supreme Court generally argues here has been called (and indeed the phrase is used in the judgment itself) the phenomenon of rights "frozen at the time of contact" (Borrows 1997). The court itself tries to wriggle out of the problem by arguing, as noted above, that its ruling does not restrict aboriginal rights to traditional subsistence activities, which would "amount to a legal straitjacket," but it does establish an "overarching limit, defined by the special nature of the aboriginal title in that land" (para. 132). In other words, aboriginal nations can change their land use practices without losing their title to the territory, but only to that point where the nontraditional uses do not amount to a land use regime that is too far removed from their traditional way of life or, to put it the other way, too similar to the way any other Canadian corporation uses its real estate. This understanding of an inherent limit to aboriginal title again connects to the paradoxical structure of indigenous rights. Land rights vanish where the indigenous claimants become too similar to other collective legal persons in the national state.

But it is important to note that this kind of limitation on indigenous land rights is not in accord with the older legal tradition on indigenous land rights we have found in the early Marshall cases. Marshall's legal pluralism was still clearly "rooted" because it was grounded in competing sovereignty over the same territory. The idea was that the land had either been ceded to the United States, in which case the Union could use it however it pleased, or it was held in Indian title, in which case the Indians could use it—without state interference—however they liked. If the United States wished to limit Indian use rights, it was able to do so, but a use limitation was not inherent in Indian title. The younger Canadian jurisprudence, however, as expressed in *Delgamuukw*, argues for an inherent limitation on aboriginal title preventing the land from being used in a way that is irreconcilable with its traditional (precontact) use.

Where does this come from? Although it may sound contradictory, I believe that this line of argumentation is a dialectic reaction to the more accommodative style of the Canadian courts, as expressed in the broadening of the standard of proof for aboriginal nations to establish the existence of aboriginal title. As we have already discussed, the sovereignty approach as an indigenous rights strategy needs to establish precontact sovereignty over the land in question. This is usually the most complicated practical problem of an indigenous rights claim because to conclusively prove precontact use and occupation "only" through oral evidence is challenging enough and becomes more challenging as time passes. Because of this, the Canadian Supreme Court loosened the standards of proof in two important ways: by allowing oral history accounts to be entered as credible evidence and by recognizing present occupation and use of the land as credible proof of occupation before the establishment of Crown sovereignty. In the words of the court: "In order to make out a claim for aboriginal title, the aboriginal group asserting title must satisfy the following criteria: (i) the land must have been occupied prior to sovereignty, (ii) if present occupation is relied on as proof of occupation pre-sovereignty, there must be a continuity between present and pre-sovereignty occupation, and (iii) at sovereignty, that occupation must have been exclusive" (para. 143). That is exactly what the Gitksan and the Wet'suwet'en did when they brought their case before Justice McEachern. They demonstrated their relationship to the land and tried to argue that there was and still is continuity between present-day land occupation and use and pre-sovereignty land occupation and use.

In this way the focus of the court shifts from sovereignty to culture. Although the basis of the Gitksan and Wet'suwet'en aboriginal title claim is pre-Canadian sovereignty, the only way to prove it is to prove precontact use and occupation. The only way to prove pre-Canadian use and occupation is to prove present use and occupation, along with a credible claim of historic continuity, which can only be proven by displaying aboriginal cultural practices that demonstrate a link to the land. In other words, to prove a legal fiction (de jure sovereignty), indigenous peoples have to perform cultural practice (de facto culture).

In *Delgamuukw* the legal fiction of sovereignty alone does not carry the day; it needs to be proven by cultural practice. To the degree that "culture as proof" is needed to bring the sovereignty argument to life, the topic shifts to culture. Only proven sovereignty is enforceable sovereignty, and only cultural practice proves such sovereignty. But the shift goes even further. I have argued that the legal fiction of "sovereignty" accommodates the indigenous paradox because an indigenous community that can claim sovereignty (however factually limited) is not completely subject to the legal system it calls on for protection: a situation of legal pluralism arises that is grounded in competing sovereignties. At the moment when sovereignty is not evident but needs to be proven by cultural practice, only factual cultural difference (and assumed historic continuity of this difference) is recognized as materialized sovereignty and the legal pluralism that comes with it. What the parties begin to talk about is factual cultural difference before the background of the legal fiction of sovereignty. In this understanding, sovereignty emerges only in its materialized form as cultural practice, while the fictional aspect of sovereignty goes out of focus.

The degree to which the legal fiction of sovereignty gets replaced by the factual phenomenon of cultural difference can be observed in the (not really dogmatically consistent) limitation of aboriginal title to traditional uses and practices. From a strict sovereignty standpoint, the legal fiction of sovereignty is sufficient to constitute legal pluralism. The idea that the cultural practice proving this sovereignty must be different from the majority culture is not compelling from that standpoint. On the contrary, to prove sovereign equality it would be important for the sovereign claimants to be able to use the land as other sovereigns do—as they see fit and according to established standards of international law. Only when they claim that the goal of indigenous rights regimes is to protect *cultural difference* rather than sovereign equality does it become imperative to preserve the very cultural difference they wish to protect. Exactly this kind of shift (although in the frame of the sovereignty approach) can be observed in *Delgamuukw v. British Columbia*.

This becomes apparent in Lamer's elaboration on the accommodation of oral history accounts by the plaintiffs. One of the larger issues in this case was the trial court's evaluation of the evidence presented by the Gitksan and Wet'suwet'en plaintiffs. Provincial Supreme Court Justice McEachern had systematically undervalued the oral evidence accounts and personal affidavits of members of the aboriginal communities. Chief Justice Lamer of the Canadian Supreme Court argued that the cultural differences in the manner and style of accounting for history "demand a unique approach to the treatment of evidence which accords due weight to the perspective of aboriginal peoples" (para. 82). He cites himself in *R. v. Van der Peet*, noting that it is necessary to bridge "aboriginal and non-aboriginal cultures" (para. 81, citing *R. v. Van der Peet*, para. 42). But to be able to bridge "cultures" instead of "legal systems," the factual (culture) begins to overcome the fictional (sovereignty).

The passage where Lamer uses examples to explain the inherent limitation of aboriginal title—that present land use may not be irreconcilable with traditional land use—is also of interest here:

> Occupancy is determined by reference to the activities that have taken place on the land and the uses to which the land has been put by the particular group. . . . For example, if occupation is established with reference to the use of the land as a hunting ground, then the group that successfully claims aboriginal title to that land may not use it in such a fashion as to destroy its value for such a use (e.g., by strip mining it). Similarly, if a group claims a special bond with the land because of its ceremonial or cultural significance, it may not use

> the land in such a way as to destroy that relationship (e.g., by developing it in such a way that the bond is destroyed, perhaps by turning it into a parking lot). (para. 128)

We can learn much from the phrasing Lamer uses—that hunting grounds may not be "strip-mined" and links to the land may not be destroyed by creating "parking lots." What reverberates through these lines is an image of the indigenous person as a spiritually engaged conservationist. As soon as indigenous communities begin to strip-mine their lands or build parking lots on them, they stop being indigenous and forfeit their aboriginal title. Moreover, to justify special protection, aboriginal land use must also remain—at least to a large extent—noneconomic and anti-capitalist: "The relationship between an aboriginal community and the lands over which it has aboriginal title has an important non-economic component. The land has an inherent and unique value in itself, which is enjoyed by the community with aboriginal title to it. The community cannot put the land to uses which would destroy that value" (para. 129).

This "special relationship" of the indigenous people to their land is a highly important argumentative feature of the inter-American case law we will investigate subsequently. Such a "special relationship"—that is, spiritual and noneconomic—would be unnecessary in a clear-cut sovereignty approach but is of huge importance in the culture approach to indigenous rights. Its most prominent elaboration can be found in an influential UN report by Erica-Irene Daes titled *Indigenous Peoples and Their Relationship to Land* (2001). This "special relationship to land" that indigenous peoples are presumed to have becomes the core of the definition of indigenous (and tribal) peoples in international law. But it is—as we can already surmise from *Delgamuukw* and as will become even more pertinent in the three following cases—inextricably bound up with Eurocentric clichés of the noble savage. It is remarkable but not surprising that these clichés are invoked in the same text that strongly denounces the Eurocentric bias manifest in the devaluation of the oral histories of aboriginal nations. The critique of ethnocentrism often remains within the same framework of ethnically grounded stereotypes—only inverted. The noble savage and the bad savage are mirror images of one another—a topic we will investigate further in the Chapter 10.

Apart from these observations it becomes evident that although aboriginal title is conceptualized as grounded in sovereignty, which was the basis of the *sui generis* nature of the land right, the focus shifts to difference in culture as it is factually performed, performable, and demonstrable. The legal fiction of sovereignty does not take the argument far enough.

* * * *

Delgamuukw v. British Columbia counts among the landmark cases of indigenous rights in Canada. Although the claim of the Gitksan and Wet'suwet'en is brought in the framework of the sovereignty approach to indigenous rights, we witness how the concept of culture becomes prominent. Generally speaking, aboriginal title is conceptualized as a *sui generis* right, mainly because it originates not only in common law but also in aboriginal law. This legal pluralism is grounded in the recognized precontact sovereignty of the indigenous nations now residing in Canada. As such, aboriginal title accommodates the indigenous paradox by establishing "rooted legal pluralism," which allows the indigenous claimant to appear in Canadian law as a legal person against whom Canadian legal principles are not completely enforceable. This is manifest in different standards of proof and allows indigenous claimants to present oral history as credible pieces of evidence. But this new evidentiary standard, which presupposes that competing sovereignty can only be proven by the performance of cultural difference, also leads to a shift of focus. The legal fiction of sovereignty takes a back seat to the factual performance of cultural difference. Dogmatically this leads to a restriction of the scope of aboriginal title to those land uses that are not irreconcilable with traditional, pre-Canadian land uses. This "culture shift" moves the goalposts of indigenous rights movements from sovereign equality to the protection of cultural difference.

CHAPTER 6

"De Facto Legal Pluralism" and the Problem of Not Being "Different Enough"

Aloeboetoe v. Suriname

The four cases we have discussed in the previous chapters have been national court cases. Our fifth case, *Aloeboetoe v. Suriname*, was decided by an international court, the Inter-American Court of Human Rights (IACtHR; "the Court"). It was the first time the then relatively young institution had to touch upon questions concerning indigenous communities. The case, however, dealt mainly with reparations to indigenous individuals after a massacre in the Surinamese civil war, a constellation not prototypical of indigenous rights cases. The claimants were a group of relatives of the massacre victims of Saramaka ethnicity, a group of African descent residing in several relatively autonomous villages of one hundred to two hundred individuals each, most of them in the rainforest of Suriname. Although they all belonged to the same Saramaka community, they did not represent the Saramakas as a whole. Nevertheless, the case is highly important for the argument I put forth in this book for two interrelated reasons.

First, the question of legal pluralism, which we have already identified as an integral part of the phenomenon of indigeneity, is discussed in the context of reparations. The Court recognized the polygamous family structure of the Saramakas—not Surinamese "official" family law—as the guideline for awarding reparations. The Court held that Suriname had to pay pecuniary damages to multiple wives of the indigenous men killed in the massacre, as well as to their children. Second, the question of collective reparations to the indigenous nations came up in trial, although the Saramakas had not presented the case as a group claim. In this context the Court discussed the possibility of indigenous self-government on the basis of Saramaka sovereignty (there had been a treaty between the Saramakas and the Dutch recognizing self-government) but dismissed the concept and denied the collective claims.

Interestingly, the Court sent two seemingly conflicting messages. It first indicated relatively clearly that it would not look into sovereignty claims of indigenous groups, but then it opened the door for indigenous rights claims by recognizing a legal pluralism involving national law and indigenous law—a legal pluralism based not on sovereignty but on factual cultural difference. This door is later opened fully with the culture approach to indigenous rights.

Indigenous Rights in the Inter-American Human Rights System

We must first take a brief look into the principles of the inter-American system for the protection of human rights. At the heart of the inter-American system for the protection of human rights is the Inter-American Court of Human Rights.[1] The Court hears and decides cases on the basis of several instruments of human rights protection in the Americas, mostly in the form of multilateral human rights treaties situated in the framework of the Organization of American States (OAS) (see Table 3).

Among these instruments, the American Convention on Human Rights ("the Convention") is the most important. In addition to a catalog of human rights guarantees, the Convention provides the legal framework for the enforcement of human rights instruments in the Americas through the Inter-American Commission on Human Rights (IACHR; "the Commission") and the Court. Of the thirty-five OAS member states, twenty-two have currently ratified the Convention (see Table 4). Among those who have abstained from the treaty are the United States and Canada.[2]

If one of the member states does not comply with the rights laid down in the provisions of the Convention, its citizens can bring a claim before the Commission. Individual or group claimants are not allowed to bring their cases directly before the Court.[3]

The Commission is the oldest body in the inter-American human rights system and was created during the Fifth Meeting of Consultation of Ministers of Foreign Affairs in Santiago de Chile in 1959. At that time it did not yet have a clear mission to protect human rights, nor was it part of

Table 3. Legal instruments in the inter-American system for the protection of human rights

Year	*Human rights instrument*	*Comments*	*Number of ratifications*
1948	American Declaration of the Rights and Duties of Man[1]	The Declaration has been adopted by the United States and Canada	Adopted by the 21 founding states of the OAS
1969	American Convention on Human Rights ("Pact of San José")	Establishes the enforcement of human rights in the inter-American system with the Commission (IACHR) and the Court (IACtHR)	22 (18 accept the IACtHR's jurisdiction)
1985	Inter-American Convention to Prevent and Punish Torture		18
1988	Additional Protocol to the American Convention on Human Rights in the Area of Economic, Social, and Cultural Rights ("Protocol of San Salvador")	The Additional Protocol adds rights to the Convention that focus mainly on "classic" political and individual rights	16
1990	Protocol to the American Convention on Human Rights to Abolish the Death Penalty		13
1994	Inter-American Convention on the Prevention, Punishment, and Eradication of Violence Against Women ("Convention of Belém do Pará")	Only the United States, Canada, and Cuba have not ratified this convention.[2]	32
1994	Inter-American Convention on the Forced Disappearance of Persons		15
1999	Convention on the Elimination of All Forms of Discrimination Against Persons with Disabilities		19

(continued)

Table 3. (*Continued*)

Year	*Human rights instrument*	*Comments*	*Number of ratifications*
2013	Inter-American Convention Against Racism, Racial Discrimination, and Related Forms of Intolerance	Ten states have signed the treaty; the ratification processes are still ongoing	0
2013	American Declaration Against All Forms of Discrimination and Intolerance	Eight states have signed the treaty; the ratification processes are still ongoing	0

Source: This list of the most important human rights instruments in the inter-American system reflects the situation as of June 2015 as it could be retrieved from the respective webpage of the OAS, http://www.oas.org/en/iachr/mandate/basic_documents.asp.

1. The American Declaration of the Rights and Duties of Man ("the Declaration") was adopted, along with the Charter of the American States, at the Ninth Inter-American Conference in Bogotá in 1948. It contains a broader range of human rights, including economic and social rights, but establishes no specific instruments for enforcement. The American Convention on Human Rights ("the Convention"), by way of comparison, contains fewer human rights but establishes the Inter-American Commission on Human Rights ("the Commission" and the Inter-American Court of Human Rights ("the Court") as the instruments of their implementation and enforcement. Those cases that come from the Organization of American States (OAS) member states that have not ratified the Convention but have adopted the Declaration are heard by the Commission on the basis of the Declaration. That is most relevant in cases concerning the United States and Canada. Because the legal scope of the Declaration is even wider than that of the Convention, the Commission usually holds these states to the same human rights standards as the member states of the Convention. The Commission is, in these situations, not entitled to refer the case to the Court. It is only able to compile a report containing nonbinding recommendations for the member state.

2. The OAS has thirty-five member states, including Cuba. With the exception of the Declaration, Cuba has not ratified any human rights instruments, partly due to its exclusion from the OAS system by veto of the United States in the course of its embargo policy against Cuba. In late 2014 the United States changed this policy and again allowed Cuba's presence at OAS meetings. Whether Cuba will now begin to further engage in the inter-American system for the protection of human rights remains to be seen.

an established system for the protection of human rights. In 1969, during the Specialized Conference on Human Rights in San José, Costa Rica, the American Convention on Human Rights established such a system (also referred to as the "Pact of San José"), with the Commission as one of its main organs. The ratification process lasted until 1978, when the Convention finally entered into force. Since then the Commission's duty has been

Table 4. Countries' status on the American Convention on Human Rights

OAS member state	*Ratification of Convention*	*Acceptance of Court jurisdiction*
Antigua and Barbuda	No	—
Argentina	Yes	Yes
Bahamas	No	—
Barbados	Yes	No
Belize	No	—
Bolivia	Yes	Yes
Brazil	Yes	Yes
Canada	No	—
Chile	Yes	Yes
Colombia	Yes	Yes
Costa Rica	Yes	Yes
Cuba	No	—
Dominica	Yes	No
Dominican Republic	Yes	Yes[1]
Ecuador	Yes	Yes
El Salvador	Yes	Yes
Grenada	Yes	No
Guatemala	Yes	Yes
Guyana	No	—
Haiti	Yes	Yes
Honduras	Yes	Yes
Jamaica	Yes	No
Mexico	Yes	Yes
Nicaragua	Yes	Yes

(*continued*)

Table 4. (*Continued*)

OAS member state	*Ratification of Convention*	*Acceptance of Court jurisdiction*
Panama	Yes	Yes
Paraguay	Yes	Yes
Peru	Yes	Yes
St. Kitts and Nevis	No	—
St. Lucia	No	—
St. Vincent and Grenadines	No	—
Suriname	Yes	Yes
Trinidad and Tobago	Yes, but denunciation in 1998[2]	—
United States	No	—
Uruguay	Yes	Yes
Venezuela	Yes, but denunciation in 2012[3]	—

Source: The information reflects the situation as of May 2019 as it could be retrieved from the respective webpage of the OAS, http://www.oas.org/dil/treaties_B-32_American_Convention_on_Human_Rights_sign.htm.

1. The Constitutional Court of the Dominican Republic declared acceptance of the jurisdiction of the Inter-American Court of Human Rights ("the Court") to be unconstitutional in 2014, and therefore ordered the national courts not to abide by the Court's jurisprudence. As of June 2015, however, the Dominican Republic had not rescinded its acceptance of the Court's jurisdiction nor denounced the Convention.

2. Trinidad and Tobago denounced the American Convention in 1998 in regard to the Commission's jurisprudence restricting the death penalty.

3. Venezuela denounced the American Convention in 2012, accusing the Commission of interfering with internal affairs.

to hear individual complaints of violations of one or several of the human rights enshrined in the Convention.

After the Commission has heard a case brought by an individual or a group, it compiles a report detailing the violations and the recommended remedies. According to article 50 of the Convention, the Commission then transmits the report to the member state. If the member state does not comply with the recommendations of the Commission and the matter is not otherwise settled within a period of three months, article 51 of the Convention

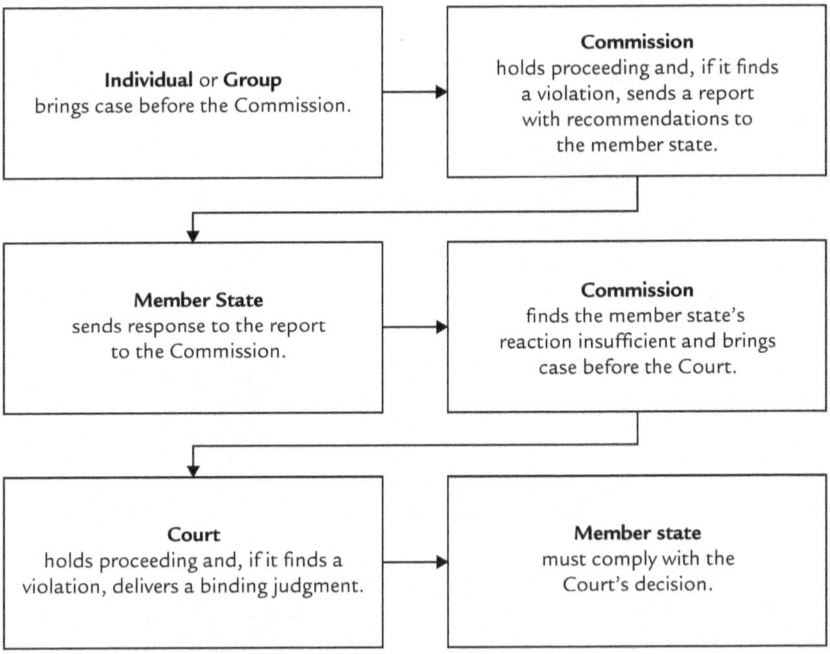

Figure 1. Complaint procedure in the inter-American system for the protection of human rights

entitles the Commission either to bring the case before the Court or simply to publish its report without further proceedings (see Figure 1).[4]

Only the Court—established after the Convention went into force in 1979—can pass a judgment that is binding for the member states under its jurisdiction. Even if individual OAS member states have ratified the Convention, they must also agree separately to the contentious jurisdiction of the Court. This means they have to accept the Court's jurisdiction in general and not just on a case-by-case basis (see Table 4).[5]

Indigenous Rights Jurisprudence before *Aloeboetoe*

The Court first came into existence in 1979. In its early phase in the 1980s its procedures were not yet fully established, and it only processed a few cases. Most of the early cases of the Court were concerned with massive human rights violations related to massacres that occurred during the numerous civil wars and armed conflicts in the 1970s and 1980s. *Aloeboetoe v. Suriname* is one such case. Generally these cases stayed within the well-established frame of individual rights and liberties. The question of special protection for indigenous peoples in the form of collective rights did not come up in the first two decades of the Court's jurisprudence. Since the 1970s, however, the Commission had been much more active than the Court in laying the groundwork for indigenous rights conceptions in the inter-American system (Davis 1988).

As early as the 1970s the Commission had elaborated on indigenous rights in several country reports on the state of human rights in the OAS member states. In these reports the Commission criticized member states for violating human rights in general, and especially with regard to indigenous peoples (Shelton 2013, 948–950). The Commission also began to address issues concerning indigenous peoples in its jurisprudence, such as in *Guhaibo v. Colombia* (1973) and *Ache v. Paraguay* (1978). In these early cases, however, the Commission, being reluctant to recognize collective indigenous rights, focused on individual human rights violations.

The first major landmark case concerning indigenous rights—and the one that also first grabbed the attention of the mass media—was *Yanomami v. Brazil* (1987).[6] In its resolution directed to the Brazilian government, the Commission clearly affirmed the need for special measures to protect indigenous peoples. The Commission found that a proposed highway through Yanomami territory violated their rights and recommended that Brazil set aside and demarcate Yanomami lands. The Commission addressed violations of the Yanomami community's rights to life, liberty, and personal security, to residence and movement, and to the preservation of health and well-being. Property rights, which would later emerge as the cornerstone of the Court's indigenous rights jurisprudence, are not yet mentioned. Nevertheless it was the first case before the Commission in which natural resource exploitation initiatives by the state were regarded as a violation of indigenous peoples' human rights (Miranda 2012, 821). The Commission itself drew a connection between natural resource development projects and the destruction of indigenous communal identity and culture (*Yanomami v. Brazil*, para. 10d).

For the Court, however, the topic remained unexplored until *Aloeboetoe v. Suriname*, when it had to deal with an indigenous rights question in the context of a massacre case. Indigenous rights came up in an unlikely context: the calculation of reparations.

The Saramakas in the Surinamese Civil War

The claimants in *Aloeboetoe v. Suriname* were Saramaka. At the time of the case, the Saramakas comprised some 22,000 people and are one of six Maroon peoples in Suriname that constitute about 10 percent of the national population. The Saramakas are the descendants of Africans brought to the Americas as slave laborers in the late seventeenth and early eighteenth centuries to work on Suriname's sugar plantations. Over time many of these slaves—whether individually, in small groups, or in collective rebellions—escaped from the plantations into the dense rainforest. There they founded villages and communities beyond the reach of the colonial forces (Price and Price 1991, viii).

In 1762 the Saramakas entered into a treaty with the Netherlands, the colonial power in Suriname. The treaty contained several provisions recognizing their territorial autonomy (para. 56).[7] When Suriname became independent in 1975, the emerging (post)colonial legal system did not acknowledge any territorial autonomy for the Saramakas or other groups of African descent in the country. In the aftermath of independence and ongoing political instability, civil war broke out, leading to a most brutal guerrilla war from 1986 to 1992, most of which took place in the rainforest. In the course of this conflict, which destabilized the Saramakas' territory, many Saramakas migrated to French Guiana.

The actions leading to the claim in *Aloeboetoe v. Suriname* took place at the high point of the armed conflict. In 1987 troops under the control of the Surinamese government massacred seven Saramaka men they suspected of belonging to the opposition guerrilla force known as the "Jungle Commando." In fact, they were civilians. The judgment describes the occurrences as follows:

> The events that gave rise to the petition apparently occurred on December 31, 1987, in [the two villages] Atjoni . . . and . . . Tjongalangapassi. . . . In Atjoni, more than 20 male, unarmed Bushnegroes (Maroons) had been attacked, abused and beaten with rifle butts by a group of soldiers. A number of them had been wounded with bayonets and knives and were detained on suspicion of belonging to the Jungle Commando, a subversive group. Some 50 persons witnessed these occurrences.
>
> . . . The Maroons all denied that they were members of the Jungle Commando. The Captain of the village of Gujaba made a point of

> informing the commander in charge of the soldiers that the persons in question were civilians from various different villages. The commander disregarded this information.
>
> . . . The soldiers allowed some of the Maroons to continue on their way, but . . . seven of them, including a 15-year-old boy, were dragged, blindfolded, into a military vehicle and taken through Tjongalangapassi in the direction of Paramaribo. . . .
>
> . . . The vehicle stopped when it came to Kilometer 30. The soldiers ordered the victims to get out or forcibly dragged them out of the vehicle. They were given a spade and ordered to start digging. Aside [one of the Saramakas] was injured while trying to escape, but was not followed. The other six Maroons were killed.
>
> . . . Aside, who had a bullet in his right thigh, pointed out [to the people who found him] that he was the sole survivor of the massacre, the victims of which had already been partially devoured by vultures. Aside's wound was infested with maggots and his right shoulder blade bore an X-shaped cut. . . . He was admitted to the Academic Hospital of Paramaribo on January 6, 1988, but died despite the care provided. (paras. 2–6)

The facts of the case were clear and the Surinamese government disputed them only at first and quite half-heartedly. After brief proceedings the Commission submitted the case to the Court in 1990. When the Court held a public hearing in 1991, Suriname acknowledged the facts presented, accepted its responsibility, and agreed to pay reparations to the relatives of the victims (para. 11). The case became controversial only after the judgment on the merits had been delivered and the Court was about to decide on the question of reparations in 1993. A question arose regarding how to determine the number of the surviving dependents of the seven men killed—with reference to official Surinamese family law or with reference to traditional Saramaka family law.

The Claim

The Commission argued before the Court that Suriname had to pay damages to the minor children of the deceased in the form of a trust fund and to their dependent adults in the form of annual payments, both on the basis of the projected life income of the victims (paras. 15–16). To determine the number of persons who would be entitled to this compensation, it would be necessary to take into account the family structure of the Saramakas:

> With regard to the persons who would be entitled to compensation for actual damages, the Commission explains that it is necessary to take into account the family structure of the Maroons, of which the Saramakas (the tribe to which the victims belonged) are a part. It is essentially a matriarchal [footnoted: "Probably a more precise anthropological term would be *matrilineal*"] structure, where polygamy is common. In Suriname, marriages must be registered in order to be recognized by the State. Due to the dearth of registry offices in the interior of the country, however, that requirement is generally not met. The Commission is of the opinion that this should not affect the right to compensation of the relatives or spouses of unregistered marriages. It is argued that the care of family members is entrusted to a communal group organized along maternal lines; this is something that should be borne in mind in determining which of the relatives should be compensated. (para. 17)

The Commission argued that the number of dependent children should be calculated in reference to Saramaka family law rather than Surinamese family law. The latter requires the public registration of marriages (which Saramaka couples almost never did) and allows only marriages between one man and one woman, thus not the polygamy common in Saramaka families. The consequence was that the number of dependents would include several wives and the offspring of these multiple marriages of the seven men.

The second point the Commission made was for collective reparations rather than individual reparations. It argued that it was not only the dependent individuals of the victims who had suffered, but the community as a whole: "In the traditional Maroon society, a person is not only a member of his own family group, but also a member of the village community and of the tribal group. In this case, the damages suffered by the villagers due to the loss of certain members of its group must be redressed. Since the villagers, in practice, constitute a family in the broad sense of that term . . . they have suffered direct emotional damages as a result of the violations of the Convention" (para. 19). In that sense Suriname would not only have to pay reparations to the victims' next of kin, but also to the community as a whole. This obligation to pay reparations would go beyond what would be necessary in other cases and would, consequently, amount to collective reparations to the community. Such a construction resembles war reparations between states after a state of war. The Commission argued in that very direction: "The deeds for which the Government accepted responsibility appear to have caused damages to the Saramaka tribe, aggravated by the Government's subsequent actions in not recognizing "*the rights of the Bush-negroes*." In the Commission's opinion, a conflictive relationship appears to have existed between the Government and the Saramaka tribe and the killings occurred as a consequence of that situation" (para. 19; emphasis in original).

The state of Suriname found the amount put forward by the Commission to be excessive. If the Commission had followed Suriname's civil law, which only recognizes one marriage at a time, the number of next of kin would have been considerably less. Consequently, Suriname argued that "the customary norms of the Saramaka tribe should not be binding in fixing the amount of compensation to be granted to the victims' next of kin," but contended that the questions of "family relationship must be determined by reference to the American Convention and the applicable principles of international law" (para. 27). With regard to the Commission's claim for collective reparations to the Saramaka community as a whole, the government referred to the fact that such a demand had not been made in the course of the proceedings before the Commission and should not be admitted in the proceedings before the Court.

The Ruling

The Court extensively elaborated on two central questions: the applicable family law and the issue of collective reparations. On the question of family law, the Court acknowledged that "in the instant case, there is some difference of opinion between the parties as to who the successors of the victims are." The Commission "urges that this decision be made with reference to the customs of the Saramaka tribe, whereas Suriname requests that its civil law be applied" (para. 55).

The Court, being, after all, an international court, clarified that the question of who the successors of a person are had to be decided according to international law. But because no international treaty (such as ILO 169) applicable to Suriname could be found and "under international law there is no conventional or customary rule that would indicate who the successors of a person are," the Court had no alternative but to apply general principles of law (para. 61).[8] According to general principles of law, the successors of a person are his or her "children," "spouse," and "ascendants." International law does not provide precise definitions of these terms; they have to be interpreted according to "local law."

But which local law should be applied—"official" Surinamese law or "traditional" Saramaka law? If Saramaka family law were to be made the reference point for the Court's decision, its body of rules would have to qualify as "local law," which would appear to confirm the existence of a legal pluralism that includes both Saramaka law and Surinamese law. As the first link to determining some form of legal autonomy of the Saramakas, the Court discusses the treaty the Saramakas made with the Dutch. "The Commission's brief affirms that the Saramakas enjoy internal autonomy by virtue of a treaty dated September 19, 1762, which granted them permission to be governed by their own laws" (para. 56). In North America such treaties had been interpreted as *quasi* international treaties between sovereign nations. The Court, however, does not go in that direction. Instead it argues as follows:

> The Court does not deem it necessary to investigate whether or not that agreement is an international treaty. Suffice it to say that even if that were the case, the treaty would today be null and void because it contradicts the norms of *jus cogens superveniens*. In point of fact, under that treaty the Saramakas undertake to, among other things, capture any slaves that have deserted, take them prisoner and return them to the Governor of Suriname, who will pay from 10 to 50 florins per slave, depending on the distance of the place where they were apprehended. Another article empowers the Saramakas to sell to the Dutch any other prisoners they might take, as slaves. No treaty of that nature may be invoked before an international human rights tribunal. (para. 57)

This argumentation is indeed remarkable. Instead of positioning itself vis-à-vis the question of "tribal sovereignty" as one would in North American cases, the Court argues that the treaty is null and void because it contains provisions not in accord with *jus cogens*, those rules of customary international law which are universally accepted and which supersede all treaty terms. The prohibition of slavery counts as *jus cogens*. Because of that, according to the Court, the treaty is null and void, and cannot be part of the Court's deliberations.

Apart from the question of the value of this particular legal argument,[9] it shows that the Court jumps at the opportunity to avoid having to take a position on the legal quality of treaties between colonial powers and indigenous nations in general. Instead, the Court takes a shortcut and simply refers to the Commission, which "has pointed out that it does not seek to portray the Saramakas as a community that currently enjoys international juridical status; rather, the autonomy it claims for the tribe is one governed by domestic public law" (para. 58). This sentence by itself could be severely damaging to the sovereignty approach to indigenous rights. But the phrasing is unclear in many ways. The Court agrees with the Commission in its wish not "to portray the Saramakas as a community which currently enjoys international juridical status." This, however, is not an unequivocal assertion by the Court that the Saramakas do not enjoy international status; it is simply an acknowledgment that the Commission had refrained from portraying them as such, whatever the term "portraying" may mean in this context. Second, the Court agrees that issues of Saramaka autonomy have to be "governed by domestic public law." That alone does not mean that the Saramakas are not a sovereign entity—in the United States and Canada, issues of indigenous autonomy are discussed as part of public law, but with the idea of sovereignty as one of the governing principles.

After stating that the Saramakas' legal status would have to be determined by Surinamese law, the Court goes on to explain that this in itself does not yet lead to the conclusion that Surinamese family law does in fact govern Saramaka family affairs:

> The Court does not deem it necessary to determine whether the Saramakas enjoy legislative and jurisdictional autonomy within the region they occupy. The only question of importance here is whether the laws of Suriname in the area of family law apply to the Saramaka tribe. On this issue, the evidence offered leads to the conclusion that Surinamese family law is not effective insofar as the Saramakas are concerned. The members of the tribe are unaware of it and adhere to their own rules. The State for its part does not provide the facilities necessary for the registration of births, marriages, and deaths, an essential requirement for the enforcement of Surinamese law. Furthermore, the Saramakas do not bring the conflicts that arise over such matters before the State's tribunals, whose role in these areas is practically non-existent with respect to the Saramakas. It should be pointed out that, in the instant case, Suriname recognized the existence of a Saramaka customary law. (para. 57)

The Court does not address the question of whether the legal pluralism of Saramaka family law and Surinamese "official" family law is grounded in the circumstance that both are sovereigns within Surinamese territory, albeit not equally powerful. This was the North American way to provide a legal basis for existing legal pluralism. Rather, the legal pluralism is treated as a factual question. The Court argues that the Saramakas govern their family-related affairs according to their family law as a matter of fact. And the state of Suriname does not impose its "official" family law on the Saramakas, also as a matter of fact. Without elaborating on the foundations of this legal pluralism, the Court restricts itself to the observation of the phenomenon in fact and attaches legal consequences to it.

The Court therefore finds that to determine the meaning of the terms "children," "spouse," and "ascendants," "here local law is not Surinamese law, for the latter is not effective in the region insofar as family law is concerned. It is necessary, then, to take Saramaka custom into account" (para. 62). But the Court makes one highly interesting addition to its finding: "That custom will be the basis for the interpretation of those terms, to the degree that it does not contradict the American Convention. Hence, in referring to 'ascendants,' the Court shall make no distinction as to sex, even if that might be contrary to Saramaka custom" (para. 62). In this single sentence the indigenous paradox appears quite clearly. Here the Court accepts—at least partially—Saramaka custom as a body of law to which the Court can refer in order to determine specific terms of international law. The Saramakas therefore appear as something similar to one of the member states of the Convention: an entity able to govern itself through law. But at that point the Court also restricts this autonomy in the same way it does that of the member states. According to matrilineal Saramaka family law, only the female ascendants are seen as belonging to the family group. Male ascendants are not seen as related in this sense. As much as the member states of the American Convention may not discriminate on the basis of sex in determining who is the heir of a deceased person, the same goes for the Saramakas. Saramaka law can supersede "official" Surinamese law, but only under the same restrictions.[10]

Suriname had further made the objection that there was no proper documentation of the victims' family members. The Court explains:

> It has proved extremely difficult to identify the children, spouses, and, in some cases, the ascendants of the victims in this case. These are all members of a tribe that lives in the jungle, in the interior of

> Suriname, and speaks only its own native tongue. Marriages and births have in many cases not been registered. . . .
>
> . . . It is true that a person's identity must, as a general rule, be proved by means of relevant documentation. However, the situation in which the Saramakas find themselves is due in great measure to the fact that the State does not provide sufficient registry offices in the region; consequently, it is unable to issue documentation to all its inhabitants on the basis of the data contained therein. Suriname cannot, therefore, demand proof of the relationship and identity of persons through means that are not available to all of its inhabitants in that region. . . . Considering the circumstances surrounding the instant case, the Court believes that the evidence supplied is credible and can be admitted. (paras. 63–64)

Here a problem presents itself that is central to many indigenous rights cases, including *Delgamuukw v. British Columbia*, the case examined in Chapter 5: special exceptions from the burden of proof for indigenous claimants. The exception here is that the Saramakas, who do not have good access to public registration offices, are exempt from the obligation to present proper official documentation. The Court links this exception to the Saramakas' concrete living conditions. We will see that these exceptions become much more relevant in larger land rights cases concerning oral history accounts about land tenure. What the Court does here is still relatively unspectacular: in the concrete situation the Court is satisfied with the proof the Saramakas have provided, but it does not generalize that indigenous rights claims are not decided by the same standards of proof as other court cases. The reasons the Court gives for allowing evidence that does not consist of official documentation are specific and not general. It is connected not to the Saramakas' indigeneity but to the fact that official documentation is simply "not available to all of its [i.e., Suriname's] inhabitants in that region" (para. 64). Consequently, the Court presents a list of wives and children of the seven victims, three of whom had two wives each, who are counted as "spouses" and are eligible for actual damages (para. 66).

Eventually the Court comes to the question of damages for the community as a whole. Against this claim Suriname had only argued on procedural grounds, because the Commission had not brought up the question of collective reparations in its proceedings. The Court rebuffs this argument. It would be legitimate for the Commission to change its plea during the Court's proceedings. The Court then addresses the Commission's arguments for collective reparations. First it examines the claim that the killings of the seven Saramakas were racially motivated, which it finds not to be proven:

> Throughout the proceedings, the statement that the soldiers acted on suspicion that the Saramakas were members of the Jungle Commando was neither amended nor challenged. Consequently, the origin of the events as described in the memorial of April 1, 1991, lies not in some racial issue but, rather, in a subversive situation that prevailed at the time. Although a certain passage of the brief dated March 31, 1992, and the testimony of an expert both refer to the conflicting relationship that appears to have existed between the Government and the Saramakas, in the instant case it has not been proved that the racial factor was a motive for the killings of December 31, 1987. It is true that the victims of the killings all belonged to the Saramaka tribe, but this circumstance of itself does not lead to the conclusion that there was a racial element to the crime. (para. 82)

A second argument the Commission had presented was that "in traditional Maroon society, a person is a member not only of his or her own family group, but also of his or her own village community and tribal group. According to the Commission, the villagers make up a family in the broad sense. This is why damages caused to one of its members also represent damages to the community, which would have to be indemnified" (para. 83).

At this point we find a genuine feature of the "culture approach" to indigenous rights. The Commission evokes Saramaka family structure as a special cultural feature that sets the Saramakas apart from "ordinary" Surinamese. Because Saramaka family structure was presumed to be much more close-knit than that of Surinamese majority society, the loss of one member hits the group as a whole much harder than does the loss of a member of Surinamese majority society. Therefore, according to the Commission's argument, the killing of a member of an indigenous community can give rise to collective reparations. The Court, however, does not agree with this reasoning. Characteristically it denies the special claim by referring to the Saramakas' similarity to the majority Surinamese society:

> As for the argument linking the claim for moral damages to the unique social structure of the Saramakas who were generally harmed by the killings, the Court believes that all persons, in addition to

> being members of their own families and citizens of a State, also generally belong to intermediate communities. In practice, the obligation to pay moral compensation does not extend to such communities, nor to the State in which the victim participated; these are redressed by the enforcement of the system of laws. If in some exceptional case such compensation has ever been granted, it would have been to a community that suffered direct damages. (para. 83)

In other words, every person, whether indigenous or not, belongs to some kind of community. This fact does not yet give rise to the obligation to compensate that community for the death of one of its members. This clearly dismisses the idea of a special right for indigenous communities in the field of reparations by stating that an indigenous individual's relationship to his or her community is no different from a nonindigenous individual's. Later decisions, as we will see in *Awas Tingni v. Nicaragua* and *Saramaka v. Suriname*, will be much more sympathetic to the idea that indigenous individuals have some kind of exceptional relationship to their communities—and especially to their land—that sets them apart from the majority population.

The third argument of the Commission for collective damages is a classic sovereignty argument, which is also rebuffed by the Court. The Commission had argued that the killings took place on Saramaka territory, and these illegal actions of representatives of the Suriname state on Saramaka land violated the Saramakas' territorial integrity, a right the Saramakas held as a whole. But the Court does not find any proof for the territorial autonomy of the Saramakas:

> According to the Commission, the third ground for payment of moral damages to the Saramakas involves the rights that the tribe apparently have over the territory they occupy and the violation of such rights by the Army of Suriname when it entered that territory. The Commission has stated that the autonomy acquired by the Saramakas, while originating in a treaty, at the present time is only governed by domestic public law, since no form of international status is sought for the tribe. At these proceedings, the Commission has only presented the 1762 treaty. . . . The Court has already expressed its opinion of this so-called international treaty. . . . No other provision of domestic law, either written or customary, has been relied upon to establish the autonomy of the Saramakas. (para. 84)

Here again the Court dismisses "tribal sovereignty" for the Saramakas. If the Saramakas had some form of territorial autonomy, such a norm would have to be found in Surinamese public law; the treaty of 1792 is not a valid source. This of course deviates substantially from the North American cases. The Court clearly hesitates to make such a far-reaching decision, which would effectively have led to establishing principles regulating how the member states of the Convention should organize their relations with indigenous communities.

Consequently the Court dismissed collective reparations to the Saramakas as a community and only awarded individual damages,[11] but did take into account Saramaka family law. The Court ordered Suriname to pay US$453,102 in individual damages and to create two trust funds and a foundation to manage the money.[12]

The IACtHR Rejects the Sovereignty Approach

The Court in *Aloeboetoe v. Suriname* made three important decisions: (1) it would not recognize indigenous peoples as actors in international law; (2) it would, nevertheless, as a question of fact rather than sovereignty, acknowledge the legal pluralism of "official" state law and indigenous law and from time to time interpret general legal terms according to indigenous law; and (3) it would not (yet) conceptualize indigenous rights as collective rights and would be very reluctant to acknowledge violations of the rights of an indigenous group as a whole, but did nevertheless provide a basis for future claims in that direction. We will investigate these three aspects and then try to analyze how the indigenous paradox presents itself in this setting.

In the previous chapters we have already characterized the basic features of the sovereignty approach to indigenous rights: from the former sovereignty of the native nations as independent states before the arrival of the Europeans there arises a legal pluralism in the newly emerged colonial nation-states and their (post)colonial successors. To a certain degree the legal systems of the (post)colonial states accommodate this existing legal sovereignty of the indigenous nations residing within their territory. This sovereignty extends first of all to the indigenous territory. Because indigenous land rights are grounded in the sovereignty of the indigenous nations, their source lies outside the legal system of the (post)colonial state; it is, in other words, "rooted legal pluralism."

Hence, the sovereignty approach to indigenous rights consists of a claim for the recognition and accommodation of indigenous sovereignty concerning land titles or the practice of certain activities. There is a built-in imbalance to this approach. Although there are two sovereigns involved in the dispute, the decision is made not by a neutral arbiter who does not stand on either side but by a court belonging to the more powerful of the two sovereigns: the (post) colonial state. Therefore the indigenous nation, which sees itself as a sovereign entity, must request recognition of this sovereignty and a form of limited incorporation of its law into the more powerful sovereign's legal system. How far this recognition goes is up to the more powerful sovereign's court.

The indigenous paradox in its peculiar shape as a sovereignty-based claim could vanish before an international court. An international human rights tribunal could be a neutral arbiter that belongs to neither the indigenous nation nor the (post)colonial state. Such a court could balance—in an impartial way—the sovereign interests of both claimants, which clash because they factually share territory. Indigenous actors in the Americas realized this potential of international institutions from the start. In the early 1920s, shortly after its creation, the League of Nations—the short-lived predecessor of the United Nations in the era between the two world wars—became the forum for indigenous claims (Niezen 2003, 31–36). The spokesperson for the Six Nations of the Grand River Land near Brantford, Ontario, and chief of the Younger Bear Clan of the Cayuga Nation, Deskaheh (also known as Levi General), went to Geneva and brought a land rights claim against Canada before the League. Although the campaign, which was well covered by the media at the time, was unsuccessful, the episode illustrates the awareness indigenous movements had for the potential of international dispute resolution bodies to deal impartially with disputes between indigenous nations and postcolonial states (Rostkowski 1995).

In *Aloeboetoe v. Suriname*, the Inter-American Court of Human Rights chose not to address indigenous sovereignty and make it part of its jurisprudence, although the opportunity presented itself. The situation of the Saramakas was similar to the North American model of indigenous rights in that a treaty between the Dutch and the Saramakas had recognized Saramaka self-government in exchange for the future extradition of escaped slaves. This treaty could have been interpreted as recognition of continuing tribal sovereignty. The Court avoided the obvious question of tribal sovereignty recognized in the treaty by referring to the slave extradition clauses. It argued that those clauses legally invalidated the treaty completely from the perspective of international *jus cogens*. Not only is the legal basis for this finding rather weak (see note 9), it is also clear that the Court used this argument to avoid having to address the question of tribal sovereignty in general. The Commission had already pointed out that "it does not seek to portray the Saramakas as a community that currently enjoys international juridical status; rather, the autonomy it claims for the tribe is one governed by domestic public law" (para. 58).

It appears that the Court was afraid of opening this particular can of worms for two reasons. The first reason was that a notion of tribal sovereignty would have to be derived from the 1792 treaty in a more explicit manner than in most of the North American cases. The Saramakas, as people of African descent, cannot claim to be native to the American continent before the arrival of the Europeans. Their existence in Suriname is a phenomenon of the slave trade and is, therefore, inextricably bound to the colonial economy. The Saramakas had clearly not been a sovereign nation before the arrival of the Europeans. Their sovereignty would have to be of more recent provenance and could only have emerged at a time when the colonial state already claimed the whole of Suriname as Dutch territory. If the Court was not willing to construct tribal sovereignty out of the international recognition as a quasi-state in 1792 by the Dutch, the classic sovereignty approach would not help the Saramakas. We will see in *Saramaka v. Suriname* that the Court would, fifteen years later, nevertheless apply indigenous rights (it then will call them "indigenous *and tribal* rights") to the Saramakas as a community of African descent, not on the basis of sovereignty, but on the basis of ongoing cultural difference.

But even if the Court had accepted Saramaka sovereignty through an interpretation of the 1792 treaty, to adopt the sovereignty approach with its elaborate common-law interpretation would have had a huge impact on the OAS member states. Although the Saramakas had a treaty with the Dutch, the practice of treaty making, common in North America, had been the exception in Latin America. The common-law interpretation that native nations retain their rights to lands not explicitly ceded to the state was already the basis for costly land settlements in Australia, New Zealand, the United States, and Canada. The repercussions for Latin American countries would have been inestimable.

But the legal problems for the Court in a more narrow sense would also have been grave. The fundamental task of the Inter-American Court of Human Rights is to resolve disputes between the member states of the Convention and their citizens. It has the authority to do that because the member states voluntarily subject themselves to the Convention and the jurisdiction of the Court. Recognizing indigenous nations as sovereign entities would mean that the Court recognized a third entity between the member states and its citizens—the indigenous communities—that had nowhere been mentioned in the institutionalization of the inter-American human rights system.

Another question would have arisen regarding the recognition of traditional family structure: would this "new" sovereign entity only be a *beneficiary* of human rights, or would it also be an *obligated party*, bound by human rights in relation to its members?[13] The Court, not even fifteen years old, did not feel that it was in a position to deal with such far-reaching questions in a case dealing with reparations. We will see that the sovereignty approach never fully develops before the inter-American human rights institutions, but that it is replaced with the culture approach accommodating the indigenous paradox in a similar though not identical fashion.

De Facto Legal Pluralism

Although the Court did not recognize Saramaka sovereignty, it did find that the community had established a family law system independent of "official" Surinamese law. Not only are there traditional ways of maintaining family relations in the Saramaka community—polygamy, a matrilineal hereditary system, and so on—but the Court sees these traditional ways as the relevant local law according to which the terms "spouse" and "child" have to be interpreted. In other words, from the perspective of the Court, Saramaka law supersedes Surinamese law when it comes to family matters.

In our first four cases the legal pluralism of indigenous law and national law was based on competing sovereignties that provided two different sources for the competing legal systems. But in *Aloeboetoe v. Suriname*, the Court dismisses the idea of Saramaka sovereignty in an international legal sense. What is the basis, then, for a Saramaka legal system? Remarkably, the Court does not clearly say what the legal basis of the Saramaka family law system is. First, the Court does not rule on whether the Saramakas "enjoy legislative and jurisdictional autonomy," which the Saramakas could only claim in two instances: if this autonomy was a manifestation of Saramaka sovereignty or if the state of Suriname had conferred such autonomy on the Saramakas explicitly (which it had not done) (para. 55). Instead, the Court identifies the existence of a Saramaka family law *as a matter of fact*. The Court observes that the Saramakas deal with their family affairs in their community exclusively and do not register their births, deaths, or marriages before Surinamese officials. On the flip side, the state of Suriname takes no measures to enforce its official family law in Saramaka territory. The Court points out that "in the instant case, Suriname recognized the existence of a Saramaka customary law" (para. 57). This sentence does not mean that Suriname's implicit recognition constituted the legal existence of Saramaka family law. The Court does not venture an opinion on whether the Saramaka legal system has been established on the basis of the Saramakas' own sovereignty or as a result of recognition by Suriname; rather, it simply treats the question as a matter of fact.

What we can observe here are two different ways of conceptualizing the legal pluralism of official national law and indigenous law. The North American cases had conceptualized the indigenous legal system as based on the ongoing sovereignty of the indigenous nation. I call this concept "rooted legal pluralism." The Inter-American Court treats the indigenous legal system as a matter of fact. We can call this concept "de facto legal pluralism." Treating the question of legal pluralism as a factual matter is, of course, a strategy to avoid having to address the far-reaching questions we already indicated above. Nevertheless, the Court puts an important constraint on its recognition of Saramaka family law. The aspect of the matrilineal hereditary system that excludes male descendants from inheriting is not recognized because such a rule would conflict with the prohibition against sexual discrimination in the Convention: "Hence, in referring to 'ascendants,' the Court shall make no distinction as to sex, even if that might be contrary to Saramaka custom" (para. 62).

Although the Court treats the question as connected to the interpretation of terms ("spouse," "ascendant," and so on), it actually touches upon the issue of whether the Saramaka community has the obligation to comply with international human rights incorporated in the Convention. Implicitly the Court's recognition of Saramaka law comes with a price tag: Saramaka family law can be the guideline for the Court in matters of family law, but only on the Court's terms: the rules of the Convention. This argumentation is due to the fact that the Court did not conceptualize indigenous rights as special group rights, as would have been the logical consequence of indigenous rights based on sovereignty. The rights of international sovereigns are always collective rights, as actors of international law are collective entities. When the Court found an existing legal system as a matter of fact, not conceptually grounded in a sovereign entity, the idea of special exceptions from the Convention did not cross the minds of the judges.

Consequently the Court dismissed all claims for collective reparations. The two arguments for collective reparations were tribal sovereignty, which the Court dismissed in general, and a racist motivation for the killings, for which the Court did not see enough evidence. The third argument we should revisit again, as it paves the way for a different approach to indigenous rights claims: difference in culture rather than difference in sovereignty.

On the Way to a Culture Approach to Indigenous Rights

The Commission argued for collective reparations and referred to the special Saramaka family structure in which "a person is a member not only of his or her own family group, but also of his or her own village community and tribal group" (para. 83). Here the Saramakas appear as a group closely bound together by social ties and kinship. The Commission's argument implied the idea that killing a Saramaka harms the Saramaka community as a whole more than killing a Surinamese hurts his or her village or neighborhood. Therefore the obligation to pay damages must be extended beyond the usual scope.

Structurally, this is an argument for the culture approach to indigenous rights. Just as the sovereignty approach justifies special considerations on the basis of the group's difference in sovereignty, the culture approach can justify special considerations on the basis of the group's difference in culture. In this way the culture approach, like the sovereignty approach, accommodates the indigenous paradox. Both approaches use the law of the (post)colonial state (either incorporated in national or international law) to claim from the state restraint in extending its law into the indigenous group's affairs. To that end both approaches must portray the indigenous claimant as "similar enough" for the law to be applied in general (for a court not to deny extending its jurisdiction), but "different enough" for the law not to be applied completely (for a court to make special exceptions). To reach this goal the culture approach must argue difference in culture.

In *Aloeboetoe v. Suriname* the culture argument did not stick. The reason was that the argument for cultural difference did not convince the Court that the Saramakas were "different enough" in regard to their close-knit social structure from Suriname majority society. Instead, the Court argued equality between the Saramakas and the Surinamese majority society. For the culture approach to be successful it must manage the indigenous paradox. Too much similarity is as fatal as too much difference. While too much difference would close the door to the national legal system and the courts, too much similarity closes the door to special protection and divergent standards. The latter is exactly what happened in this case.

Nevertheless, the argumentative basis was put to the test and was not dismissed completely like the sovereignty approach was. After *Aloeboetoe v. Suriname*, cultural arguments in indigenous rights claims would go on to win significant indigenous rights landmark decisions in the Inter-American Court of Human Rights.

* * * *

Aloeboetoe v. Suriname can be considered the first, albeit incomplete, indigenous rights case to come before the Inter-American Court of Human Rights. Most important, the Court decided not to entertain indigenous rights cases on the basis of sovereignty. The Court still found an existing legal pluralism of "official" state law and indigenous law, but by treating it as a factual phenomenon—de facto legal pluralism—avoided grounding it in a concept of indigenous or tribal sovereignty. For the same reason the Court did not develop a clear concept of collective group rights for indigenous communities. For the first time in the Court's history, a fully developed culture argument was put to the test and failed because the cultural difference in which it was grounded was not recognized. While the decision made clear that the sovereignty approach "North American style" would not be successful in the future, the culture approach was not dismissed out of hand and would become the predominant approach to indigenous rights in the inter-American system for the protection of human rights.

CHAPTER 7

The Invention of the Culture Approach to Indigenous Rights

Awas Tingni v. Nicaragua

Awas Tingni v. Nicaragua is "the" indigenous rights landmark case of the Inter-American Court of Human Rights ("the Court"). In it the Court recognized that indigenous land and resource rights are protected under article 21 of the American Convention on Human Rights ("the Convention"), which guarantees the right to property. In elaborating on its decision, the Court explained that indigenous land rights originate in the special relationship that indigenous communities maintain with their homelands and that these land rights are protected regardless of whether "their" OAS member states have recognized such rights or not. As such *Awas Tingni v. Nicaragua* is a case in which the culture approach to indigenous rights proves to be successful.

The Awas Tingni Community on Its Way to the IACtHR

Awas Tingni v. Nicaragua was brought before the Inter-American Commission on Human Rights ("the Commission") in 1995 by the Awas Tingni community from the Nicaraguan Atlantic coast. In 1998 the Commission decided to bring the case before the Inter-American Court of Human Rights, which delivered its judgment on the merits in 2001. The Awas Tingni community consists of several hundred members whose territory lies in the Región Autónoma de la Costa Caribe Norte (RACCN).[1] The community governs itself through an assembly composed of all the adult male members of the community, which elects a board of directors consisting of the town judge, the syndic (who represents the community in dealings with Nicaraguan state officials), the deputy syndic, and a person responsible for the forest. The community's subsistence is mainly based on family farming, hunting, fishing, and the gathering of fruits and medicinal plants. The members of the Awas Tingni community identify themselves ethnically as Mayagna (sometimes also called Sumo). Most of them speak Miskito, which is also spoken by other communities along the Nicaraguan Atlantic coast.

Contact with European settlers intensified at the turn of the twentieth century, when Moravian missionaries began to establish settlements. Following that, the Nicaraguan state started expanding into the region, leading to conflicts over territory and constant negotiations over regional autonomy (Hale 1994). Nicaragua takes the position that the territories of the indigenous communities in the northern Atlantic coastal region belong to the state unless the state decides to grant property title to the respective communities. In the case of the Awas Tingni, Nicaragua had not granted such a title. However, articles 5 and 98 of the 1995 Nicaraguan Constitution recognize indigenous peoples and communal land and autonomy rights.[2] One visible consequence was the creation of two autonomous regions along the Atlantic coast, of which the RACCN, where the Awas Tingni territory lies, is one. Law No. 28 governs the authority of these autonomous regions.[3]

In the early 1990s the Nicaraguan Ministry for the Environment and Natural Resources (MARENA) made preparations to grant a logging concession to the commercial logging company Maderas y Derivados de Nicaragua, S.A. (MADENSA). As part of the process, the company and MARENA entered into consultations that were part of a larger project for sustainable logging in the region in which the World Wildlife Fund was involved. The result was a contract between the Awas Tingni and MADENSA for the comprehensive management of the forest, signed in 1992, and a forest management agreement between MADENSA and MARENA concluded in 1994. Part of the latter agreement entailed a commitment from MARENA, hence the Nicaraguan state, to legally define the communal lands of the Awas Tingni. The state did not follow up on this promise.

In 1995 MARENA decided to grant a logging concession to another firm, a Korea-based company named Sol del Caribe, S.A. (SOLCARSA), to extract timber from those lands the Awas Tingni regard as their territory. A forest management plan was drawn up and approved by the Regional Council of the RAAN (the former name of the autonomous region now called RACCN; see note 1), but was not discussed with the Awas Tingni. In 1996 MARENA granted a thirty-year logging concession to SOLCARSA, again without consulting the Awas Tingni and also without the approval of the Regional Council of RAAN.

When it became apparent that Nicaragua was about to grant a logging concession to SOLCARSA, the Awas Tingni community decided in 1995 to bring an *amparo* action before the Matagalpa Appellate Court.[4] The court dismissed the case. In the same year the community also decided to present a petition to the Inter-American Commission on Human Rights, in which it lodged two complaints:[5] first, the community asserted that the state of Nicaragua had no right to grant a logging concession on their territory without their consent; second, the Commission should find that Nicaragua had an obligation under the American Convention on Human Rights not only to refrain from granting such concessions, but also to legally demarcate the Awas Tingni territory and recognize their property rights. Lengthy proceedings began before the Commission, including several meetings in the following months and years.

In 1997 the Regional Council of RAAN brought an *amparo* action against MARENA, complaining that it had not been consulted in the course of granting the logging concession. The Nicaraguan Constitutional Court declared the logging concession to be unconstitutional. The government, however, did not comply with that decision. MARENA argued instead that the unconstitutionality was only based on a procedural error that was later corrected. Later in 1997 the Awas Tingni community filed a second *amparo* action before the Matagalpa Appellate Court and before the Nicaraguan Supreme Court, but the action was dismissed for the same reasons as in 1995. In early 1998, due to growing political pressure, the Nicaraguan government finally canceled the logging concession to SOLCARSA.

But the Inter-American Commission did not end the proceedings at that point because one of the main issues, the legal recognition of Awas Tingni lands, had not been resolved. The Commission compiled a report in which it found that Nicaragua had violated the Awas Tingni's rights as enshrined in several articles of the American Convention on Human Rights[6]—most notably their right to property (article 21)—by granting logging concessions in Awas Tingni territory without their consent, denying them legal recognition of their territory through a demarcation process, and ignoring their right to judicial protection (article 25) by not providing a regime of legal protection against violations of their property rights.[7] The Commission requested that the Inter-American Court order Nicaragua to demarcate the Awas Tingni's territory, legally recognize it, and abstain from granting further concessions for natural resource exploitation activities on their lands as long as their property status remained unresolved and appropriate legal safeguards were still not in place. Additionally, the Commission asked the Court to order Nicaragua to pay compensation to the Awas Tingni community for damages resulting from the logging activities already carried out by SOLCARSA. Because it found Nicaragua's reaction to its final report to be insufficient, the Commission decided on May 28, 1998, to present the case to the Inter-American Court of Human Rights. The Court found in favor of the Commission.

For their case the community enlisted the help of the prestigious Indian Law Resource Center, a U.S.-based NGO providing legal assistance to indigenous communities. James Anaya, a reputable professor of federal Indian law at the University of Iowa (subsequently at the University of Colorado), served as their legal representative before the Inter-American Commission and head of the legal team.[8] This kind of backing changed the way such legal proceedings are conducted in the inter-American system. First, public attention to the case was considerably higher than in the past. The community's legal representatives managed to turn the Awas Tingni's struggle for land recognition into a test case for indigenous rights for the whole of the Americas, as is demonstrated by the list of indigenous organizations from all over the Americas that submitted amicus curiae briefs: the Organization of Indigenous Syndics of the Nicaraguan Caribbean (OSICAN), the Canadian Assembly of First Nations (AFN), the National Congress of American Indians (NCAI), and the Mohawk Indigenous Community of Akwesasne. These as well as another amicus curiae brief submitted by the International Human Rights Law Group indicate the degree to which the outcome of the case was considered relevant in the international legal community.

What is more, for the first time the Court held an extensive public hearing over the course of two days to hear the evidence of expert witnesses, among them indigenous leaders, Nicaraguan officials, and anthropologists.[9] It is obvious from the transcript of the hearing that the Nicaraguan government was not prepared for a case of this magnitude. The representatives of the Commission, hence for the Awas Tingni, were eloquent lawyers accustomed to the adversarial style of a public hearing, while the Nicaraguan legal representative had clearly underestimated the performative power of the plaintiffs' evidence. Nicaragua did not manage to call witnesses to refute the expert opinions brought by the Awas Tingni community because it waited too long and missed the respective deadline (para. 53).[10] In fact, it was the Court that called one Nicaraguan official responsible for indigenous land titling (para. 55), who seemed unprepared and was not a good witness for the state of Nicaragua (transcript of the public hearing, 265–286).[11]

The exquisite performance by the plaintiffs and the international visibility of the case exerted considerable pressure on the Court, which was already eager to produce an indigenous rights landmark case, not least to consolidate its position as a human rights institution to be taken seriously. And so it did—the Awas Tingni community won its case and the Court provided a basis for the guarantee of indigenous land rights in the American Convention on Human Rights.

Negotiating Indigeneity in a Public Hearing

During its hearing held on October 16–18, 2000, the Court heard from twelve witnesses, four of whom were called as expert witnesses: three anthropologists and an expert on Nicaraguan law. Jaime Castillo Felipe was the first witness and testified as a member of the Awas Tingni community. From 1991 to 1996 he had served as syndic for the community: "The Syndic is the person in charge of resolving conflicts which might arise within the community, as well as of taking steps, in coordination with the communal authorities, before State entities" (para. 83a). He introduces the Awas Tingni community as follows (we hear the voice of the translator referring to the witness in the third person):

> It is true that there are persons in the Community who are not of the Mayagna ethnic group, but they are few, having come to live there or having members of the Community as spouses. They have been in Awas Tingni for over fifty years, and before they lived in Tuburús. He does not know exactly in what year the hamlet of Awas Tingni was established. They are the owners of the land which they inhabit because they have lived in the territory for over 300 years, and this can be proven because they have historical places and because their work takes place in that territory. There were members of the Tilba-Lupia Community who lived in Awas Tingni. He could indicate the persons who constitute the Community. (para. 83a)

The Awas Tingni community is presented as a homogeneous entity: only a few inhabitants living on their territory do not belong to the Awas Tingni ethnic group. This statement has to be seen in the context of Nicaragua's claim that the Awas Tingni territory overlapped to a great extent with the territory of other indigenous communities in the region. The witness also presents the Awas Tingni as a genetically monolithic community in which interethnic marriages are the exception.

The witness told the Court of the community's futile attempts to gain land recognition from the Nicaraguan state and then went on to portray the community's subsistence strategy, which would be endangered by the logging concession. The Awas Tingni "make their living from agriculture, hunting, and fishing, among other activities. To hunt they make a 15-day trip. The Community selects what is to be consumed, so as not to destroy the natural resources" (para 83a). Included here are two important "indigenous articulations." First, the community is presented as going on very long hunting trips, which will later serve to justify the Awas Tingni's claims to large tracts of land extending far beyond the area immediately surrounding their villages. (The extent of the claim had been a central objection of the Nicaraguan state in the proceedings.) Second, the community is presented as conservationist and noncommercial in its use of natural resources. This image of the "Indian as conservationist" is of great importance in indigenous articulations and performances (see, e.g., Hames 2007).

The witness subsequently explains the Awas Tingni's land tenure system, emphasizing that the community as a whole holds the territory as collective property, which, as we shall see, will become a central feature of the Court's reasoning:

> The lands are occupied and utilized by the entire Community. Nobody owns the land individually; the land's resources are collective. If a person does not belong to the Community, that person cannot utilize the land. There is no right to expel anyone from the Community. To deny the use of the land to any member of the Community, the matter has to be discussed and decided by the Community Council. When a person dies, his or her next of kin become the owners of those things that the deceased person owned. But since lands are collective property of the community, there is no way that one member can freely transmit to another his or her rights in connection with the use of the land. (para. 83a)

The description of the Awas Tingni's land tenure system highlights two important features of their case: communality and exclusivity. In the sovereignty approach to indigenous rights, indigenous nations portray their land as their "territory" rather than as "property," as we have seen in the North American cases (see Chapter 2). Their land is only "property" from the perspective of the (post)colonial state, not from their own perspective. As we have seen in *Delgamuukw v. British Columbia*, indigenous territory can usually only be recognized as collective property in a national legal system if the indigenous nation uses it exclusively and has used it exclusively in the past. This is precisely what the Awas Tingni witness contends.

The second witness, Charly Webster Mclean Cornelio, who was the secretary of the Awas Tingni Territorial Committee, summarizes the central facts necessary to substantiate the Awas Tingni's claim. First he reiterates the homogeneity of the Awas Tingni community: "The Community he belongs to has 1,016 inhabitants, and is formed by 208 families; only four families are formed by marriages of Miskito men and Mayagna women" (para. 83b). He again recounts the community's futile attempts to obtain title to their lands, and then describes their project to map their territory—with the help of a U.S. anthropologist—in order to document their territorial claim in the negotiations with the state. After highlighting the fact that other ethnic communities in the region do not live in Awas Tingni territory (the feature of exclusivity), he again presents the important points for the claim: "The territory of the Mayagna is vital for their cultural, religious, and family development, and for their very subsistence, as they carry out hunting activities (they hunt wild boar) and they fish (moving along the Wawa River), and they also cultivate the land. It is a right of all members of the Community to farm the land, hunt, fish, and gather medicinal plants; however, sale and privatization of those resources are forbidden" (para. 83b).

The witness mentions the cultural and religious significance of the land to the Awas Tingni community, an argument that becomes very important in the context of establishing the "special relationship to land," which will be at the center of the Court's reasoning in support of the recognition of indigenous property rights. The second two points we have already noted in the first witness's testimony: the features of the hunt as a subsistence strategy requiring a large territory and the communal nature of land and resources among the Awas Tingni. Finally, the witness closes by highlighting the cultural significance of the land for the community as a whole:

> The territory is sacred for them, and throughout the territory there are several hills which have a major religious importance, such as Cerro Mono, Cerro Urus Asang, Cerro Kiamak and Cerro Quitiris. There are also sacred places, where the Community has fruit trees such as pejibaye, lemon, and avocado. When the inhabitants of Awas Tingni go through these places, which go back 300 centuries, according to what his grandfather said, they do so in silence as a sign of respect for their dead ancestors, and they greet Asangpas Muigeni, the spirit of the mountain, who lives under the hills. (para. 83b)

This emphasis on the cultural significance of land and resources is a characteristic feature of the Awas Tingni case and will become important in the development of future indigenous rights cases. Land claims begin to be based on the special cultural significance the land has for the indigenous community, which is what distinguishes it from other communities that cannot claim the land they collectively live on as communal property. In other words, indigenous rights come to be based on the ongoing cultural significance of the land rather than on the legal fiction that the land belongs to them.

Another witness was the anthropologist Theodore Macdonald Jr., who had conducted fieldwork in the Awas Tingni territory in 1991 and again in 1996.[12] The result of his research was an ethnographic study that included a map of the Awas Tingni lands.[13] Macdonald's involvement in the case is important for two conflicting reasons: on the one hand, his testimony was valuable for the Awas Tingni's case because expert testimony is a form of evidence familiar to the Court, so Macdonald therefore made a credible and compelling witness;[14] on the other hand, the involvement of a nonindigenous outsider in compiling the documents in which the community presented itself can potentially endanger the appearance of authenticity. The culture argument is based on special cultural features distinguishing the indigenous claimant from the majority society. The suspicion that this "authentic culture" is being fabricated by North American outsiders to win a court case can severely weaken the argumentative basis of the claimants.

Macdonald therefore insists that he only assisted the community in the compilation of the map, and that the community members themselves did all the work: "The Awas Tingni Community prepared a map, roughly in 1992, without his advisory assistance; they made it on their own and showed it to him when he began the study of the witness." Afterward Macdonald assisted them in making a map using a computer-based geographic information system (GIS): "To carry out the work of locating reference points so as to make the map, two young members of the Community were trained. In this way, fieldwork for the map was carried out by indigenous people of Awas Tingni. Once this information is included in the point positioning system, there is no way to manipulate it" (para. 83c).

Subsequently Macdonald describes the history of the Awas Tingni community, all according to established anthropological theory:

> To refer to the Mayagna as a community, one has to see everything as a process. Currently it is a group with its own leadership, its own form of social organization, and it recognizes itself as an indigenous community. As regards current land tenure in the Awas Tingni Community, the witness believes that first one must talk about history. The Community has identified itself as a Mayagna community, but gradually, through demographic growth and also continuous communication with people from other areas, it came to identify itself as an independent community, around its spiritual leaders called *caciques*. In this way it took shape and strengthened its feeling of community, with its own limits and boundaries. (para. 83c)

He identifies two Awas Tingni communities and again reiterates that there is no evidence that another ethnic group had occupied the territory prior to the Awas Tingni. According to Macdonald's testimony, "the Community's perception of its boundaries has been strengthened through interactions with their neighbors. The only evidence that can be used to determine the existence of the Community before 1990 is oral tradition. There are research studies on the history of the Community, and some experts were also consulted at Harvard University, in the United States, and in Central America, and no data were found that contradicted the oral tradition on which his study is based" (para. 83c).

Finally, Macdonald also highlights the cultural significance of the land for the Awas Tingni:

> The hills located in the territory of the Community are very important. The "spirits of the mountain," *jefes del monte*, which in Mayagna are called "Asangpas Muigeni," live in them, and it is they who control the animals throughout that region. To make use of

> those animals, one must have a special relationship with the spirits. Oftentimes the *cacique*, who is a sort of "chaman" called *Ditelian*, can maintain such a relationship with the spirits. Therefore, the animals' presence and the possibility of hunting them is based on their cosmovision and has much to do with the boundaries, because according to them these masters of the mountain own the animals, especially the wild boars which move in packs around the mountains. There is then a strong tie with the surroundings, with those sacred places, with the spirits that live within, and the brothers who are members of the Community. (para. 83c)

Macdonald presents here the indigenous community in close spiritual and cultural relation to their territory in a much more eloquent and explicit way than the indigenous witnesses themselves. This may simply be the result of differences in the characteristic manner of expression of the two categories of people: the indigenous witnesses are perhaps more inclined to highlight the importance of their land for subsistence purposes (hunting, logging) and only mention a spiritual connection en passant, while the anthropologists focus on spirits, sacred sites and cemeteries, the cultural relevance of markers in the landscape, and so forth.

The fourth witness is Rodolfo Stavenhagen, an anthropologist and sociologist who was at that time the special rapporteur for indigenous peoples at the United Nations. As an expert witness, Stavenhagen presents his knowledge from the ethnographic literature he has studied. He explains that indigenous peoples of various countries suffer from systematic discrimination and marginalization and are generally economically disenfranchised. He follows with a definition of indigenous peoples:

> Indigenous peoples are defined as those social and human groups, culturally identified and who maintain a historical continuity with their ancestors, from the time before the arrival of the first Europeans to this continent. That historical continuity can be seen in their forms of organization, in their own culture, in their self-identification, and in the use of a language the origin of which is pre-Hispanic. These peoples are known in our countries because they maintain forms of life and of culture which set them apart from the rest of society, and they have traditionally been placed in a subordinate and marginal position by discriminatory economic,

> political, and social structures, which practically have kept them in a condition of second-class citizenship, despite the fact that in legislation, in formal terms, indigenous people have the same rights as non-indigenous people. But in reality, that citizenship is as if it were imaginary, because they continue to suffer structural forms of discrimination, social exclusion, and marginalization. (para. 83d)

This definition is indeed remarkable if we bear in mind the indigenous rights cases we have looked at so far. The fact that indigenous peoples inhabited the continent before the arrival of Europeans (presumably as independent nations, although this is not mentioned explicitly) becomes the point of departure for the definition rather than its main feature. Two further points in this definition of indigenous peoples emerge as much more central: first, indigenous peoples are different not in law (as sovereigns) but in fact (as culturally distinct communities); second, from this cultural difference arises a systematic discrimination, "a subordinate and marginal position." Indigeneity here is presented as consisting of three features: (1) indigenous peoples were in a given place before the arrival of Europeans; (2) they are culturally different from the majority society; and (3) they are discriminated against and marginalized. As the second and third of these features become more dominant, the first feature eventually drops out completely when the Court applies indigenous rights arguments to communities of African descent, as we shall see in *Saramaka v. Suriname* in Chapter 8.

Concerning land rights, Stavenhagen expounds on how this cultural difference as a definitional feature of indigenous nations manifests itself in their special relationship to the land:

> A fundamental theme in the definition of indigenous peoples is how they relate to the land. All anthropological, ethnographic studies, all documentation which the indigenous peoples themselves have presented in recent years, demonstrate that the relationship between indigenous peoples and the land is an *essential tie which provides and maintains the cultural identity of those peoples*. One must understand that the land is not a mere instrument of agricultural production, but part of a geographic and social, symbolic and religious space, with which the history and current dynamics of those peoples are linked. Most indigenous peoples in Latin America are *peoples whose essence derives from their relationship to the land*, whether as farmers,

> hunters, gatherers, fishermen, etc. Their tie to the land is essential for their self-identification. Physical health, mental health, and social health of indigenous peoples is linked to the concept of the land. (para. 83d; emphasis added)

The cultural relationship between indigenous peoples and their land is presented here as "essential" to their identity. The indigenous community, its physical and cultural survival, is primarily connected with the land. If the land disappears, so does the indigenous community. Stavenhagen said one more thing during the hearing that was not reproduced in the judgment, but can be found in the hearing transcript. It states the point he wishes to make as clearly as possible: "There is an old saying that says that the Indian without land is a dead Indian. And I think that is valid for many of the indigenous populations of our countries" (transcript of the public hearing, 177).

The witness then follows with an explanation of indigenous peoples' land tenure systems in Latin America generally, which tend to be communal in nature. In his view, the Awas Tingni follow a land tenure system that he calls "the lowland model," which he describes as follows:

> There are two concepts of collective land: the territory, generally, which the community considers common, although internally there are mechanisms to allocate temporary occupation and use by its members and which does not allow alienation to persons who are not members of the community; and the areas which are only used collectively, the "commons" which are not divided into plots. Almost all indigenous communities have a part used collectively as "commons," and then another part which can be divided and allocated to families or domestic units. Nevertheless, the concept of collective property remains, even if it is disputed by others, often the State itself, when there is no title. When there are problems, the need for property titles arises because the community risks losing everything. (para. 83d)

What Stavenhagen describes here resembles very much the property system of an independent state. In such a system the state gives some parts of the territory to private persons for their use and keeps other parts as commons for the use of the general population. If Nicaragua were to recognize this land tenure system, it would imply state recognition of Awas Tingni "territory" as "property," similar to the North American cases we have looked at. Territory becomes translated into communal property as a matter of perspective: for the Awas Tingni, it is their territory; for the state of Nicaragua, recognition means that it becomes the Awas Tingni's communal property, which they allocate as they wish. Stavenhagen, however, presents the tenure system in the context of cultural difference rather than that of competing sovereignty. The witness presents communal property not as a legal translation of (former) territorial sovereignty but as a form of property specific to indigenous peoples.

Stavenhagen closes by highlighting the need to establish new norms and rules to deal with indigenous peoples that take into consideration cultural difference as the basis of their identity and the rights they claim: "The international community and human rights law face the challenge of developing new concepts and new norms which, without in any way damaging or curtailing the individual's human rights, are able to enrich the way of life of indigenous peoples by recognizing the social and cultural reality in which those rights are breached" (para. 83d).[15]

Is Indigenous Territory the Community's Property?

The Commission argued during the proceedings that by not demarcating and titling the Awas Tingni's lands and by granting a logging concession to SOLCARSA on their territory, Nicaragua had violated the community's right to property. It was operating on the assumption that the Awas Tingni have communal property rights to their territory within the Nicaraguan property system—regardless of whether Nicaragua had recognized such rights or not:

> The Mayagna Community has communal property rights to land and natural resources based on traditional patterns of use and occupation of ancestral territory. There [*sic*] rights "exist even without State actions which specify them." Traditional land tenure is linked to a historical continuity, but not necessarily to a single place and to a single social conformation throughout the centuries. The overall territory of the Community is possessed collectively, and the individuals and families enjoy subsidiary rights of use and occupation. (para. 140a)

This contention reflects the established legal view on indigenous land rights as we have already investigated them in the North American cases. The land rights of the indigenous communities come from traditional use (as in common law), and they originate not in the national legal system of the (post)colonial state, but "exist even without State actions." In *Delgamuukw* we have seen that this is the main reason why the Canadian courts define "aboriginal title" as *sui generis*—because it originates outside the national legal system. The Commission also argued that the Awas Tingni community owns its territory collectively, another common characteristic of indigenous land rights. As we have seen in the other cases, communal property is the right within a national property system that most closely resembles international territory.

The Commission further argued that indigenous land rights, even if they are not recognized within the legal order of the state, are nevertheless property rights in the sense of article 21 and thus are protected by the Convention: "Traditional patterns of use and occupation of territory by the indigenous communities of the Atlantic Coast of Nicaragua generate customary law property systems, they are property rights created by indigenous customary law norms and practices which must be protected, and they qualify as property rights protected by article 21 of the Convention" (para. 140b). Although indigenous land rights would not need to be recognized by national law to come into existence and to be protected by the Convention, Nicaragua had in fact recognized these land rights in its Constitution (para. 140c). That indigenous peoples have rights to their ancestral territory would also be—in addition to its protection by the Convention—a norm of customary international law (para. 140d).

The Commission argued, therefore, that the right of the Awas Tingni community to their territory was protected under article 21 of the Convention. In the proceedings Nicaragua expressed the view that the Awas Tingni did not inhabit their ancestral territory, but had moved to the lands they claimed in the 1940s (para. 141d). The Commission rebuffed this argument, stating that "most inhabitants of Awas Tingni [had] arrived during the 1940s to the place where they have their main residence, having come from their former ancestral place: Tuburús. There was a movement from one place to another within their ancestral territory; the Mayagna ancestors were here since immemorial times" (para. 140h).

Nicaragua argued that while it recognized indigenous land rights in principle, special circumstances precluded the Awas Tingni's claim in the concrete case:

> There are "particularistic circumstances which place this claim outside the normal scope of indigenist law." The Community is a small group of indigenous people which resulted from a communal

> separation and successive geographic shifts; their presence in the region has not been sufficiently documented; they possess lands which are not ancestral and on part of which title has been obtained by other indigenous communities, or other communities claim that they have ancestral possession rights predating the alleged right of Awas Tingni. Land claims by various ethnic groups have led to the existence of complex conflicting interests, which require careful analysis by national authorities and a delicate process of solution of those conflicts to generate legal certainty. The Community recognized that its population includes persons coming from the Tilba-Lupia indigenous community, which received title deed from the State. (para. 141a)

Nicaragua furthermore argued that the Awas Tingni's land claim was excessive in relation to their population:

> The area of land claimed by the Community is disproportionate to the number of members of the Community, for which reason it does not have the right under the terms stated in its claim. The Mayagna Community states that it has about 600 members, and it irrationally claims an area of roughly 150,000 hectares, a claim that exceeds the subsistence needs of its members. The area's biodiversity does not justify the long distances covered for hunting and fishing, which seems to be an argument used by the Community to increase the area they are claiming. Furthermore, a 1995 census indicates that the number of members of the Community is 576 persons, of whom only 43% are Mayagna. (para. 141g)

The line of argumentation, which becomes clear in the last sentence, can be observed throughout the entire case: the question of the degree of genetic purity of the Awas Tingni community. Although it is never at the center of either party's argument, it becomes evident that while the community wished to portray itself as ethnically homogeneous, Nicaragua tried to argue that Awas Tingni was an ethnically diverse community.

This discourse is also connected to the indigenous paradox, which demands what many scholars have called "strategic essentialism" (Hale 2006). The paradoxical nature of indigeneity demands that the indigenous community be different enough from the majority society to constitute an exception from the standards of equal treatment demanded by the liberal rule of law but still be able to invoke the rule of law against the state and confront it as a legal subject equal to others. To constitute this "difference in equality," the indigenous community must appear as distinct: either legally distinct (in the sovereignty approach) or culturally distinct (in the cultural approach). If cultural distinctiveness is the key argument for special rights, internal cultural diversity jeopardizes the legal strategy. Therefore, the indigenous claimant will try to appear culturally (and in reference to certain conceptions of culture also genetically) homogeneous, while the state will try to portray the claimant as culturally (and ethnically) diverse, no different from any nonindigenous community.

The Court decided to agree with the Commission. It invoked its established guidelines for the interpretation of the rights laid down in the Convention: the "autonomous meaning" of the human rights enshrined in the Convention, and the Convention as a "living instrument." The "autonomous meaning" of the Convention's human rights refers to the idea that the Convention has to be interpreted primarily in reference to international law—the scope and content of the rights cannot be determined in reference to national law. If in Nicaraguan national law indigenous interests in their land were not conceptualized as "property," that would not mean that "property" in the sense of article 21 of the Convention could not include such indigenous land rights. The Convention as a "living instrument" refers to the historical development of rights. When the scope and content of certain human rights have been determined by the Court for the purposes of one case, it does not mean that the interpretation of those same rights cannot change if sociopolitical circumstances and international legal opinion change. The two concepts—the "autonomous meaning" of human rights and the Convention as a "living instrument"—allow the Court, like its European counterpart (Mowbray 2005), to interpret human rights with the fewest legal restrictions possible and to deviate over time from its own determinations in the past.

According to these principles the Court sees indigenous land rights as protected under article 21 of the Convention:

> Through an evolutionary interpretation of international instruments for the protection of human rights, taking into account applicable norms of interpretation and pursuant to article 29(b) of the Convention—which precludes a restrictive interpretation of rights—it is the opinion of this Court that article 21 of the Convention protects the

> right to property in a sense which includes, among others, the rights of members of the indigenous communities within the framework of communal property, which is also recognized by the Constitution of Nicaragua. (para. 148)

After generally recognizing that indigenous land and resource rights are protected by the Convention's right to property in article 21, the Court elaborates on the specific configuration of such indigenous rights:

> Given the characteristics of the instant case, some specifications are required on the concept of property in indigenous communities. Among indigenous peoples there is a communitarian tradition regarding a communal form of collective property of the land, in the sense that ownership of the land is not centered on an individual but rather on the group and its community. Indigenous groups, by the fact of their very existence, have the right to live freely in their own territory; the close ties of indigenous people with the land must be recognized and understood as the fundamental basis of their cultures, their spiritual life, their integrity, and their economic survival. For indigenous communities, relations to the land are not merely a matter of possession and production but a material and spiritual element, which they must fully enjoy, even to preserve their cultural legacy and transmit it to future generations. (para. 149)

This sounds very different from the phrasing we have come to recognize in indigenous land rights cases. The most striking difference is that no reference whatsoever is made to former or ongoing sovereignty of indigenous peoples as persons of international law. We have already seen in *Aloeboetoe v. Suriname* that the Court had an opportunity there to refer to indigenous sovereignty, but then rejected the concept. The feature that makes indigenous rights different from "regular" property rights is not the fact that it is grounded in precolonial sovereignty but something else: a special cultural and spiritual relationship to the land.

Indigenous identity is portrayed as inextricably linked to the land. This cultural significance of the land makes indigenous peoples' property something other than the real estate of nonindigenous persons. It is not merely economic but cultural and, above all, spiritual. What resonates through these lines is the implicit comparison with "regular" property and the assumption that indigenous peoples' "ownership" of their land differs from that of non-indigenous peoples—it is somehow "fuller," with more dimensions attached to it (cultural and spiritual ones). Indigenous groups have a connection to their territory (to nature) that nonindigenous groups or individuals do not have (any more).

This close connection of indigenous peoples to their land is of course quite culturalist and serves several legal purposes. This kind of legal reasoning brings cultural issues into the center of the land rights discussion and opens up the possibility of asserting other indigenous rights to engage in certain cultural activities (hunting, fishing, religious ceremonies, and so forth) and at the same time linking those activities to the obligation of states to grant land title to indigenous peoples. We will see in *Saramaka v. Suriname* that this kind of definition allows for the land claims of groups of African descent to also be incorporated under the umbrella of article 21 of the Convention. But this culturalization of indigenous property brings with it new restrictions, which we have already examined in *Delgamuukw v. British Columbia* in our discussion of "culture as constraint." How strong these culturalizing tendencies are can be observed in the separate opinions.

Three Separate Opinions: What Is Indigenous Property?

The three judges—the president of the Court Antônio Cançado Trindade, as well as Justices Máximo Pacheco Gómez and Aliriu Abreu Burelli—take advantage of the possibility of issuing separate opinions to further characterize the nature of indigenous property and its distinction from "regular" property. The judges place an even stronger emphasis on the cultural component of indigenous property. One aspect is of particular interest to the judges: "the intertemporal dimension of the communal form of property prevailing among the members of the indigenous communities" (Joint Separate Opinion of Judges Cançado Trindade, Pacheo Gómez, Abreu Burelli, para. 1). The judges refer to the public hearing to make their point:

> At the public hearing held in the headquarters of the Inter-American Court on 16, 17 and 18 November 2000, two members and representatives of the Community Mayagna (Sumo) Awas Tingni pointed out the vital importance of the relationship of the members of the Community with the lands they occupy, not only for their own

> subsistence, but also for their family, cultural and religious development. Hence their characterization of the territory as sacred, for encompassing not only the members of the Community who are alive but also the mortal remains of their ancestors, as well as their divinities. Hence, for example, the great religious significance of the hills, inhabited by those divinities. (Joint Separate Opinion of Judges Cançado Trindade, Pacheo Gómez, Abreu Burelli, para. 2)

This summary of the hearing is particularly interesting when one takes a closer look at the transcript of the hearing—the strongest statement of the sacred and spiritual relationship of indigenous peoples to the land was made not by the indigenous witnesses but by the anthropological expert witnesses. However, the judges refer not to the expert witness reports but to the accounts of indigenous persons. What they seem eager to highlight is that this special relationship is authentically indigenous.

The judges further want to highlight the anti-capitalist nature of indigenous property:

> As it can be inferred from the testimonies and expertises rendered in the aforementioned public hearing, the Community has a tradition contrary to the privatization and the commercialization and sale (or rent) of the natural resources (and their exploitation). The communal concept of the land—including as a spiritual place—and its natural resources form part of their customary law; their link with the territory, even if not written, integrates their day-to-day life, and the right to communal property itself has a cultural dimension. In sum, the habitat forms an integral part of their culture, transmitted from generation to generation. (Joint Separate Opinion of Judges Cançado Trindade, Pacheo Gómez, Abreu Burelli, para. 6)

The way the judges describe the indigenous people's special relationship to the land seems to paint an idealistic picture of a life untainted by "privatization and commercialization and the sale (or rent) of the natural resources (and their exploitation)." Indigenous peoples are close to nature in a way nonindigenous peoples and their law cannot clearly comprehend (anymore). They are essentially connected with their land: "The feeling which can be inferred is in the sense that, just as the land they occupy belongs to them, they in turn belong to their land. They thus have the right to preserve their past and current cultural manifestations, and the power to develop them in the future" (Joint Separate Opinion of Judges Cançado Trindade, Pacheo Gómez, Abreu Burelli, para 8). They go on to explain:

> Hence the importance of the strengthening of the spiritual and material relationship of the members of the Community with the lands they have occupied, not only to preserve the legacy of past generations, but also to undertake the responsibilities that they have assumed in respect of future generations. Hence, moreover, the necessary prevalence that they attribute to the element of conservation over the simple exploitation of natural resources. Their communal form of property, much wider than the civilist (private law) conception, ought to, in our view, be appreciated from this angle, also under Article 21 of the American Convention on Human Rights, in the light of the facts of the *cas d'espèce*. (Joint Separate Opinion of Judges Cançado Trindade, Pacheo Gómez, Abreu Burelli, para. 9)

The judges explicitly state here what the judgment had only indicated: indigenous property is a fuller, more complete, form of property than the property of nonindigenous people, "much wider than the (civilist) private law conception." This difference is grounded in the closer and more complete relationship indigenous communities have with nature: "The concern with the element of conservation reflects a cultural manifestation of the integration of the human being with nature and the world wherein he lives. This integration, we believe, is projected into both space and time, as we relate ourselves, in space, with the natural system of which we are part and that we ought to treat with care, and, in time, with other generations (past and future), in respect of which we have obligations" (Joint Separate Opinion of Judges Cançado Trindade, Pacheo Gómez, Abreu Burelli, para. 10).

What the judges propagate here is a transformation of the legal discussion of indigenous property into a general debate on the value of nature in capitalist society. The judges' writing style creates a concept of indigeneity that serves as a foil to project romanticized notions of being reconnected to nature. The judges highlight the importance of the Awas Tingni case: "However, in this Judgment on the merits in the case of the *Community Mayagna (Sumo) Awas Tingni*, the Court, for the first time, goes into greater depth in the analysis of the matter, in an approximation to an integral interpretation of the indigenous cosmovision, as the central point of the present Judgment"

(Joint Separate Opinion of Judges Cançado Trindade, Pacheo Gómez, Abreu Burelli, para 13).

After a short guilty acknowledgment of the universality of human rights in multicultural societies and their rejection of the "distortions of cultural relativism," the judges close by highlighting the historic importance of this new style of legal interpretation in considering the "indigenous cosmovision":

> The interpretation and application given by the Inter-American Court to the normative content of Article 21 of the American Convention in the present case of the *Community Mayagna (Sumo) Awas Tingni* represent, in our view, a positive contribution to the protection of the communal form of property prevailing among the members of that Community. This communal conception, besides the values underlying it, has a cosmovision of its own, and an important intertemporal dimension, in bringing to the fore the bonds of human solidarity that link those who are alive with their dead and with the ones who are still to come. (Joint Separate Opinion of Judges Cançado Trindade, Pacheo Gómez, Abreu Burelli, para. 15)

Other judges, such as Hernán Salgado Pesantes, take the same line: indigenous property "transcends the right to property in the traditional sense" because it is more cultural. "The anthropology of the XX century made it abundantly clear that indigenous cultures have a very unique bond with their ancestral lands. They rely upon the land for their survival and look to it for moral and material fulfillment" (Separate Opinion of Judge Salgado Pesantes, paras. 2–3).

Judge Sergio García Ramírez, however, does not agree with this culturalist rhetoric. He does not find that indigenous property is somehow to be measured by a different standard than any other property interest:

> The language in which this right [to property] is framed was meant to accommodate all subjects protected by the Convention. Obviously, there is no single model for the use and enjoyment of property. Every people, according to its culture, interests, aspirations, customs, characteristics and beliefs, can institute its own distinctive formula for the use and enjoyment of property. In short, these traditional concepts have to be examined and understood from the same perspective.

> . . . A number of countries in the Americas are home to indigenous ethnic groups whose ancestors—this hemisphere's aborigines—built legal systems that predate the conquest and colonization and that are to some extent still in effect. These ethnic groups established special *de facto* and *de jure* relationships with the land that they possessed and from whence they obtained their livelihood. Since the conquest, their legal institutions—which reflect their framers' way of thinking and have the full force of law—have withstood countless attempts to undermine them and have managed to survive to this day. In a number of countries, these indigenous legal institutions have been adopted into the national legal systems and are backed by specific international instruments that assert the lawful interests and traditional rights of the original inhabitants of the Americas and their descendants. (Separate Opinion of Judge García Ramírez, paras. 11–12)

This is indeed the classic sovereignty argument: the fact that indigenous nations were there before European colonization as independent sovereign nations gives rise to a legal pluralism in the Americas. This legal pluralism is grounded in competing sovereignties: those of the indigenous nations and the postcolonial states. Some states accommodate this competing sovereignty more than others.

García Ramírez makes careful arguments for the collective nature of indigenous rights, but only as a careful and considerate application of the established principles of international law, not as the incorporation of a whole new cosmovision (paras. 13–16). Consequently he closes with a plea that indigenous peoples be granted equal rights, not special rights: "The American Convention, applied in accordance with the interpretation that it authorizes and in accordance with the rules of the Law of Treaties, must be and is a system of rules that affords the indigenous people of our hemisphere the same, certain protection that it affords to all people of the American countries who come under the American Convention's umbrella" (Separate Opinion of Judge García Ramírez, para. 17).[16]

García Ramírez's approach is clearly different from that of the majority of the court. We are reminded of *Aloeboetoe v. Suriname*, where the Court recognized legal pluralism in Suriname, but only as a factual phenomenon and not as the product of competing sovereignties. In the opinion of the majority of the Court, it is now the prominence of the "special relationship" of indigenous peoples to their land, the distinction between "regular" property and indigenous property that "goes beyond" regular property, that grounds indigenous legal pluralism not in sovereignty but in culture. The source of the legal pluralism of indigenous law and "official" state law is not competing sovereignties but multiculturalism.

The Culture Approach, the Indigenous Paradox, and the Noble Savage

In *Awas Tingni v. Nicaragua*, the Inter-American Court carves out the conceptual basis for the recognition of indigenous land rights in Latin America. The Court refuses to follow the sovereignty approach that had been developed in common law but finds a concept based on cultural difference.

In North America the idea had been, simply put, that indigenous peoples had been independent nations before the arrival of the Europeans and as such possessed complete international sovereignty over their territory. The consequence is a model of "rooted legal pluralism" (grounded in sovereignty), which provides the basis for the sovereignty approach and accommodates the indigenous paradox. It allows the indigenous claimant to bring its case before a national court and request the protection of the rule of law, all the while remaining in a position to reject the national legal system by claiming the precedence of its own law over the one the court applies.

That, however, is not the solution of the Inter-American Court. We have seen in *Aloeboetoe v. Suriname* that the Court acknowledges the existence of a legal pluralism of national law and indigenous law, but this legal pluralism is not rooted in sovereignty. The question of which legal fiction underlies this legal pluralism remains unasked: legal pluralism is simply recognized as existing de facto. This de facto legal pluralism is the basis of the culture approach because it, like rooted legal pluralism, is able to accommodate the indigenous paradox. The indigenous claimant uses the legal pluralism to claim rights before the national courts without being completely bound by national law. As in rooted legal pluralism, the indigenous claimant is able to ask the court to order the state not to apply its own law but to give priority to indigenous law. Without being rooted in sovereignty, however, de facto legal pluralism cannot easily be established in reference to a legal fiction (sovereignty); it can only be established in reference to factually existing cultural difference.

Sovereignty in principle does not require cultural difference. On the contrary, as we have discussed in the context of *Worcester v. Georgia*, the concept of sovereignty is deeply connected with the idea of the equality of sovereigns in the realm of international law. De facto legal pluralism in turn can only be "de facto" if there is an observable difference in how the majority society and the indigenous group manage their affairs. The main feature, or discursive formation, in which this difference crystallizes is the so-called "special relationship" that indigenous peoples maintain with the land they regard as their territory. The practical consequences of the heightened need to establish cultural difference to win an indigenous rights claim are indigenous articulations, performances, and translations of such cultural difference. In *Delgamuukw v. British Columbia* we have seen that indigenous rights claims based on sovereignty also need to portray cultural difference, just not as an end in itself but as a means to prove ongoing sovereignty. The practical consequences for a trial strategy may be similar, but the underlying concepts are different.

Anthropological studies have revealed that, when going to court, indigenous communities have to essentialize and culturalize their image as distinct communities in order to win their trials (Clifford 1986; French 2009; Donahoe 2012). One can also observe this in the testimonies in the Awas Tingni hearing. The witnesses called by the Awas Tingni community articulate and perform their indigeneity as essentialized. They are ethnically pure: "It is true that there are persons in the Community who are not of the Mayagna ethnic group, but they are few, having come to live there or having members of the Community as spouses" (para. 83a). They maintain their genetic distinctiveness vis-à-vis neighboring groups: "The Community . . . has 1,016 inhabitants, and is formed by 208 families; only four families are formed by marriages of Miskito men and Mayagna women" (para. 83b).

But this cultural difference is also articulated and performed in a way that is understandable to the nonindigenous audience, in our case, the Court. Among the most important of these "understandable" articulations are the long-established discourses on the noble savage. There is a great deal of literature on the images of savagery transported in European thought since the earliest phases of colonialism (and even before), how this has shaped European self-conceptions (Said 1978; Fink-Eitel 1994; Ellingson 2001; Williams 2012), and how anthropology as a discipline has been—and still is—complicit in the creation of such fictions of the savage, noble or otherwise (Wagner 1981; Kuper 1988; Fabian 2002).

One of the first, most prominent proponents of the "noble savage" in European literature is Michel de Montaigne and not, as is often assumed, the French philosopher Jean-Jacques Rousseau.[17] In one of his essays titled "Of Cannibals," Montaigne discusses the Tupinambá, a native community from the eastern coast of Brazil who greatly fascinated him:[18]

> This is a nation . . . in which there is no sort of traffic, no knowledge of letters, no science of numbers, no name for a magistrate or for political superiority, no custom of servitude, no riches or poverty, no contacts, no successions, no partitions, no occupations but leisure ones, no care for any but common kinship, no clothes, no agriculture, no metal, no use of wine or wheat. The very words that signify lying treachery, dissimulation, avarice, envy, belittling, pardon—unheard of. (2005, 186)

Such Eurocentric imagery of native Americans is still powerful. An example of the use of the "noble savage" for social and political movements is the idea of the eco-friendly indigenous person (Krech 1999; Hames 2007; Davidov 2011); such ecology discourses are perhaps most evident in the frame of the far-reaching *buen vivir* debate in Latin America (Fabricant 2013).

All the prevalent features of the noble savage are mentioned by the witnesses: ecological sustainability ("The Community selects what is to be consumed, so as not to destroy the natural resources"); disregard for private property ("Nobody owns the land individually; the land's resources are collective"); peacefulness ("There is no right to expel anyone from the Community"); anti-capitalism ("Sale and privatization of those resources are forbidden"); spirituality ("When the inhabitants of Awas Tingni go through these places, which go back 300 centuries, according to what his grandfather said, they do so in silence as a sign of respect for their dead ancestors, and they greet Asangpas Muigeni, the spirit of the mountain, who lives under the hills") (para. 83a–b).

In Chapter 3, we have seen how the Cherokees also had to perform their indigeneity to the Supreme Court in a way that was understandable to their audiences. While they performed European-style civilization that could be understood in the context of contemporary Lockean-inspired property theory, the Awas Tingni community also had to link their claims to contemporary discourses of multiculturalism, environmentalism, and so forth. In both instances, the indigenous articulation cannot gain full independence from the audience to which it is directed.

Sui Generis Revisited: Indigenous Peoples and Their Special Relationship to the Land

In their concurring opinion, Chief Justice Trindade and the two other judges of the Court engage in an implicit critique of Eurocentric property conceptions. They contend that indigenous peoples' "communal form of property" is "much wider than the civilist (private law) conception" (para. 9). The idea that there is some form of fundamental difference between "regular" real estate property and indigenous land rights connects to the debate on the *sui generis* nature of aboriginal title in Canadian law, which we investigated in the *Delgamuukw v. British Columbia* case. This common-law debate was—as I have argued—concerned with the source of aboriginal title in indigenous sovereignty, which differentiates it from other rights originating in common law only. I would argue that the idea that there is something "special" about indigenous land rights in the context of the culture approach is in some ways similar to this debate.

As I have said, the conceptualization of indigenous rights in the framework of the culture approach is ultimately based on a blind spot: where the legal pluralism in the sovereignty framework is rooted in sovereignty, the question of where the legal pluralism of national and indigenous law comes from is left out of the culture approach. I believe the question of the source of de facto legal pluralism comes in through the back door in the guise of the "special relationship to the land." Where sovereignty provides a legal fiction as the basis for indigenous rights, "the special relationship to land" as the main feature of cultural difference provides an extralegal and, one could even say, *mythical* fiction as the basis for indigenous rights.

According to the Court, the relationship the indigenous peoples maintain to the land they live on is not only a result of the fact that indigenous peoples inhabit a certain space. It seems dialectically linked to the existence of the indigenous community itself. As Stavenhagen phrased it in the public hearing, "An Indian without his land is a dead Indian." Since *Awas Tingni* and even before, we find the phrase "special relationship to land" everywhere in the literature and jurisprudence on indigenous rights in the inter-American system (Madariaga Cuneo 2005; Pasqualucci 2006; Tramontana 2010; Odello 2012; Olivares Alanís 2013). The idea of a somehow special relationship of indigenous peoples to their land was elevated to a more general principle by Erica-Irene Daes's study for the UN Subcommission on Promotion and Protection of Human Rights titled *Indigenous Peoples and Their Relationship to Land* (2001). In a related article she explains the concept:

> Indigenous peoples have repeatedly emphasised the urgent need for understanding by non-indigenous societies of the spiritual, cultural, social, political and economic significance to indigenous societies of their lands, territories and resources for their continued survival and vitality. In order to understand the profound relationship that indigenous peoples have with their lands, territories and resources, there is a need for recognition of the cultural differences that exist between them and non-indigenous people, particularly in the countries in which they live. Indigenous peoples have urged the world community to attach positive value to this distinct relationship. It is difficult to separate the concept of indigenous peoples' relationship with their lands, territories and resources from their cultural values and differences. (Daes 2005, 76)

If we follow Daes's explanation, the relationship of indigenous peoples to their land is somehow fuller than a "regular" (read: nonindigenous) relationship between a person or a collective of persons and real estate. It is presented as holistic ("spiritual, cultural, social, political and economic"). To "understand the profound relationship," according to Daes, "there is a need for recognition of the cultural differences" between indigenous and non-indigenous people. There is a need to "attach positive value" to this "distinct relationship." The whole explanation of the idea of the special relationship to the land appears at best dialectical, maybe even circular: indigenous people maintain a special relationship to the land because they are culturally different, and what makes them culturally different is the special relationship they have to the land. The special relationship to land is at the same time reason for and manifestation of cultural difference.

In this structure the idea of a special relationship to land resembles the legal fiction of sovereignty but with an important difference: the cultural difference manifested and grounded in the special relationship between indigenous peoples and their land is not conceptualized as "legal" but as "extralegal," in this case as "cultural," therefore "factual." The fictionality of the special relationship to land is veiled and marked as factual. While sovereignty is thought of as a legal potential for sovereign equality that happens to be factually suppressed, the culturally different relationship to the land is thought of as a factual phenomenon that is grounded in a mythical, spiritual, cultural difference.

On Culturalized Property

It is also remarkable that the Inter-American Court develops the culture approach in the dogmatic context not of a human right to culture, which is not codified in the Convention, but in the context of the right to property in article 21. Dinah Shelton explains that the inter-American system has "an overwhelming focus on the right to property as the pre-eminent juridical guarantee of the rights of indigenous peoples." Other rights that are usually subsumed under indigenous rights, such as the rights to culture, religion, political participation, and self-determination, are understood as "subsumed in or dependent on the land and resource rights. . . . Indeed, property is defined in cultural terms" (Shelton 2013, 968).

As we have seen, in *Awas Tingni* the Court declares that the land is culturally inseparable from the indigenous community and is, therefore, the very basis for self-determination (para. 79). Shelton contends that the Court and the Commission framed indigenous rights in terms of the right to property in order to be able to address these rights at all within the framework of the American Convention, and so as not to be limited to the enforcement of rights already guaranteed by the member states. An approach that was limited to enforcing indigenous rights the members states had already recognized and granted would have worked in the case of Nicaragua because Nicaragua recognizes indigenous land rights in its constitution. Such an approach, however, would not have helped those indigenous communities who face less favorable national legal systems.

This approach is not unproblematic. The right to property can more easily be infringed upon by the state than other rights. According to the Convention, the right to property can be infringed upon by the state if the state can show that the right to property can legitimately be "subordinated by law to the interest of society." This "infringement test" is of special relevance in resource conflicts between indigenous nations and the state. Because of the special construction of property rights, it is much easier to compensate infringements on property rights monetarily instead of in kind, which is the usual way that rights violations are compensated. However, if property rights are construed as incorporating other rights such as subsistence rights or the right to freedom of religion, it is not possible to really protect them within the standard property rights framework, especially if sacred sites are lost and subsistence practices rendered impossible.

Moreover, the phenomenon of "culture as constraint" comes up when indigenous land rights are culturalized, as we have already seen in *Delgamuukw v. British Columbia* when we discussed the phenomenon of rights "frozen at the time of contact." Shelton summarizes: "This freezes economic and beneficial uses of property in the past, rather than allowing the communities to develop new uses for resources on their lands, a restriction not generally imposed on non-indigenous landowners" (2013, 970). It is not a far step to imply that this "wider" notion of property can easily be turned against indigenous communities and severely narrow their land rights claims if they are not able to make these special spiritual and cultural connections plausible to the legal system. The workings of culturalized property will be one important topic in our discussion of *Saramaka v. Suriname* in Chapter 8.

* * * *

Awas Tingni v. Nicaragua is an example of a successful culture approach to indigenous rights claims. The Inter-American Court establishes the existence of a legal pluralism encompassing indigenous law and national law, a model that recognizes indigenous land rights as originating outside the national legal system, in the indigenous land tenure system itself. This makes land rights claims possible even if the rights are not granted by the postcolonial state. The legal pluralism is not grounded in sovereignty; it is, rather, a de facto legal pluralism whose legal source rests on the extralegal fiction of cultural difference. This cultural difference manifests itself in the assumption that indigenous communities maintain a special spiritual and cultural relationship to their homeland. To prove this culturally different special relationship to the land, they must essentialize their cultural identity before the Court. The "special relationship to land" can also be connected to Eurocentric discourses on the noble savage, and both serves as the reason for indigenous rights and marks out the boundaries of these rights. The approach of the Inter-American Court of Human Rights results in a concept of "culturalized property."

CHAPTER 8

Expansions and Limits of the Culture Approach

Saramaka v. Suriname

While the Inter-American Court of Human Rights ("the Court") ruled in *Awas Tingni v. Nicaragua* that indigenous land and resource rights are protected under article 21 of the American Convention on Human Rights ("the Convention"), later cases were more concerned with matters of procedure. Generally indigenous rights—like all rights—are not absolute; they can be infringed upon by the state under certain circumstances. For this reason, there are legal "infringement tests" that provide the rules governing such infringement. These usually stipulate that there must be an overriding public interest to justify the state measure. When it comes to resource rights another complication arises. Indigenous communities, even if they hold their land in legal title, are not necessarily protected against state-instigated initiatives to exploit subsurface resources. This, by the way, is also the case for full real estate property such as fee simple. Most Latin American constitutions, like most legal systems in the world, exclude certain subsurface minerals from full property rights.[1] *Saramaka v. Suriname* serves as an example of such discussions. The Court in this case elaborated on the conditions under which a member state may exploit natural resources on indigenous territories. What is more, the Court used indigenous land rights arguments in support of the Saramakas, who had also been at the center of *Aloeboetoe v. Suriname* (see Chapter 6). As a community of African descent, their ancestors had not been native inhabitants of the Americas prior to colonization. What we will observe is how the culture approach to indigenous rights is able to embrace more than just native American communities because its point of reference is not precolonial sovereignty, but cultural difference vis-à-vis the majority society.

The Saramakas on Their Way to the IACtHR

Due to its suffering economy in the 1990s, the state of Suriname began to expedite the extraction of natural resources from Saramaka lands.[2] In the course of this new policy, Suriname began to grant logging and mining concessions to private companies, allowing them to extract timber and subsurface minerals from Saramaka territory. Between 1997 and 2004, Suriname issued at least four logging concessions and a considerable number of mining concessions on territory traditionally owned by the Saramaka community to both Saramaka and non-Saramaka persons, as well as to foreign companies. Because the government did not consult with the Saramakas nor seek their consent, several Saramaka clans filed a complaint before the Inter-American Commission on Human Rights ("the Commission") in 2000.

Suriname issued the logging and mining concessions on the basis of article 41 of the Surinamese Constitution, which declares that all natural resources belong to the state. The Saramakas took the position that this constitutional provision did not apply to their territory. The community had made their first treaty with the Netherlands, the colonial power at the time, in 1762. When the treaty was renegotiated in 1835, the state agreed to demarcate the Saramaka territory and acknowledged their right to exploit natural resources for subsistence activities, which mainly included (and still include) hunting, fishing, and woodworking.

When in 2006 all means for an amicable settlement with the state of Suriname had been exhausted, the Commission referred the case to the Inter-American Court of Human Rights. It argued before the Court that Suriname had violated the Saramakas' right to property as protected under article 21 of the Convention by refusing to effectively recognize the Saramakas' land rights. By not providing a legal framework for the recognition of their traditional land rights and thereby denying the Saramakas access to justice, the state had also violated their right to judicial protection as stipulated in article 25 of the Convention. After a public hearing, the Court ruled on the preliminary objections, merits, costs, and reparations in 2007.

Are the Saramakas a Tribal Community?

The Court had decided in *Awas Tingni v. Nicaragua* (Chapter 7) that indigenous land rights are protected as property in the sense of article 21 of the

American Convention on Human Rights. As a result of this decision, member states are obligated to secure these land rights by legally recognizing them. In *Awas Tingni* the Court had always used the term "indigenous community" to describe the legal person entitled to special land rights. In *Saramaka v. Suriname* the Court adopted the language of ILO Convention No. 169, which speaks of "indigenous *and tribal* peoples." The Court explained that the collective land rights not only of "indigenous" communities but also of "tribal communities" are protected by the right to property in article 21 of the American Convention. If the Saramakas could qualify as a tribal community, then their claim for legal demarcation of their lands by Suriname would have merit.

The Court first acknowledges that the Saramakas are not indigenous to the region they currently occupy. As their ancestors had been former African slaves brought to Suriname in order to work in the colonial sugar plantations in the late seventeenth and early eighteenth centuries, they are—unlike the Mayagna (Sumo) in the case of *Awas Tingni v. Nicaragua*—not the descendants of America's native inhabitants. The Saramakas' ancestors fled from their owners—in some cases individually but also in larger groups—and founded autonomous communities, mostly in the dense rainforests of Suriname. Nevertheless, the Court stated that the Saramakas "share similar characteristics with indigenous peoples, such as having social, cultural and economic traditions different from other sections of the national community, identifying themselves with their ancestral territories, and regulating themselves, at least partially, by their own norms, customs, and traditions" (para. 79).[3] The Court explained that the Saramakas' social structure is different from that of the other sectors of Suriname's society: "The Saramaka people are organized in matrilineal clans (*lös*), and they regulate themselves, at least partially, by their own customs and traditions. Each clan (*lö*) recognizes the political authority of various local leaders, including what they call Captains and Head Captains, as well as a *Gaa'man*, who is the community's highest official" (para. 81).

The Court highlighted the fact that the Saramakas also share a cultural feature that is of utmost importance for the legal recognition of land rights: a special relationship to their land.

> Their culture is also similar to that of tribal peoples insofar as the members of the Saramaka people maintain a strong spiritual relationship with the ancestral territory they have traditionally used and occupied. Land is more than merely a source of subsistence for

> them; it is also a necessary source for the continuation of the life and cultural identity of the Saramaka people. The lands and resources of the Saramaka people are part of their social, ancestral, and spiritual essence. In this territory, the Saramaka people hunt, fish, and farm, and they gather water, plants for medicinal purposes, oils, minerals, and wood. Their sacred sites are scattered throughout the territory, while at the same time the territory itself has a sacred value to them. In particular, the identity of the members of the Saramaka people with the land is inextricably linked to their historical fight for freedom from slavery, called the sacred "first time." During the public hearing in this case, Head Captain Wazen Eduards described their special relationship with the land as follows: "The forest is like our market place; it is where we get our medicines, our medicinal plants. It is where we hunt to have meat to eat. The forest is truly our entire life. When our ancestors fled into the forest they did not carry anything with them. They learned how to live, what plants to eat, how to deal with subsistence needs once they got to the forest. It is our whole life." (para. 82)

Finally, the Court also characterized the Saramaka economy as tribal: "According to the expert testimony of Dr. Richard Price, for example, 'the very great bulk of food that Saramaka eat comes from . . . farms [and] gardens' traditionally cultivated by Saramaka women. The men, according to Dr. Price, fish and 'hunt wild pig, deer, tapir, all sorts of monkeys, different kinds of birds, everything that Saramakas eat.' Furthermore, the women gather various fruits, plants and minerals, which they use in a variety of ways, including making baskets, cooking oil, and roofs for their dwellings" (para. 83).

On the basis of these three factors (social structure different from the majority society, special relationship to the land, tribal economy) and "because they regulate themselves, at least partially, by their own norms, customs, and/or traditions," the Court came to the conclusion that the Saramakas are indeed a tribal community (para. 84). When extrapolated to a general principle, this implies that descent from precolonial populations in the Americas is not a necessary prerequisite to qualify as a tribal community.

The Court had decided in *Awas Tingni v. Nicaragua* that, in light of article 1(1) of the Convention guaranteeing the full exercise of the human rights protected by the Convention without undue discrimination, member states are obligated to protect indigenous and tribal peoples' rights by enacting special measures. This is especially the case regarding the protection of indigenous and tribal property rights, which are seen as the basis of their physical and cultural survival. In *Moiwana v. Suriname* the Court had already decided that a Maroon society, under which the Saramakas are subsumed, is entitled to these legal protections developed for indigenous peoples, despite the fact that they are not indigenous to the region:

> The Court sees no reason to depart from this jurisprudence in the present case. Hence, this Tribunal declares that the members of the Saramaka people are to be considered a tribal community, and that the Court's jurisprudence regarding indigenous peoples' right to property is also applicable to tribal peoples because both share distinct social, cultural, and economic characteristics, including a special relationship with their ancestral territories, that require special measures under international human rights law in order to guarantee their physical and cultural survival. (para. 86)

Can Peoples of African Descent Hold Indigenous Property?

After recognizing the Saramakas as a tribal community and reiterating the general applicability of article 21 of the Convention to collective tribal land rights, the Court elaborated on the specifics. In its jurisprudence the Court had held in *Awas Tingni v. Nicaragua* and reiterated in *Sawhoyamaxa v. Paraguay* (2006) that article 21 of the Convention protects indigenous and tribal property rights even though the property is owned communally, not individually. The Court again clarified in *Yakye Axa v. Paraguay* (2005) that the Convention protects both the individual property of the community's members and the communal property of the community as a whole (para. 89).

Suriname had argued before the Court that, although its domestic law did not recognize the Saramakas' land rights, legal recognition of a use privilege to their territory did exist. The state furthermore alleged that the land tenure system of the Saramakas was so unclear that recognition of demarcated property presented great logistical problems. The Court, however, did not share this view:

> From the evidence and testimonies submitted before the Court, it is clear that the *lös*, or clans, are the primary land-owning entities within

> Saramaka society. Each *lö* is highly autonomous and allocates land and resource rights among their constituent *bëë* (extended family groups) and their individual members in accordance with Saramaka customary law. Pursuant to this customary law, the Captains or members of a *lö* may not alienate or otherwise encumber the communal property of their *lö*, and a *lö* may not encumber or alienate their lands from the collectively held corpus of Saramaka territory. On this last point, Head Captain and *Fiscali* Eddie Fonkie explained that "[i]f a *lö* tried to sell its land, the other *lö* would have the right to object and to stop [such transaction] because it would affect the rights and life of all Saramaka people. The *lö* are very autonomous and . . . do not interfere in each other's affairs unless it affects the interests of all Saramaka people." This is because the territory "belongs to the Saramakas, ultimately. [That is,] it belongs to the Saramakas as a people." (para. 100)

If the situation lacked clarity in the concrete case, then the state would be obligated to seek clarification of concrete land tenure issues by engaging in a process of consultation with the Saramakas. Suriname further contended that recognizing special property rights for the Saramakas could constitute or at least be perceived as discrimination against nonindigenous and nontribal Surinamese. The Court rejects this argument:

> The State's argument that it would be discriminatory to pass legislation that recognizes communal forms of land ownership is also without merit. It is a well-established principle of international law that unequal treatment towards persons in unequal situations does not necessarily amount to impermissible discrimination. Legislation that recognizes said differences is therefore not necessarily discriminatory. In the context of members of indigenous and tribal peoples, this Court has already stated that special measures are necessary in order to ensure their survival in accordance with their traditions and customs. . . . Thus, the State's arguments regarding its inability to create legislation in this area due to the alleged complexity of the issue or the possible discriminatory nature of such legislation are without merit. (para. 103)

This passage is interesting regarding our analytical framework of the indigenous paradox. The indigenous community makes a claim using the national law to ensure that the national law is not applied to them. This paradoxical endeavor is based on a legal pluralism model that emerges out of the cultural differences between the indigenous community and the majority society. Special rights are granted to a community because of its difference.

After finding that the Saramakas have a communal land right to their territory, the Court addressed the question of whether this includes the right to use and enjoy the natural resources that are connected with the land. Suriname had argued that, according to its constitution, all interests in subsoil resources are excluded from individual land rights and are vested in the state. The Saramakas argued that the use and enjoyment of subsoil resources is a necessary condition for their use and enjoyment of their land and, according to their customary law, those natural resources belong to them.

First the Court stated that other courts had acknowledged that natural resources are in principle part of indigenous land rights, such as the Canadian Supreme Court in *Delgamuukw v. British Columbia* and the South African Constitutional Court in *Alexkor Ltd. and the Government of South Africa v. Richtersveld Community* (2003). According to this jurisprudence, however, these resource rights are not absolute, but can be restricted by the state. The Court had held in *Yakye Axa v. Paraguay* and *Sawhoyamaxa v. Paraguay* that indigenous and tribal communities have a right to those of their own natural resources that they have used traditionally within their territory. The Court argued that the right to occupy the land they have traditionally occupied and the right to use the resources they have traditionally used both would be directed toward the same goal: "to guarantee that they may continue living their traditional way of life, and that their distinct cultural identity, social structure, economic system, customs, beliefs and traditions are respected, guaranteed and protected by States" (para. 121). The Court explained this view further:

> Accordingly, the right to use and enjoy their territory would be meaningless in the context of indigenous and tribal communities if said right were not connected to the natural resources that lie on and within the land. That is, the demand for collective land ownership by members of indigenous and tribal peoples derives from the need to ensure the security and permanence of their control and use of the natural resources, which in turn maintains their very way of life. This connectedness between the territory and the natural resources necessary for their physical and cultural survival is precisely what

> needs to be protected under Article 21 of the Convention in order to guarantee the members of indigenous and tribal communities' right to the use and enjoyment of their property. From this analysis, it follows that the natural resources found on and within indigenous and tribal people's territories that are protected under Article 21 are those natural resources traditionally used and necessary for the very survival, development and continuation of such people's way of life. (para. 122)

Consequently, the Court had to identify which natural resources in and on Saramaka land are "essential for the survival of their way of life, and are thus protected under article 21 of the Convention" (para. 123). These natural resources are surely those connected to their traditional subsistence activities such as hunting, fishing, and cultivation. As Saramakas traditionally had not engaged in large-scale logging operations or mining, these resources were not part of their property rights. The Court nevertheless acknowledged that "traditional resources" (game, fish, and so on) and "non-traditional" resources (subsurface minerals, timber in large quantities, and so on) are tightly interconnected. Large-scale logging and mining operations could compromise clean water resources, which are integral to Saramaka traditional subsistence activities. This interconnectedness, however, does not lead to the strict conclusion that the state is generally precluded from issuing licenses for resource extraction on Saramaka land:

> Article 21 of the Convention states that the "law may subordinate [the] use and enjoyment [of property] to the interest of society." Thus, the Court has previously held [in *Yakye Axa v. Paraguay*] that, in accordance with Article 21 of the Convention, a State may restrict the use and enjoyment of the right to property where the restrictions are: a) previously established by law; b) necessary; c) proportional; and d) with the aim of achieving a legitimate objective in a democratic society. In accordance with this Article, and the Court's jurisprudence, the State will be able to restrict, under certain circumstances, the Saramakas' property rights, including their rights to natural resources found on and within the territory. (para. 127)

In addition to this usual "justification test," the states are only allowed to infringe on tribal and indigenous property in light of another factor:

"Furthermore, in analyzing whether restrictions on the property right of members of indigenous and tribal peoples are permissible, especially regarding the use and enjoyment of their traditionally owned lands and natural resources, another crucial factor to be considered is whether the restriction amounts to a denial of their traditions and customs in a way that endangers the very survival of the group and of its members" (para. 128).

In the concrete case of the Saramakas, the Court found that the state had two general obligations when extracting natural resources from tribal or indigenous land: consultation (and, where applicable, also obtaining consent) and benefit sharing. The right to consultation encompassed a series of procedural issues such as respecting tribal and indigenous decision-making processes in good faith (para. 134), but, more important, the Court elaborated on the question of when consultation is sufficient and when obtaining consent from the community is necessary:

> In addition to the consultation that is always required when planning development or investment projects within traditional Saramaka territory, the safeguard of effective participation that is necessary when dealing with major development or investment plans that may have a profound impact on the property rights of the members of the Saramaka people to a large part of their territory must be understood to additionally require the free, prior, and informed consent of the Saramakas, in accordance with their traditions and customs. (para. 137)

In other words, the larger the project, the greater the obligation to consult. If the project has a "profound impact" on a "large part" of the territory, the community must give its consent. The member state is further obligated to share the benefits of the resource extraction. If states infringe on the right to property in article 21(2) of the Convention, the property holder is entitled to "just compensation": "In the present context, the right to obtain 'just compensation' pursuant to Article 21(2) of the Convention translates into a right of the members of the Saramaka people to reasonably share in the benefits made as a result of a restriction or deprivation of their right to the use and enjoyment of their traditional lands and of those natural resources necessary for their survival" (para. 139).

The Court reiterated that, although article 21 of the Convention did not preclude the state from issuing concessions for natural resource extraction on tribal or indigenous land per se, if the state wanted to legitimately restrict Saramaka property rights, it had to consult with the indigenous or tribal community first (para. 143). Regarding the logging concessions, then, the Court first examined the question of whether timber was one of the resources traditionally used by the Saramakas and is important for their cultural survival. It found that taking wood was of great importance for the community and cited from the transcripts of the public hearing. "Another witness addressed the importance of wood-cutting for the Saramaka people and how they care about their environment: 'When we cut trees, we think about our children, and our grandchildren, and future generations. . . . When we go into the forest for any purpose, we think about what we're doing, we think about saving the environment. We are very careful not to destroy anything that is in the forest. We take the wood that we need for our purposes, and we are very careful not to destroy the environment'" (para. 144).

The Court found that besides the wood needed to build houses and canoes, the Saramakas were also traditionally engaged in selling wood for subsistence purposes. Individual Saramakas had in the past applied for logging concessions with the state to legally solidify this practice. The Court therefore found that "the State should not have granted logging concessions within Saramaka territory unless and until the three safeguards of effective participation, benefit-sharing, and prior environmental and social impact assessments were complied with" (para. 146).

But Suriname had not engaged effectively in a participation process with the Saramakas, in part because the state was under the impression that the areas for which concessions had been granted did not infringe on tribal interests—there were not any sacred sites, cemeteries, or agricultural plots in those areas. The state had also failed to complete an environmental and social impact assessment before issuing the concessions. Such an impact assessment was necessary because the extraction of timber through logging had a great impact on the forest ecosphere. The Court cites several witness testimonies to that effect, among them this one: "This statement is also supported by the declaration of Mr. Hugo Jabini, who added that these companies 'left a totally ruined forest where they worked. Big parts of the forest cannot be used anymore for farming, and animals will stay away from these areas as well. The creeks are all blocked and the area is flooded and turning into a swamp. It is useless and the spirits are greatly offended'" (para. 150). The Court was convinced by the evidence that the logging on Saramaka land was done in a manner that was exceptionally harmful to the forest, especially as the companies were not compelled to observe even minimum standards of sustainable forest management.

Finally, the concessions did not include any benefit-sharing measures: "Not only have the members of the Saramaka people been left with a legacy of environmental destruction, despoiled subsistence resources, and spiritual and social problems, but they received no benefit from the logging in their territory. Government statistics submitted into evidence before the Court prove that a considerable quantity of valuable timber was extracted from the territory of the Saramaka people without any compensation" (para. 153). Because of these omissions, according to the Court, the state had violated the Saramakas' right to property under article 21 of the Convention by issuing the logging concessions. With regard to the gold-mining concessions, the situation was different because gold mining was not seen as a traditional practice of the Saramakas. Although it could be argued that the justification standard should in that case be lower, the Court generally sets the same parameters:

> According to the evidence submitted before the Court, the members of the Saramaka people have not traditionally used gold as part of their cultural identity or economic system. Despite possible individual exceptions, members of the Saramaka people do not identify themselves with gold nor have demonstrated a particular relationship with this natural resource, other than claiming a general right to "own everything, from the very top of the trees to the very deepest place that you could go under the ground." Nevertheless, as stated above . . . , because any gold mining activity within Saramaka territory will necessarily affect other natural resources necessary for the survival of the Saramakas, such as waterways, the State has a duty to consult with them, in conformity with their traditions and customs, regarding any proposed mining concession within Saramaka territory, as well as allow the members of the community to reasonably participate in the benefits derived from any such possible concession, and perform or supervise an assessment on the environmental and social impact prior to the commencement of the project. The same analysis applies regarding other concessions within Saramaka territory involving natural resources which have not been traditionally used by members of the Saramaka community, but that their extraction will necessarily affect other resources that are vital to their way of life. (para. 155)

Although only small-scale mining operations had taken place on Saramaka land, these concessions also did not meet the requirements of prior consultation, prior impact assessment, and benefit sharing.

Cultural Difference as an Extralegal Fiction

In the *Awas Tingni v. Nicaragua* case analyzed in Chapter 7, it became evident how the feature of prior sovereign occupation of the Americas has lost relevance in the definitional concept of indigenous communities. Instead, cultural difference—dialectically entangled with the experience of discrimination that further intensifies this cultural difference—comes into focus. What makes indigenous communities special is the profound relationship they maintain with the land they live on. This special relationship is charged with several features reminiscent of noble savage imagery: ecological sustainability, disregard for private property, peacefulness, anti-capitalism, spirituality. When cultural difference manifested in a special relationship to land becomes the prevalent feature of indigeneity and the source of special rights, it also becomes possible to recognize indigenous rights for those communities that are not composed of descendants of the native inhabitants of the Americas—in the case of the Saramakas, communities of African descent.

The Court tells us that not only do the Saramakas, as a community of African descent, maintain a relationship to the land that is similar to that of indigenous communities, but this relationship to the land is also the very core of their being—in the words of the Court, "a necessary source for the continuation of the life and cultural identity of the Saramaka people." We can see that the main definitional feature of indigenous communities has shifted from "they were here first" to "they have a spiritual and cultural relationship to the land." The terms "indigenous" and "tribal" are not to be understood as synonymous, but as two different terms that overlap to a large extent. The Saramakas may not be indigenous, but they are tribal. And what makes them tribal is the spiritual and cultural relationship to the land.

In *Awas Tingni v. Nicaragua* we have seen that cultural difference, like sovereignty, is able to accommodate the indigenous paradox. The indigenous paradox, in which the indigenous (and tribal) claimant must appear at the same time as part of and dissociated from national law, requires that the claimant be in a position to evoke the rule of law of the (post)colonial legal system, but only to demand that it not extend its rule of law to the claimant.

The culture argument says that because indigenous and tribal groups are culturally different—especially with regard to the special spiritual and cultural as well as economic relationship they maintain to the land—this cultural difference must be protected by the state. I have tried to show that this argument has, like sovereignty, a fictional structure, but with the difference that this fiction is conceptualized as extralegal (de facto), while sovereignty is conceptualized as a legal category.

As such, cultural difference in the form of a "special relationship to land" serves as a source of de facto legal pluralism and provides the basis for a successful indigenous rights approach. The Court has implicitly stated that Suriname is obligated to protect the cultural difference it is confronted with: the Saramakas and their special relationship to the land they live on, which is the basis of their "way of life." To protect the Saramakas' way of life, they have to be able to decide on how to use their land and natural resources—every infringement by Suriname must be justified. This gives rise to a right to regulate their own affairs, because they already do so—following their culturally different "way of life." De facto legal pluralism allows the Saramakas to claim from the state protection and enforcement of a right that does not originate in the law of the state. As such, "cultural difference" is able to serve the same function as sovereignty.

Culture as Constraint Revisited: Procedural Questions

At the beginning of this chapter I indicated that the legal debates on indigenous rights have largely shifted to procedural matters. After *Awas Tingni v. Nicaragua*, which was concerned with establishing the doctrinal basis for indigenous land and resource rights, the question of the circumstances under which these indigenous rights can be infringed upon by member states came into focus. In *Saramaka v. Suriname* we can see that the existence of indigenous land rights demands that a state that wishes to take actions infringing on those land rights (in our case, to grant concessions for resource extraction) has to justify those actions.

In this regard indigenous rights are no different from other fundamental rights in the national legal context. Because a state is obligated to treat its citizens fairly and equitably, every state action that benefits some citizens and adversely affects others must be justified. To that end the state must balance the legitimate rights and interests of all actors involved. The recognition of indigenous land rights therefore puts the onus on the state to include those rights in its legal calculations. The consequence is that indigenous land rights are neither absolute nor can they be completely ignored. Every concrete case demands a justified solution.

The Court clarifies in *Saramaka v. Suriname*, however, that in this balancing of rights and interests, certain factors have to be considered that are specific to indigenous (and tribal) communities. Concerning resource rights, the Court takes a narrow interpretation regarding which resources are protected by article 21 of the Convention: "Natural resources found on and within indigenous and tribal people's territories that are protected under Article 21 are those natural resources traditionally used and necessary for the very survival, development and continuation of such people's way of life" (para. 122). What we find here is the concept that is often identified with the term "frozen rights." Because the basis of indigenous land and resource rights is the culturally different way of life, only those resources necessary to maintain this traditional way of life are recognized as protected. Culture, which serves as the basis of indigenous rights in the culture approach, functions therefore at the same time as a constraint on the scope of indigenous rights.

We have already analyzed in *Delgamuukw v. British Columbia* this phenomenon of "culture as constraint." But there it was embedded in a claim based on the sovereignty approach to indigenous rights and came into tension with it. This tension does not emerge in *Saramaka v. Suriname*. As cultural difference is the reason for the state's obligation to protect indigenous communities, the state is not obligated to abstain from regulating those issues that do not concern the culturally different lifestyle of the indigenous and tribal community.

The same concept applies with regard to the justification of concrete state actions. How high the standard for justification is depends on how intensely the state action touches on traditional and culturally specific features of the indigenous and tribal community. The community is faced with two choices: either to stay culturally distinct and maintain considerable space for self-rule and protection from the state, or to become more similar to the majority society and narrow this space.

* * * *

In *Saramaka v. Suriname* we can observe many of the features and consequences of the culture approach to indigenous rights. In this case cultural difference alone—and not the legal fiction of sovereignty—emerges as the conceptual basis for the rights of communities. This cultural difference between the Saramaka claimants and the majority society in Suriname serves at the same time as the source of and constraint on property rights. In this context questions of procedure to protect against the infringement of these rights revolve around culture and the "way of life" of the Saramakas. Although the culture approach, with its conceptual basis of de facto legal pluralism, is not conceptualized as rooted in a legal fiction (sovereignty), I contend that the cultural difference itself—especially in its manifestation in the special relationship to the land—serves as an extralegal fiction to constitute indigenous and tribal rights.

CHAPTER 9

Sovereignty, Culture, and the Indigenous Paradox

Indigeneity is a somewhat elusive phenomenon. It is, furthermore, inextricably entangled with the legal field: indigeneity as a cultural phenomenon emerges in the interaction between disenfranchised minority communities and national and international courts. What makes indigeneity such an elusive phenomenon is the paradox underlying every indigenous rights claim: it demands that the indigenous claimant embody contradictory propositions. The claimant must, on the one hand, count as a legal person in the eyes of the (post)colonial state, at least from the perspective of the court. Otherwise it would be barred from bringing a case before such an institution. On the other hand, the indigenous claimant must also stand outside the realm of the very national law that guides the decisions of the court whose help the indigenous claimant seeks. Otherwise the claimant would not be able to claim rights beyond those granted by the (post)colonial state.

We have now thoroughly examined several court decisions in landmark indigenous rights cases in the Americas and gained some insights into the structures of indigenous rights strategies and hence into the discursive structure of indigeneity. We have seen that the production of legal pluralism is essential for an indigenous rights strategy because, I contend, some understanding of legal pluralism is necessary to be able to accommodate the indigenous paradox. A model of legal monism leaves no room to argue for any kind of special group rights apart from those the (post)colonial state (and thus the majority society) is willing to grant and guarantee (see Figure 2). We have identified at least two different ways to conceive of such legal pluralism:

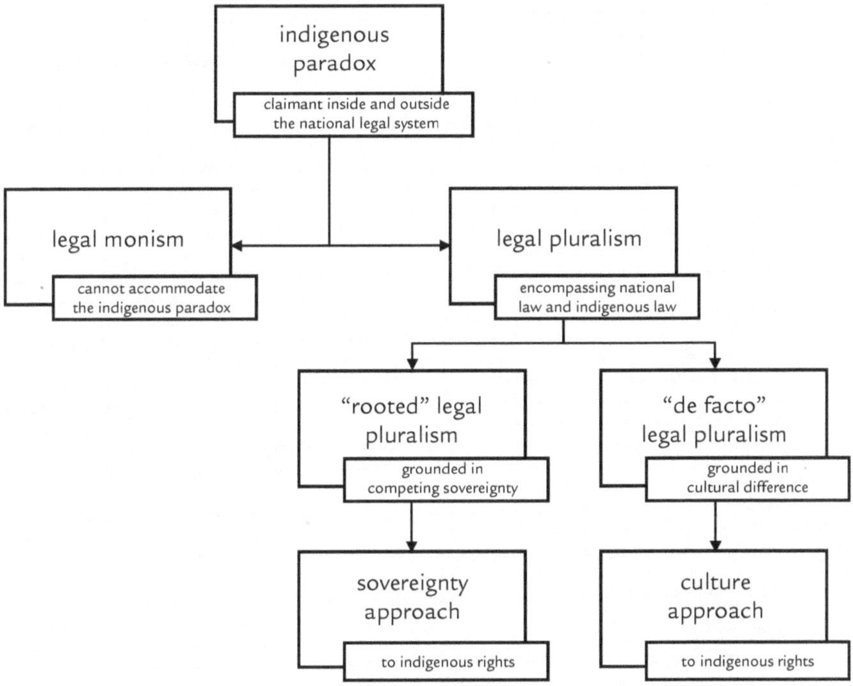

Figure 2. A systematization of indigenous rights strategies

rooted legal pluralism grounded in the legal fiction of sovereignty and de facto legal pluralism grounded in the extralegal fiction of cultural difference. From these two varieties of legal pluralism two indigenous rights strategies emerge: the sovereignty approach and the culture approach. Both strategies accommodate the indigenous paradox and are structurally similar, but they have important conceptual differences.

Johnson v. McIntosh develops indigenous land rights out of a complex model whereby indigenous territorial sovereignty is translated into and recognized by U.S. law following a detour into international customary law. In *Cherokee Nation v. Georgia* we have seen that Indian tribes are conceptualized as retaining ongoing sovereignty from precolonial times as nations in the sense of international law. This sovereignty legitimizes their own legal systems and protects them, as we have seen in *Worcester v. Georgia*, from state intrusions into their territory. In *Delgamuukw v. British Columbia*, we have seen that the indigenous land rights concept of aboriginal title is categorized as *sui generis* to indicate that it originates outside of common law in a parallel indigenous legal system. In *Aloeboetoe v. Suriname*, we have seen that the Inter-American Court of Human Rights recognized Saramaka family law as a form of "local law" existing parallel to "official" Surinamese family law and used it to determine who should be eligible for reparations. In *Awas Tingni v. Nicaragua*, the special relationship that indigenous communities maintain with the land they live on was seen as the manifestation of their own land tenure system, which exists independent of the law of the state. And in *Saramaka v. Suriname* we have seen how the de facto legal system (including land tenure and land use regulations) of a group of people of African descent is considered similar enough to indigenous legal systems to warrant the application of legal standards initially developed for indigenous communities.

The three "Marshall trilogy" cases—*Johnson v. McIntosh*, *Cherokee Nation v. Georgia*, and *Worcester v. Georgia*—as well as the Canadian case *Delgamuukw v. British Columbia*, are based on the model I have called "rooted legal pluralism." The legal pluralism of national law and indigenous law is based on the fact that the indigenous nations had been legal persons under international law before the arrival of Europeans and that they did not lose their sovereignty when the colonial state and its legal system were established. I have defined "sovereignty" as the legal fiction that the sovereign entity is the source of its own legal system. The sovereign entity is therefore bound only by its own rules or by those rules that can be traced back to its own sovereignty. Because the sovereignty of indigenous nations persists, it competes with the sovereignty of the (post)colonial state for the same territory. Whose sovereignty is legitimately executed depends on the legal perspective (from national law and from indigenous law) and—in practice—on negotiations between the sovereignty holders. One recognizes and accommodates the other's sovereign rights in a situation characterized by unequal power relations. Rooted legal pluralism is thus grounded in the legal fiction of competing sovereignties.

In *Aloeboetoe v. Suriname*, *Awas Tingni v. Nicaragua*, and *Saramaka v. Suriname*, indigenous law is not conceptualized as deriving from international sovereignty. The Inter-American Court has confined itself to determining the existence of parallel legal systems—"official" national law on the one hand and indigenous law on the other—as a matter of empirical fact. This de facto legal pluralism differs from rooted legal pluralism in how its origin is conceptualized (or perhaps more precisely, whether the issue is even addressed at all). While rooted legal pluralism emerges from the legal fiction of competing sovereignties, the origin of de facto legal pluralism remains unasked; it is a black box. That the existence of legal pluralism is an empirical question means that it becomes evident only in those cases where the indigenous (or tribal) community governs its own affairs in a way that is demonstrably different from "official" law. De facto legal pluralism is thus grounded in cultural difference.

In analyzing *Awas Tingni v. Nicaragua* and *Saramaka v. Suriname*, however, I have argued that the "origin question" for de facto legal pluralism comes in through the back door. The clearest manifestation of the cultural difference that gives rise to de facto legal pluralism is the so-called special relationship indigenous (and tribal) communities maintain with their land. I have argued that the explanations and descriptions of this special relationship have a fictional structure, but one that is different from the fiction of sovereignty. The cultural difference between indigenous peoples and the majority society, manifested in their special relationship to land, is an extralegal fiction marked as a de facto phenomenon. While sovereignty is a fiction grounded in international law conceptions derived from Europe, I argue that the culturally specific relationship of indigenous peoples to the land is a fiction easily connectable to Eurocentric discourses of the "noble savage."

The concept of the indigenous paradox posits that if the indigenous community is either too similar to the rest of the nation or too different from the rest of the nation, the indigenous rights claim will fail.

In *Cherokee Nation v. Georgia*, the Cherokee Nation had to prove that it is a "foreign state," one of the categories of legitimate claimants before the Supreme Court as enumerated in the U.S. Constitution. The Cherokees lost their case because they did not fit that category. But with the model I have proposed, I contend that they could not have won even if they had been able to prove that they were a foreign state. In Justice Johnson's minority opinion we can see why: if the indigenous community is conceptualized as completely outside the legal realm of the (post)colonial state (in this case conceptualized as a "foreign state"), the paradoxical nature of the indigenous cannot be accommodated. In this case the national law that binds the court does not demand recognition or accommodation of indigenous law beyond what is demanded by international law. When the indigenous claimant is a foreign state, it is simply too foreign to claim the rights guaranteed by another state's legal system. The great danger is that the national court will see the case as outside its own jurisdiction—as part of international relations, which are in the political realm of the executive.

On the other hand, the indigenous rights claim will also fail when the claimant is conceptualized as being too similar to the majority society. In

Aloeboetoe v. Suriname, the claim for collective reparations after a massacre was not successful. The Inter-American Commission argued that killing a member of an indigenous community had a more devastating effect on the community as a whole than the murder of a nonindigenous person would have on his or her community. This reasoning was based on the articulation of the cultural difference between indigenous communities and other communities in the majority society. Because indigenous communities are presumed to have such a close-knit social and kinship structure, the loss of a person weighs much more heavily than in other communities.

The Inter-American Court rejected this argument because it found that the difference between indigenous and nonindigenous communities with regard to the embeddedness of individuals was not stark enough to justify a special standard. In *Aloeboetoe v. Suriname*, the Saramaka were not able to articulate their cultural difference and therefore were not able to occupy the paradoxical position necessary for a successful indigenous rights claim.

To be recognized as indigenous it is not enough merely to convince the court of the negative condition—that is, for the indigenous claimant to appear *not* too similar on the one hand and *not* too foreign on the other. To complete the paradoxical phenomenon, the indigenous community must also be able to convince the court of the affirmative: that it is in fact both similar *and* foreign at the same time. This can be observed in a number of the legal notions we have investigated. The term "domestic dependent nation," coined by Chief Justice Marshall in *Cherokee Nation v. Georgia*, grammatically embodies the indigenous paradox. The indigenous claimant is "domestic" and "dependent" and is therefore part of the common-law system and the legal order of the United States. But it is also a "nation," therefore foreign to the legal system of the United States, which is a nation itself. A "domestic dependent nation" is therefore both foreign and domestic.

The idea of the *sui generis* nature of aboriginal title in Canadian law is another example. Aboriginal title is seen as a property interest of Canadian law, a common-law right enforceable before a common-law court. It also originates outside of the Canadian common-law legal system, in the aboriginal legal systems rooted in the indigenous nations' ongoing sovereignty. Aboriginal title is therefore a common-law right and not a common-law right.

The concept of indigenous land and resource rights protected in article 21 of the Inter-American Convention also has a paradoxical character. The OAS member states must protect indigenous (and tribal) land and resource rights inside their own legal systems, as they do any other property of nonindigenous people. But the indigenous land rights are also inherently different from nonindigenous property rights in the sense that they do not derive from the national legal system but come from the special relationship the indigenous peoples have with the land. This special relationship gives rise to property that exists independent of state recognition but is at the same time a national property right the state is obligated to protect.

The Differences Between the Sovereignty and Culture Approaches to Indigenous Rights

Karen Engle (2010) has made some observations on the different approaches to indigenous rights (what we have characterized under the headings "sovereignty" and "culture" approaches, Engle speaks of in terms of "self-determination" and a "human right to culture," respectively). Her argument is that indigenous rights movements the world over have shifted from a focus on self-determination to the right-to-culture strategy. Engle posits a connection between the two analytical approaches and the different colonial law discourses that were prevalent in the former British and former Spanish colonies. Following scholarship that proposes different discourses for the different European colonial powers (Pagden 1995), she ties "indigenous demands for a right to self-determination and land to former British colonies, while connecting legal and political strategies aimed at internal autonomy and collective cultural rights to former Spanish colonies" (Engle 2010, 19).

We have already observed that the indigenous rights debates starting in the 1970s were initially dominated by indigenous movements from North America. They promoted the arguments they were most comfortable with—those based on sovereignty—while indigenous movements from the global South were underrepresented in the respective forums of international law. Beginning in the 1990s, this North–South gap began to close. Indigenous movements—especially from South and Central America—gained more and more influence (Niezen 2003; Engle 2010). In this view the rise of the culture argument is linked to the rise of Latin American indigenous movements, and the different indigenous rights strategies in North America and Latin America are grounded in the *longue durée* of the different legal histories of their respective experiences of colonization. I find this an intriguing idea, and there are some very good arguments to be made for such a view. It might go too far, however, to understand the culture approach to indigenous rights as having historically superseded the sovereignty approach. Following the contentions I have made thus far on the paradoxical nature of indigeneity, I believe that the sovereignty and the culture approaches are not mutually exclusive concepts but different modes of indigenous rights strategies that can, and often do, overlap. Each has its strengths and weaknesses, but in different ways.

The sovereignty argument is in one important aspect stronger than the culture argument. I have already explained that the sovereignty argument is grounded in the legal fiction of competing sovereignties. Indigenous claimants who follow the sovereignty approach still have to prove their claims to the land—namely, their sovereign occupation and use of the territory from a time before the establishment of the postcolonial state. The claimants must do this by means of indigenous articulations, performances, and translations, but the legal fiction adds to these cultural performances. In other words, claimants in the sovereignty framework still must "play themselves," but the legal fiction of sovereignty can help in situations where indigenous "authenticity" is being questioned.

In the course of the culture approach, the articulation and performance of cultural difference is not aided by a legal fiction. We can illustrate this by comparing the conceptualization of resource rights in *Delgamuukw v. British Columbia* and *Saramaka v. Suriname*. Where cultural difference is the decisive factor for establishing the de facto existence of legal pluralism, only the proven and demonstrably "traditional" and "authentic" indigenous practices give rise to special protections: culture is at the same time the source of the legal protection and a constraint on the scope of these protections. This consequently leads to the phenomenon of "frozen rights," where only those practices existing at the time of contact or at least at the time of the establishment of the colonial legal order are protected. In *Saramaka v. Suriname*, the Inter-American Court explicitly states that only those resources that were used "traditionally" are part of indigenous resource rights; gold mining, for instance, is not a resource use protected for indigenous communities under article 21 of the American Convention. Only if the claimant can prove that a resource use is "traditional" can it claim its indigenous rights against an infringement by the state.

In *Delgamuukw v. British Columbia*, the Canadian Supreme Court elaborated on the question of "frozen rights" and came up with a more conciliatory solution. Because it is not only traditional practices but, above all, aboriginal sovereignty that is protected, aboriginal nations must be allowed the space to develop their land use practices as they see fit. Culture emerges as a constraint in this context, but only as an absolute limit on the development of land use practices. Aboriginal communities can change their land use patterns, but only as long as the nontraditional land use does not become irreconcilable with the traditional way of life of the indigenous nation. The initial recognition of aboriginal sovereignty occurred with the establishment of the Crown's sovereignty and was reinforced through the various treaties the Crown entered into with aboriginal nations. This "baseline" sovereignty still determines the scope of the legal space within which indigenous nations can change their practices and still be able to claim protection for those practices. In other words, Canada recognizes aboriginal sovereignty as long as the outer limits of this legal space are not transcended.

The culture argument functions differently. The culturally different traditional practices themselves are seen as protected. Their ongoing existence must be proven without the aid of a legal fiction, and the corridor for change of cultural practice is much narrower than in the sovereignty concept. Although I have argued that cultural difference and the special relationship of the indigenous communities to their land have a fictional structure, this fiction is extralegal and does not provide an additional legal assumption for the existence of protected rights. In this sense the culture model is weaker than the sovereignty model.

The sovereignty approach, however, has an important weakness. The concept of ongoing indigenous sovereignty entails, first of all, the idea that the present-day community either consists of the descendants of the native inhabitants of the American continent before European colonization or that they somehow achieved or were granted sovereignty later (through a treaty, for example). Those communities not descending from precolonial inhabitants of the Americas, such as the Saramakas, have the greatest difficulty in deploying a sovereignty approach. Another prerequisite for a successful sovereignty claim is that the community can prove an unbroken chain of sovereignty from precontact times to the present. This becomes more difficult the more time has elapsed since the beginning of the colonial endeavor. This problem is even greater for those communities who no longer live on the same territory where their ancestors lived when the Europeans arrived.

The culture argument has an important advantage over the sovereignty argument: it is more inclusive with respect to the number of communities able to claim rights in its framework. As we have seen in *Saramaka v. Suriname*, the culture approach is able to incorporate other communities that are not native in that they are not descendants of the precolonial inhabitants of the Americas. In this case the Inter-American Court extended indigenous rights to communities of African descent by broadening the category to "indigenous and tribal rights" (in reference to ILO 169). Where cultural difference is the point of reference to determine whether a community is entitled to special protections, other culturally different communities can also be included as long as they can prove that they conform to the extralegal fiction of having a "special relationship to the land."

In that sense both the sovereignty and the culture arguments open up spaces for special rights that go beyond those provided by the (post)colonial states' legal systems. But both approaches also foreclose some space for rights, either because they limit the scope of such special rights or because they limit the number of communities entitled to them.

Finally, a question presents itself: Why do both the sovereignty and the culture strategies work? In the first chapter we have established that indigenous articulations, performances, and translations depend as much on the expectations of nonindigenous audiences as they do on indigenous self-conceptions. It is therefore important that both arguments be understandable for the nonindigenous legal discourse, which is heavily influenced by the *longue durée* of Eurocentric conceptions of law, culture, and identity.

I contend that the sovereignty approach appeals to clearly established conceptions of international public law derived from Europe. The analogy to the European nation-state taps into established (often highly Eurocentric) discourses. These connections to European public international law discourses are quite explicit in Marshall's various references to such scholars as Francisco de Vitoria and Emmerich von Vattel. But the culture argument is also understandable in the framework of Eurocentric legal discourse. The idea of the exceptional value of indigenous communities' special relationship to land is—as we have observed in *Awas Tingni v. Nicaragua*, *Saramaka v. Suriname*, and even in *Delgamuukw v. British Columbia*—also connected to the very Eurocentric discourses on the noble savage. Both sovereignty and culture as basic arguments for indigenous rights are able to accommodate the indigenous paradox by providing the foundation for a conceptualization of legal pluralism while at the same time being grounded in discourses that speak to the nonindigenous public.

* * * *

Indigeneity presents itself as a paradox. A community, being independent from the state in which it resides, is dependent on this very state to bring to life its independence. In the legal-political encounter between the indigenous community and the state, some conception of legal pluralism is invoked that allows for this paradox to be practiced: the indigenous community is both subject to the (post)colonial legal system and it is not. Such an indigenous rights claim can be based on the legal fiction of sovereignty, the extralegal fiction of cultural difference, or a combination of these. All of these approaches to indigenous rights are functionally similar in one aspect: they are all able to accommodate the indigenous paradox.

CHAPTER 10

Indigeneity and the Politics of Recognition

In the first chapter of this book I argued for thinking of indigenous rights judgments as ethnographic texts and for investigating the intertextuality in which they emerge as a mélange of yet other ethnographic and autoethnographic texts. Now that we have delved deeper into some landmark judgments on indigenous rights in the Americas, whether it be more recent decisions such as *Delgamuukw v. British Columbia*, with its passionate plea for the common-law recognition of culturally specific accounts of aboriginal nations' oral history, and *Awas Tingni v. Nicaragua*, with its evocation of the spiritual, noneconomic relationship between indigenous peoples and their land, or much older cases such as *Cherokee Nation v. Georgia*, with its strong assertions of indigenous national sovereignty, we cannot help but be struck by the many passages whose engaged language and tone far exceed the usual detached tenor of legal texts. These decisions read like the emic accounts of indigenous self-conceptions we would expect to find in ethnographic literature.

One might also be tempted to identify the more recent prominence of "culture talk" in global indigenous rights debates as a symptom of this new understanding of indigenous cosmovisions. The legal conceptualization of ongoing sovereignty alone, derived from European ideas of legal personality and oriented toward the nation-state, appears no longer to be an apt concept for indigenous peoples. A new relativism has created space for new, more indigenous views and concepts, as well as a new valuation of cultural difference. When reading these judgments, especially the newer ones, one is tempted to think that after centuries of legal discrimination and being written out of the law, the indigenous voice has finally been heard. Lawyers and, perhaps more important, judges have begun to listen to indigenous communities and to incorporate their cosmovisions into the law.

I hope it has become clear that things are not that simple. The interpretation of indigenous rights conceptualizations (and the indigenous articulations, performances, and translations that bring them about) that I have presented thus far questions such assumptions. My contention is that indigeneity and indigenous rights movements, as well as their legal strategies and concepts, emerge in a paradoxical structure. In this view the more recent prevalence of culturally sensitive language in indigenous rights judgments represents no fundamental difference from the sovereignty approach. Rather, as I have discussed in Chapter 9, the two approaches are similar in their function of conceptualizing a legal pluralism that can account for the paradoxical structure of indigeneity. Having established this, we are now in a position to better assess ongoing debates on the question of the transformative potential—or lack thereof—of indigenous rights movements.

The Politics of Recognition and Its Critics

In the political theory literature, indigenous rights movements are often seen as manifestations of a politics of recognition. A politics of recognition is often associated with the so-called new social movements that emerged in the second half of the twentieth century in Western Europe and North America (Larana, Johnston, and Gusfield 1994), such as second-wave feminism, environmentalist movements, civil rights movements, anti-war movements, and so forth. Beginning in the 1980s, political theorists started discussing on a theoretical level the importance of the production and reproduction of identities for political processes (Laclau 1994; Hall and du Gay 1996) and the prevalence of "the cultural" (rather than "the economic") in political debates (Jordan and Weedon 1995).

In the 1990s the multicultural project as a model for the recognition of cultural diversity in liberal democracies gained prominence (Kymlicka 1995, 2007; Shapiro and Kymlicka 1997) and influenced debates in the Americas (Nuijten 2010). The movement of indigenism in national and international law that I have been discussing in this study has also been interpreted as part of the multicultural project (Anaya 2004b). As the multicultural project is directed at the legal and political recognition of different cultural identities, the term "politics of recognition" has been used to describe it (Gutmann and Taylor 1992).

According to Bhikhu Parekh (2004), the politics of recognition is characterized by three factors: (1) it makes an underlying anthropological assumption about the relationship between the individual and its culture; (2) it formulates an implicit and explicit critique of the norms and values of majority society; and (3) it derives from this assumption and this critique a concrete politico-juridical project directed to the national and international legal systems. The underlying anthropological assumption of the politics of recognition is that all human beings are culturally embedded. This means that an individual's identity is profoundly shaped by his or her cultural surroundings (meanings, values, ideals).[1] Culture permeates all parts of life, including the political; therefore, it cannot be confined to the private sphere. From this underlying assumption, a politics of recognition derives a critique of the majority society: the majority society (including its legal system) is also, like all aspects of life, permeated by culture; therefore, it cannot be free of cultural assumptions and values. Because the legal system needs "some conception of the good life to structure its institutions," the majority "unwittingly adopts, institutionalizes and enforces the categories, practices, and values of the dominant culture" (Parekh 2004, 201). The majority society and its legal system are, therefore, by definition culturally biased, even if it does not realize it. From this critique of majority society, the politics of recognition derives a politico-juridical project that aims at taking full account of cultural, religious, and other differences in its laws, institutions, practices, and policies, instead of relegating the negotiation of those differences exclusively to the private sphere.

The politics of recognition is hence connected to a very basic normative understanding of how society should be. Social philosopher Axel Honneth (1992), for instance, has made the "struggle for recognition" a cornerstone of his proposition on how to morally organize contemporary society. Based on Hegel's early writings, Honneth argues that modern liberal democratic society becomes manifest in the constant struggle over how to recognize the other in all its difference and negotiate commonality at the same time. What Honneth and other theorists of recognition show is how much is at stake in the discussion regarding the politics of recognition: no less than a basic understanding of "modern liberal democratic society"—with all the (empty) signifiers this phrase entails.

The politics of recognition has been heavily criticized from several sides (Figure 3). Two of these criticisms are very basic. First, although most authors see the politics of recognition as a product of the liberal theoretical tradition

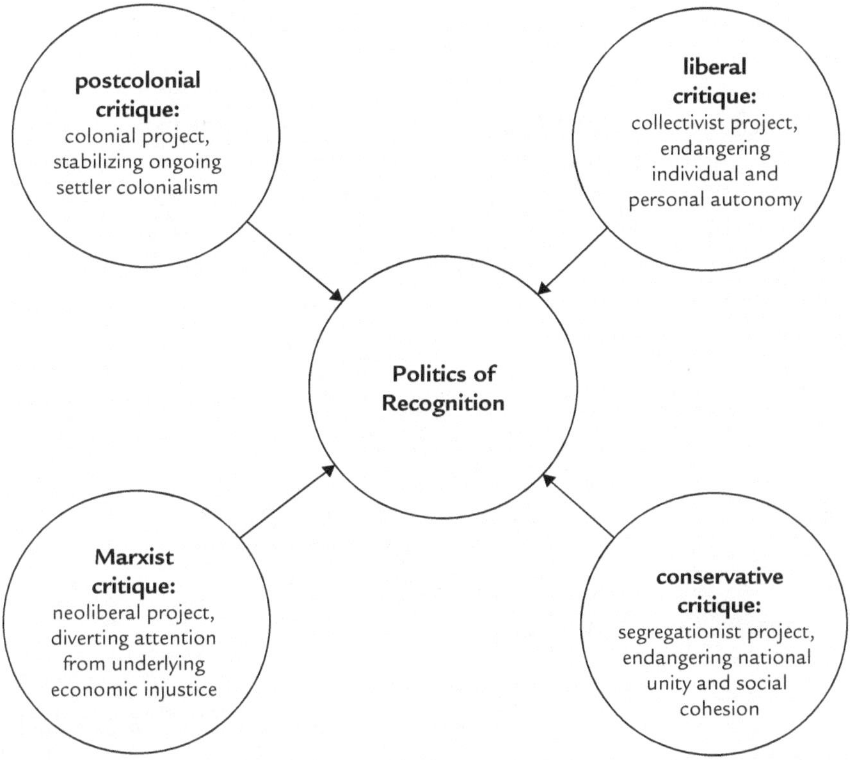

Figure 3. Critical approaches to a politics of recognition

(e.g., Povinelli 2002), there is a very prominent liberal (or maybe intraliberal) critique of the concept. This liberal critique sees the politics of recognition as overly collectivist. By arguing for collective rights or group rights, the politics of recognition threatens basic liberal values of individual and personal autonomy as well as the basic idea of the universality of human rights. There is also a conservative critique of the politics of recognition. The basic argument of conservatives is that a legal system that recognizes different sociocultural identities by granting them special rights endangers national unity and social cohesion. These two extreme critiques agree in a very basic denunciation of special group rights. For them, the struggle for indigenous rights as group rights is in and of itself erroneous. Instead, indigenous communities should struggle for equal rights from within the national body politic—not as indigenous people, but as citizens of the nation-state. For our purposes, we will leave aside these two positions and focus more on two strands of criticism that generally sympathize with indigenous movements but are skeptical of their mode of engagement.

A Marxist critique contends that the issue of the recognition of cultural identity diverts attention from the underlying problem of social and economic injustice. Most prevalent in the literature on the politics of recognition in regard to ethnic minorities and indigenous peoples is the "recognition versus redistribution" debate (Fraser 1995; Tully 2000). Critics from the left generally, but not exclusively, favor a politics of redistribution over a politics of recognition. In this view, legal recognition will not improve the situation of ethnic minorities and indigenous peoples as long as the economic and social inequalities underlying and effectuating their discrimination are not addressed. A focus on culture instead of economics not only deflects attention from the underlying economic inequalities, but also emphasizes (cultural) difference instead of equality and therefore weakens solidarity with other economically disenfranchised actors (Barry 2002). A multiculturalism that loses the focus on economic redistribution could even support and stabilize discriminatory inequalities in capitalism, as a limited recognition of cultural rights is already an integral part of neoliberal governance (Hale 2005).

In its purest form, the redistributionist critique boils down to the argument that a politics of recognition is only concerned with "symbolic issues," while a politics of redistribution focuses on "real economic issues." I believe that this analysis posits too stark a contrast between "the symbolic" and "the economic." I am inclined to agree with those post-Marxist approaches that emphasize that the economic sphere is also symbolically grounded and that it is a misconception to differentiate between a discursive political sphere (where identities are negotiated) and a purportedly nondiscursive economic sphere (where objective laws are presumed to govern development and change) (Laclau and Mouffe 1985; Ortner 2006). Therefore, those who make an argument addressing economic inequalities must also address symbolically negotiated identities. Some people have tried to bridge the two positions by suggesting greater sensitivity to economic imbalances and to the Marxist critique within the framework of a politics of recognition, and point to indigenous land and resource rights struggles as examples where recognition may very well entail economic redistribution (Parekh 2004). Recently, Mark Goodale (2016) has renewed the call for including political economy in indigenous rights research by providing more in-depth ethnographic studies in that direction. One example is Isabel Altamirano-Jiménez's (2013) exciting comparative study on indigenous identity in Canada and Mexico in the context of neoliberal environmental policies.

Another strand of critique draws on postcolonial theory and focuses more explicitly on this point. In this view, the politics of recognition, because it is so much based on the political and legal system of the settler state, cannot accommodate indigenous communities' interests (see, e.g., Howard-Wagner, Bargh, and Altamirano-Jiménez 2018). Glen Coulthard argues that "the politics of recognition in its contemporary liberal form promises to reproduce the very configurations of colonialist, racist, patriarchal state power that Indigenous peoples' demands for recognition have historically sought to transcend" (2014, 3). As such, both the Marxist and the postcolonial approaches derive from their analysis of the politics of recognition a critique of the blind spots of the modern liberal democratic state. Based on similar insights drawn from postcolonial theory, Elizabeth Povinelli (2002), who sees her work as a "critique of late liberalism," points to the "cunning of recognition" as an example of "the possibility that liberalism is harmful not only when it fails to live up to its ideals, but when it approaches them" (2002, 13).

On the Master's Tools and His House

A critical or skeptical take on the politics of recognition has become mainstream in scholarship on indigenous rights. The Marxist and the postcolonial strands of critique frequently merge with each other, and I basically agree with them. These approaches make visible the degree to which the politics of recognition is deeply connected to the political philosophy of liberalism and sometimes hint, albeit often inchoately, at some kind of radical democracy as an alternative.[2] That is all well and good. The question that I believe must be asked in light of the propositions I have made in this book is the following: Is there a radical alternative form of recognition waiting beyond the narrow confines of the "modern liberal democratic state"? Are any group rights conceivable without the paradoxical practice that seems to result from them? I am skeptical. To phrase the question differently: Is the indigenous paradox unique insofar as it is a result of judicialized settler colonialism, or does it point to a more fundamental paradox grounded in the process of recognition beyond the modern nation-state? I am inclined to think the latter is true. However one answers, I would always advise that such questions of political theory and practice be approached from a broad perspective on both the productive and the repressive potential of recognition.

One important point of convergence between Marxist and postcolonial critiques of the politics of recognition, particularly in indigenous rights movements, is the risk of frozen identities. Critics observe that indigenous movements in their cultural politics are under pressure to essentialize cultural identities for political mobilization, which tends to "freeze" identities and therefore forecloses the possibility of cultural change and economic development (Fraser 2000). This is an issue we have observed in our reading of the cases. We have seen it in *Cherokee Nation v. Georgia*, in which the Cherokee Nation, in order to buttress its claims to sovereign equality, had to prove that it could pass a "civilization" test based on Anglo-American conceptions of Lockean property theory. We have observed the phenomenon of "culture as proof" and "culture as constraint" in *Delgamuukw v. British Columbia* and *Saramaka v. Suriname*, in which cultural articulations are needed to give evidence of indigenous rights, but serve at the same time as a means to limit those rights.

It is in this context that many scholars discuss the problem of "strategic essentialism" in indigenous politics. The widely cited but very disparately outlined concept of "strategic essentialism" is derived from postcolonial theory and is often attributed to Gayatri Spivak (1984/85, 1985), who very early on distanced herself from the concept. It roughly refers to the paradoxical task of knowingly essentializing and even exaggerating cultural identities for the purposes of political and legal mobilization and recognition. Some scholars and activists argue for such a strategic essentialism in the context of cultural arguments in indigenous rights struggles and make a case for consciously constructing and deconstructing cultural identities in the political struggle as a strategic measure (Hale 2006). Others are skeptical of "strategic essentialism" and argue for incorporating less essentializing concepts of culture into the legal debates (Engle 2010; Zenker 2016). I believe this debate on strategic essentialism, which, I contend, cannot be resolved, is already indicative of the more basic paradox that is inherent not only in indigenous politics but in all kinds of politics of recognition.

In the first chapter I discussed the theoretical ramifications of indigenous articulations, performances, and translations. From that perspective indigeneity always entails a complex dialectics of identity processes, whereby indigenous "displays" are as much part of non-indigenous expectations as of indigenous self-conceptions. Most theories of identity widely used in anthropological research—with their origins in, among other fields, classical sociology, psychoanalysis, structuralist and poststructuralist philosophies, postcolonial theory, and so on (Du Gay, Evans, and Redman 2001)—highlight the fact that "self" and "other" are deeply interconnected. In this view, identity emerges in a dialectical process of exclusion of the other and formation of the self. Therefore, indigenous discourses have to be understood, as Pratt puts it, as processes that occur in the contact zone, and the various legal texts we have referred to should be approached as "arts of the contact zone" (1991).

In the previous chapters I have conducted an analysis of the "special relationship to land," which is, in my opinion, the most important component of the extralegal fiction of cultural difference underlying the culture approach to indigenous rights. I have contended that these conceptions of indigenous communities maintaining a noneconomic, spiritual, and cultural relationship to their land are presented as indigenous self-conceptions. At the same time, however, these concepts fit just as neatly into Eurocentric discourses of the "noble savage." These noble savage discourses do not come across (at least not obviously) as tools of oppression, however, but as tools wielded by progressive social and political movements. However, tapping into the Eurocentric conception of the noble savage for strategic purposes cannot circumvent the dialectical entanglement of the noble savage with the bad savage. As Hinrich Fink-Eitel observes in his analysis of passages from Christopher Columbus's logs from the late fifteenth century: "The bad savage and the noble savage constitute *one* phantasmagoria of dominance. Both have to be enslaved. The noble savage is not even saved by the fact that he has a capacity for Christianity equal to the European; he is wonderful but, of course, still in the state of nature. According to the inner ambivalence of this underlying fantasy, the good is simultaneously bad and the bad simultaneously attractively good" (1994, 101; my translation).

When we apply the theoretical instruments laid out here to understand indigenous articulations, performances, and translations, we see that this unfolding story is much more than the simple explication of indigenous self-conception. Like "sovereignty," the "special relationship to the land" is a concept deeply embedded in the discourses of the West. And while these legal arguments (sovereignty and culture) are deployed to criticize mainstream notions of Western policies of exclusion, they are inextricably bound up with the very notions they criticize. In this view the idea of the indigenous paradox I have put forth in this book also emerges on the conceptual level of the culture argument to indigenous rights. We must understand indigenous rights strategies as connected to and disconnected from, critical of, and dependent on the very formations they strive to overcome: the postcolonial state, Western law, and neoliberal governance and its strategies of exclusion.

Audre Lorde (2003) has reminded us that "the master's tools will never dismantle the master's house." This study on legal arguments for and discourses of indigenous rights may have revealed how limited the transformative potential of indigenous rights movements is. I have argued that the legal strategies and arguments of indigenous rights, whether based on conceptualizations of competing sovereignty or cultural difference, are structurally similar. They have to fulfill a paradoxical task: to somehow use the rule of law to open up a space in which this very rule of law does not apply. Indigenous movements are, in the final analysis, entirely dependent on the state they need to negate in order to exist. This dependence of indigenous movements on the state does not allow for a complete and radical break with the national legal system.

On a discursive level the situation is the same. The idea of sovereignty is a concept derived from Eurocentric ideas of international law. The "special relationship with the land" is as much a part of Eurocentric savagery discourses as it is an indigenous articulation. Both indigenous rights strategies are, of course, "the master's tools," and, as Lorde noted, they will never be able to "dismantle the master's house." The reason for this lies in the paradoxical structure of indigeneity. When one understands indigeneity as a paradoxical formation of dependence in independence, both of the indigenous rights strategies we have discussed are already structurally strategies of "reform" rather than of "revolution." A complete break from the legal, political, and economic system disenfranchising indigenous communities is not possible with an indigenous rights strategy that depends on this very system to come to life.

Thus, indigenous rights strategies, and especially the culture argument, have their limits. But their paradoxical nature entails that indigenous rights strategies, as dependent as they may be on the very structures they criticize, are able to better the conditions of indigenous communities and to tackle existing legal, social, and economic inequalities. How much room indigenous peoples occupy in the master's house is still a matter of negotiation and struggle, in which the discursive ramifications of the concepts of indigenous rights play an important part.

Indigenous rights movements have not completely changed the landscape of national and international law, nor will they ever be able to. The strategies of indigenous movements "work" because they refer to the very same discursive structures that disenfranchise them, but with the aim of opening up space in the master's house. That the rule of national and international law also enshrines the instruments used to suspend it is the very reason that there are legal strategies that can open up at least some room for maneuver. But the paradoxical nature of indigeneity also enables indigenous movements to open up spaces of resistance, because as much as their strategies depend on the state, they are also independent of it. To that end indigenous movements emerge, with all of the inherent paradox they entail, ultimately embracing both hopelessness and hope.

NOTES

Chapter 1

1. A number of metaphors have been proposed to highlight the relationality of indigeneity. In the North American context, Richard White (1992) speaks of a "middle ground," while Kevin Bruyneel (2010) proposes a "third space." I find such descriptive language to be both evocative and productive. I elaborate elsewhere how the terminology I propose here, i.e., the "paradox" of indigeneity, relates to these metaphors (Bens 2018).

2. The Négritude was a circle of black intellectuals and activists and a literary-philosophical movement that focused on the cultural and political emancipation of black Africans. One focal point of their literary and political activities was the journal *Présence Africaine*, which was founded in 1947 in Paris and is published in French to this day. The term *négritude* was first used by Aimé Césaire in his *Cahier d'un retour au pays natal* (1939; the English version, *Notebook of a Return to the Native Land*, was published in 2001). The movement gained broader prominence when French existentialist philosopher Jean-Paul Sartre wrote a preface to Léopold Sédar Senghor's edited volume *Anthologie de la nouvelle poésie nègre et malgache de langue française* (1948). See also Ellen Kennedy's *The Negritude Poets: An Anthology of Translations from the French* (1975).

3. This proliferation of human rights regimes is complemented by a liberal political theory that has intensified and honed rights-based approaches to the promotion of liberal values of social equality, democracy, and individual freedom. In recent years not one prominent protagonist of rights-based, contractualist political theory has let slip by the chance to elaborate extensively on the importance of the implementation and intensification of human rights discourses (Dworkin 1977; Nussbaum 1997; Rawls 1999; Habermas 2004; Beck 2012).

4. The United States' entanglement with international human rights regimes is, in comparison to most Latin American states, relatively weak. The U.S. Supreme Court's record of refusing to consider the case law of international courts is exceptional, and its compliance with international court decisions is therefore relatively low. However, Martin Shapiro notes that "American politics has been Constitution-centered from the very beginning, and lawyers play a disproportionate role in political life" (1994, 101). Shapiro underpins this observation with a historical analysis. He views the American Revolution as focused on "a natural law/social contract ideology" and therefore as "particularly legalistic," and supports this with the assertion that "the revolution was not expressed as an assault on the existing legal system of law and courts but as an assertion of legal and constitutional rights of Englishmen against an overbearing Parliament" (1994, 101). Furthermore, he interprets the disproportionate role of lawyers in American politics as "probably the result of deeper socio-economic causes, such as the absence of a hereditary aristocracy, the prevalence of small, market-oriented agricultural land holdings, and the rapid

economic development experienced through competitive corporate capitalism" (1994, 102). This political-economic interpretation is intriguing and invites one to transfer this idea to Latin American developments. From this perspective it may be suggested that recent judicialization processes in Latin America can be attributed to the expansion of capitalist structures clinging to the coattails of neoliberal reforms in the 1980s (Margheritis and Pereira 2007). The findings of Comaroff and Comaroff (2007) seem to point in that direction as well. Nevertheless, the historical roots of judicialization in early colonial times suggest that it could be enlightening to broaden the political-economic analysis. There are significant differences between the political economy of early colonial times in Latin America and today's capitalism. Following this line of thought, it would be a worthwhile project to conduct a historically deep analysis of the political-economic conditions in which judicialization processes emerge, rather than assuming that they all have similar historical origins and root causes.

5. Of course, constitutional legal discourse plays a major role in Latin America as well as in postcolonies in general. Comaroff and Comaroff count 105 national constitutions written or heavily revised between 1989 and 2005, most of them in postcolonies (2007, 141). There is a "rise of world constitutionalism" that has important discursive consequences. As Bruce Ackerman puts it, "faith in constitutions is sweeping the world" (1997, 2). Constitutional language is therefore an important part of "rights talk" and is both a symptom of and a contribution to the judicialization of politics.

6. The family as a group is protected in ICCPR, Article 23(1), and ICESCR, Article 10.

7. ILO 107 still applies to those states that have not ratified ILO 169 but were party to the older convention. Many provisions of ILO 107 are interpreted in light of the new convention. Only a few legal differences remain.

8. A similar formulation can also be found in Article 1 of both ICCPR and ICESCR.

9. Karen Engle has argued that the culture approach has superseded the sovereignty approach as the dominant line of argumentation for indigenous rights movements. She concludes that "not only were [the advocates of the sovereignty approach] unable to convince states to support such a right, but they did not persuade enough other indigenous groups to follow their lead in what was thought by many to be a futile attempt to affect international law too dramatically" (Engle 2010, 2). I believe this conclusion goes too far. When referring to the phrasing of international legal texts, the language of the culture approach does indeed appear to be dominant, but in activist circles the sovereignty argument still predominates. Academic interest in the sovereignty argument likewise remains high, especially in the North American context (see Wilkins and Lomawaima 2002; Corntassel and Witmer 2008), and sovereignty continues to be a concern that connects the Americas as a whole (Barker 2005; Cheyfitz, Duthu, and Huhndorf 2011; Negrón-Muntaner 2017). I discuss the relationship between the sovereignty and culture approaches to indigenous rights in relation to the politics of recognition in Chapter 10.

10. Mary Louise Pratt has elaborated on the kind of textual genre emerging in the (post) colonial encounter. One of her central terms is "contact zone," which she describes as those "social spaces where cultures meet, clash, and grapple with each other, often in contexts of highly asymmetrical relations of power, such as colonialism, slavery, or their aftermaths as they are lived out in many parts of the world today" (Pratt 1991, 34). The courtroom in indigenous rights cases is often a contact zone in this sense. In it, complex negotiations—deeply connected to the colonial encounter—take place. National and indigenous identities are negotiated and power struggles are fought. Pratt calls those texts that emerge in the contact zone "autoethnographic

texts," defined as texts "in which people undertake to describe themselves in ways that engage with representations others have made of them. Thus if ethnographic texts are those in which European metropolitan subjects represent to themselves their others (usually their conquered others), autoethnographic texts are representations that the so-defined others construct *in response to* or in dialogue with those texts" (1991, 35; emphasis in original).

11. In linguistic anthropology there is a growing body of literature on the living construction of groups by means of text, discourse, and language (see, e.g., Dinwoodie 1998, 2013; Silverstein 2005). In the wider sense, this book can be seen as a contribution to that project.

Chapter 2

1. Page numbers in parentheses in this chapter without a reference to author and year refer to the pages of the judgment *Johnson v. McIntosh*, 21 U.S. 543 (1823).

2. Influential legal handbooks on federal Indian law include Getches et al. (2012); and Newton and Anderson (2012). For an overview, see Canby 2009. For historical works on the Indian policies of the United States, see Debo (1970); Tyler (1973); Washburn (1975); Prucha (1995). For a legal history of the case law in federal Indian law, see Wilkinson (1987).

3. In the United States, Indian affairs are under the authority of the Union. According to the so-called commerce clause in article 1, section 8, clause 3 of the U.S. Constitution, all authority "to regulate commerce with foreign Nations, and among the several States, and with Indian Tribes" lies at the federal level. The commerce clause therefore serves as the constitutional basis for the Indian Non-Intercourse Acts. For the history and relevance of the commerce clause for federal Indian law, see Clinton (1995).

The other highly relevant constitutional provision in federal Indian law is the so-called advice and consent clause in article 2, section 2, clause 2 of the U.S. Constitution, which establishes the president's authority to make treaties, a prerogative that the federal government exercised many times in the first decades of the United States by making treaties with Indian tribes. The treaty era ended in 1871 when Congress passed a statute on future treaties with Indian tribes, which ordered the president to stop entering into treaties with Indians.

4. For a comprehensive account on the Non-Intercourse Acts and their legal significance, see Prucha (1962). The general principle that land purchases from Indians require the federal government's consent is still in force and is part of the United States Code, 25 U.S.C. § 177.

5. The decisive passage of the Royal Proclamation of 1763 by King George III reads:

> And whereas great Frauds and Abuses have been committed in purchasing Lands of the Indians, to the great Prejudice of our Interests and to the great Dissatisfaction of the said Indians: In order, therefore, to prevent such Irregularities for the future, and to the end that the Indians may be convinced of our Justice and determined Resolution to remove all reasonable Cause of Discontent, We do with the Advice of our Privy Council strictly enjoin and require that no private Person do presume to make any purchase from the said Indians of any Lands reserved to the said Indians, within those parts of our Colonies where, We have thought proper to allow Settlement: but that if at any Time any of the Said Indians should be inclined to dispose of the said Lands, the same shall be Purchased only for Us, in our Name, at some public Meeting or Assembly of the said Indians, to be held for that Purpose by the Governor or Commander in Chief of our Colony respectively within which they shall lie: and in case they shall.

6. The historical circumstances leading to the issuing of the Royal Proclamation of 1763 in the aftermath of the French and Indian War are explained in Getches et al. (2011, 59–61). For its impact on federal Indian law in the United States generally, see Clinton (1989).

7. Robert Williams describes how the legal arguments against British legislation in the colonies were framed as Saxon-derived natural law ideas, also represented in the natural law discourses of John Locke, in contrast to Norman-derived feudalist law. "The theory of the Norman Yoke boiled down to the opinion that before 1066 the Anglo-Saxons of England lived as free and equal citizens under a form of representative government that was inspired by divine principles of natural law and common rights of all individuals. The Norman conquest, however, had destroyed this Saxon model of government" (Williams 1990, 253). The North American colonists were depicted as the free Saxons who had to shake off the illegitimate Norman yoke. This discourse was intended to invalidate British legislation in the colonies by revealing it to be an unjustified imposition on the settlers and their legitimate economic interests.

8. In this action, a fictive tenant of the plaintiff seeks to evict a fictive tenant of the defendant from the property. The eviction action in this constellation is an archaic English common-law action no longer used in U.S. courts.

9. In 1924 Congress passed a statute that conferred citizenship on all Indians born in the United States (8 U.S.C.A. § 1401b). In 1887 the so-called General Allotment Act, also called the Dawes Act (24 Stat. 388), already opened up the opportunity for Indians to become U.S. citizens if they applied for an allotment. In 1924 all those Indians who had not yet become citizens by virtue of being "allotees" were conferred U.S. citizenship unilaterally by Congress.

10. In Canada the concept of Indian title (there usually called "aboriginal title") and its alienability exclusively to the Crown has—in contrast to the Marshall decision—been seen as originating in the Royal Proclamation of 1763 itself. See Chapter 5 for a discussion of this important difference.

11. For reasons of clarity in my line of thought I have omitted from the passage a few sentences that are often cited as among the more racist statements in Marshall's judgment: "Its vast extent offered an ample field to the ambition and enterprise of all, and the character and religion of its inhabitants afforded an apology for considering them as a people over whom the superior genius of Europe might claim an ascendency. The potentates of the old world found no difficulty in convincing themselves that they made ample compensation to the inhabitants of the new, by bestowing on them civilization and Christianity in exchange for unlimited independence" (573). I am not convinced that this passage is a clear indication that Marshall agrees with the premise of the inferior character of Indians (as indicated in Getches et al. 2011, 70). First we must see that Marshall here refers to the legal arguments of the old European nations, not his own. Later he calls the thinking underlying the discovery doctrine "extravagant" (591), and in this passage he uses the phrase "had no difficulty in convincing themselves," which suggests a critical take on this kind of self-serving justification. Nevertheless, as he explains later, he feels bound to it by legal tradition. The first part of the passage, though, where he says "the character and religion of its inhabitants afforded an apology for considering them . . . ," has no explicit phrasing of dissociation, although the sentence is embedded in other sentences that indicate Marshall's desire to distance himself from this kind of reasoning. However one interprets this passage, one has to admit that Marshall does not make it absolutely clear whether he really thinks of Indians as inherently inferior to people of European descent or not. And that ambiguity is indicative of a style of argumentation that is completely different from other authors of the time, including the arguments by McIntosh that we have investigated above.

12. Lindsay Robertson has pointed out that Marshall's derivation of the discovery doctrine from the legal documents he cites was by no means free of questionable methodological moves: "John Marshall knew that these sources were methodologically deficient at the time he issued the opinion" (1997, 765). Robertson contends that "Marshall ignored alternative histories in drafting the *Johnson* opinion" (1997, 766). Stuart Banner points out that "the transition from ownership to occupancy," as he calls it, "would have been hard to predict in the early 1790s" (2005, 150). The idea of full ownership of Indian land had then been the government's position, including prominent statements by Henry Knox, Thomas Jefferson, and Alexander Hamilton (Banner 2005, 151). Banner also refers to a 1795 decision of the Pennsylvania Supreme Court confirming the Indians' full property title to the land on which they live (2005, 151).

13. Banner questions Marshall's assertion that the idea that Indians possessed only a right of occupancy in conquered territory was customary law during colonial times. "The idea that the Indians possessed only a right of occupancy in their unsold land was a concept that was only three decades old in 1823. English colonial law had included no such concept, nor had American law before the 1790s" (Banner 2015, 179).

14. Marshall suggests that both "discovery" and "conquest" are able to establish title for the discovering and conquering nation respectively, and in the middle of the judgment the terminology switches from "discovery" to "conquest." This switch is interpreted by Banner as a rhetorical trick Marshall applies to underline the fact that conquest, more than discovery, was outside the jurisdiction of the courts and was the most "political question" of all. Banner argues that "if Marshall wanted to avoid responsibility for the outcome of *Johnson*, it was convenient to slip from discovery to conquest as the basis for the opinion" (Banner 2005, 186).

I believe mentioning conquest has two functions for Marshall. The legal consequences of conquest were clear, while those of discovery had yet to be established. By conflating conquest and discovery, Marshall explains that discovery was seen *as if* the land had actually been conquered. Second, Marshall also sees conquest as a possibility to extinguish Indian title after discovery. Eric Kades phrases Marshall's view as the "black letter rule that the United States could divest the Indians of title only via purchase or conquest" (2000, 1096–1097): the government either acquires Indian lands peacefully or, because the Indians resist, by military means. In Felix Cohen's words, "the sovereign could extinguish Indian title by treaty or by war" (1947, 48).

15. I am especially grateful to Richard Monette, who discussed this passage in his course "American Indians and the Law" at the University of Wisconsin–Madison Law School in 2014. This course expanded my knowledge of federal Indian law more than any other.

16. Banner (2005, 150–90) has shown how important it was for Marshall to find a model in which the state was said to hold Indian land in fee simple in addition to territory. He interprets this as the need to legitimize the market for "preemption rights," in which Marshall was involved himself.

17. But the important complication is that the state is not allowed to extinguish Indian title because the U.S. Constitution has vested this authority exclusively in the Union. This aspect will become more important in *Worcester v. Georgia.*

18. In *Tee Hit Ton Indians v. United States*, the Supreme Court held that Indian title not recognized by the United States is not compensable under the takings clause of the Fifth Amendment to the U.S. Constitution.

19. Karen Engle analyzes the question of alienability of land for the strategies of indigenous movements as follows: "Indigenous rights advocates are understandably ambivalent about alienation. Those who argue for maintaining the possibility of independence or statehood, or even

strong forms of autonomy connected to specific territory, have a stake in maintaining the prohibition on alienation. If alienability of land were permitted, it would foreclose discussion of such arrangements now and in the future. At the same time, the prohibition comes from the state and expresses itself as a limitation on indigenous autonomy at both the group and individual level" (2010, 181). Lindsay Robertson, like many scholars, criticizes the inalienability of indigenous lands in the United States as a great hindrance to indigenous development. He argues that "because the tribes cannot freely sell their lands, they cannot mortgage them, thus complicating capital accumulation" (2005, 30). It is important to note that there is no legal obstacle for a bank to mortgage land held in Indian title; it is merely a question of policy. Similar to loans private banks give to states, such loans would depend on the level of trust the credit institution has in the financial stability of the tribe or in the tribal court system to rule according to established legal principles in case of a dispute.

20. The second important factor Banner identifies as influencing this discursive shift is a growing market for preemption rights in Indian country.

Chapter 3

1. Two excellent overviews of the history and context of this case and *Worcester v. Georgia* are Rennard Strickland's article "The Tribal Struggle for Indian Sovereignty: The Story of the Cherokee Cases" (2011); and Jill Norgren's book *The Cherokee Cases: Two Landmark Federal Decisions in the Fight for Sovereignty* (2004). I have relied heavily on these two sources for much of the information in this chapter.

2. This principle means consequently that legal sovereignty *over* Indian tribes is derived *from* Indian tribes themselves, who presumably transferred sovereignty and authority to the United States, usually in a treaty. This principle still governs federal Indian law today, although not consequentially (see Collins 1989).

3. The most radical manifestation of this legal idea was the nullification doctrine, which led to the so-called nullification crisis between North Carolina and the Union.

4. Treaty with the Cherokee, November 28, 1785, 7 Stat. 18.

5. In 1828 the Georgia legislature passed an act titled "An act to add the territory lying within this state and occupied by the Cherokee Indians, to the counties of Carroll, De Kalb, Gwinnett, Hall, and Habersham, and to extend the laws of this state over the same and for other purposes." The act was followed by an 1829 act titled "An act to add the territory lying within the chartered limits of Georgia, and now in the occupancy of the Cherokee Indians, to the counties of Carroll, De Kalb, Gwinnett, Hall, and Habersham; and to extend the laws of this state over the same and to annul all ordinances made by the Cherokee nation of Indians, and to provide for the compensation of officers serving legal process in said territory, and to regulate the testimony of Indians, and to repeal the ninth section of the act of 1828 on this subject."

6. All page numbers in parentheses in this chapter without reference to an author indicate the documents of the case *Cherokee Nation v. Georgia* as they are reprinted in Peters (1831).

7. John Locke nonetheless makes an appearance in this passage in the last sentence, albeit indirectly. The Cherokee's former territory, according to Marshall (and it was their territory from the perspective of international law), was too large for them, at least from the perspective of natural law. Now they may only retain "a remnant" of their former lands, but after several cessions "they retain no more of their formerly extensive territory than is deemed necessary for their comfortable subsistence" (15). Here Marshall's rootedness in Lockean property theory, which connects property rights to productive use, becomes visible. In *Johnson v. McIntosh*,

where such property conceptions also appeared in the text, those kinds of arguments were not at the center of Marshall's ruling. He was, rather, oriented toward international customary law as the source of Indian title. I believe that is also true for *Cherokee Nation v. Georgia*.

8. Article 12 of the Treaty of Hopewell reads: "That the Indians may have full confidence in the justice of the United States, respecting their interests, they shall have the right to send a deputy of their choice, whenever they think fit, to Congress" (Treaty with the Cherokee, November 28, 1785, 7 Stat. 18).

9. "The political-question doctrine is rooted in prudential concerns and separation-of-powers principles. As one of the Court's self-crafted restrictions on its jurisdiction, the doctrine permits the Supreme Court to avoid political controversies that lack manageable judicial standards and that the Constitution has clearly committed to Congress and the president" (Green 2005, 724). The first case in which the Supreme Court came up with the political question doctrine was *Marbury v. Madison*, 5 U.S. 137 (1803). For a historical and doctrinal study, see Strum (1974). The Supreme Court has invoked the political question doctrine when it comes to the abrogation of treaty rights by Congress. The so-called plenary power doctrine gives Congress sole authority over Indian affairs, including the abrogation of treaty rights without Indian consent. The Supreme Court decided in *Lone Wolf v. Hitchcock*, 187 U.S. 553 (1903) that "plenary authority over tribal relations of the Indians . . . has always been deemed a political one, not subject to be controlled by the judicial department of the government. . . . As with treaties made with foreign nations . . . the legislative power might pass laws in conflict with treaties made with Indians" (*Lone Wolf*, 565–566). For *Lone Wolf* and its importance for federal Indian law, see Estin (1984). The transference of the political question doctrine to federal Indian affairs is a consequent application of the principles derived from the Cherokee cases. The similarities between Indian affairs and foreign affairs, based on the (impaired) sovereignty of Indian tribes, made it seem appropriate to apply the judicial restraint exercised in political questions concerning foreign affairs to the adjudication of Indian affairs.

Chapter 4

1. For a biography of Worcester, see Bass (1996).

2. Page numbers in parentheses without reference to author and year in this chapter refer to *Samuel A. Worcester, Plaintiff in Error v. the State of Georgia*, 31 U.S. 515 (1832).

3. On December 22, 1830, the Georgia legislature passed an act titled "An act to prevent the exercise of assumed and arbitrary power by all persons, under pretext of authority from the Cherokee Indians." Section 7 of the act stated that "all white persons, residing within the limits of the Cherokee nation on the 1st day of March next, or at any time thereafter, without a license or permit from his excellency the governor, or from such agent as his excellency the governor shall authorise to grant such permit or license, and who shall not have taken the oath hereinafter required, shall be guilty of a high misdemeanour, and upon conviction thereof, shall be punished by confinement to the penitentiary at hard labour, for a term not less than four years" (cited in *Worcester v. Georgia*, 521–523).

4. The other missionaries who were arrested along with Worcester are Elizur Butler, James Trott, Samuel Mays, Surry Eaton, Austin Copeland, and Edward D. Losure. Following their arrest in March, they had to be set free because Worcester and his fellow missionaries were in the service of the postmaster and were, therefore, federal employees. The law in question (see note 2) explicitly allowed federal agents to reside on the reservation without a permit. With that exemption Georgia accommodated the fact that Indian affairs were, after all, under federal authority. President Andrew Jackson, sympathetic to Georgia's policies, intervened and

dismissed the missionaries from federal service. After he sent a letter to Georgia's governor George Gilmer declaring that the missionaries were no longer employed by the federal government, Worcester and his collaborators were arrested again (Strickland 2011, 73).

5. Article 6, clause 2 of the U.S. Constitution states that "all treaties made, or which shall be made, under the Authority of the United States, shall be the supreme Law of the Land."

6. Some of Worcester's letters are reprinted in Worcester (1968).

7. Whether Jackson actually said this or not is uncertain (see Chroust 1960).

8. Strickland makes a historical comparison: "In historical perspective, it is as if President Eisenhower had sent federal troops to Little Rock to support Governor Faubus *against* the Supreme Court decision in *Brown v. Board of Education*" (2011, 76; emphasis in original).

9. For historical accounts on Cherokee removal, see W. L. Anderson (1991); and Perdue and Green (1995).

10. The general principle of tribal sovereignty began to change with two cases where state courts were granted criminal jurisdiction over crimes committed on Indian country in which both victim and perpetrator were non-Indians. These cases were *United States v. McBratney*, 104 U.S. 621 (1881); and *Draper v. United States*, 164 U.S. 240 (1896). Although the principle of no state jurisdiction on Indian country still exists (federal jurisdiction is easier to establish), it was significantly watered down in the twentieth century (Canby 2009, 156–168).

11. Marshall generally disapproves of following the wording of treaties to the letter when doing so would be to the disadvantage of the Indians:

> Is it reasonable to suppose, that the Indians, who could not write and most probably could not read, who certainly were not critical judges of our language, should distinguish the word "allotted" from the words "marked out"? The actual subject of contract was the dividing line between the two nations, and their attention may very well be supposed to have been confined to that subject. When, in fact, they were ceding lands to the United States, and describing the extent of their cession, it may very well be supposed that they might not understand the term employed as indicating that, instead of granting, they were receiving lands. If the term would admit of no other signification, which is not conceded, its being misunderstood is so apparent, results so necessarily from the whole transaction, that it must, we think, be taken in the sense in which it was most obviously used.
>
> So with respect to the words "hunting grounds." Hunting was at that time the principal occupation of the Indians, and their land was more used for that purpose than for any other. It could not, however, be supposed, that any intention exhibited of restricting the full use of the lands they reserved. (552–553)

Chapter 5

1. See Chapter 2 for a discussion of the Royal Proclamation of 1763.

2. According to section 35(2) of Canada's Constitution Act of 1982, "'aboriginal peoples of Canada' includes the Indian, Inuit and Métis peoples of Canada." The term "Indian" is generally felt to be more pejorative than in the United States, which is why the term "First Nations" is more frequently used. Inuit and Métis, however, are not referred to as "First Nations."

3. For an analysis of the configurations of the Canadian constitutional reform process regarding aboriginal rights, see Sanders (1987, 184).

4. In *Guerin v. The Queen*, [1984] 2 S.C.R. 335, the Canadian Supreme Court found the existence of a "fiduciary obligation" between the Crown and indigenous peoples parallel to the "trust relationship" in U.S. federal Indian law. In *Simon v. The Queen*, [1985] 2 S.C.R. 287, the Canadian Supreme Court reaffirmed the principle that aboriginal title exists without legal acknowledgment as long as it has not been extinguished. To establish the extinguishment of aboriginal title by the Crown, the court applies the "strict proof" test. The judgment is parallel in its content to the U.S. Supreme Court decision *United States v. Santa Fe Pacific Railroad*, 314 U.S. 339 (1941), which it explicitly cited. In *Sparrow v. R.*, [1990] 1 S.C.R. 1075, the Canadian Supreme Court required a "justification test" for the extinguishing of aboriginal title and at least a prior consultation with the indigenous group. In *R. v. Van der Peet*, [1996] 2 S.C.R. 507, the Canadian Supreme Court acknowledged that "aboriginal title" originated in the precontact occupation of the land by indigenous peoples and was accepted in common law, which brings the legal conceptualization of "aboriginal title" close to the principles laid out in the U.S. Supreme Court decision *Johnson v. McIntosh*, 21 U.S. 543 (1823).

5. I here use the notation for both indigenous nations as they are used the court documents, although there are several other recognized forms of spelling. I mainly wish to avoid confusion when quoting from the judgment. In the late 1980s the Gitksan numbered some 4,000 to 5,000 individuals, the Wet'suwet'en approximately 2,000. About 30,000 non-aboriginals resided in the area.

6. The Indian Act (R.S.C., 1985, c. I-5) had significant influence on the definition of Indianness in Canada. Disregarding traditional kinship systems, the Indian Act imposed a registration scheme under which "band" membership was determined on the basis of descent from the male line. Such band members are called "status Indians" and are assigned to one of 609 bands, each of which was allocated a small portion of its traditional territory as reserve land. Those indigenous people who for different reasons are not registered under the Indian Act are called "non-status Indians" (Imai 1999, 155–164).

7. In the *Handbook of North American Indians* (vol. 7, *Northwest Coast*), the Gitksan and Wet'suwet'en are counted among the Tsimshian peoples in the Pacific Northwest, all of whom share certain cultural features. Among the Tsimshian peoples the seminal *Handbook* counts the Coast Tsimshian, Southern Tsimshian, Nishga, and Gitksan (Halpin and Seguin 1999).

8. The matrilineal kinship system of the Gitksan and Wet'suwet'en follows the Iroquois type (Halpin and Seguin 1990, 274). In Gitksan and Wet'suwet'en society every individual is born into the mother's "house" and her "clan," which comprises several houses. The "house" is a corporate matrilineage and traditionally referred to the blood-related family inhabiting the same dwelling with affines, adopted children, slaves, and so forth. Today, belonging to the same house does not necessarily require residing together. "Each house owned fishing, hunting, and gathering territories and locales, which it exploited under the direction of the house chief (the man, and in exceptional circumstances, the woman, who bore its highest-ranking name). The house owned crests, songs, names, and other privileges, also under control or stewardship of the chief" (Halpin and Seguin 1990, 274). There are four Gitksan clans: Lax Gibuu (Wolf), Lax Xskiik (Eagle), Giskaast (Fireweed), and Lax Seel/Lax Ganeda (Frog). The five Wet'suwet'en clans are Gitdumden (Wolf), Gilserhu (Frog), Laksilyu (Small Frog), Laksumushu (Fireweed), and Tsayu (Beaver) (Monet and Skanu'u 1992, 26). Clans are exogamous groups. As a basic rule it is considered inappropriate to marry inside one's own clan (Halpin and Seguin 1990, 274).

9. This situation is similar to Alaska, where there had also never been treaties with Alaskan natives or large-scale extinguishment of Indian title. The legal situation was partly stabilized by

the Alaska Native Claims Settlement Act (ANCSA), a huge settlement the United States entered into with several groups of Alaska Natives in 1971 (see Huhndorf and Huhndorf 2011).

10. Monet and Skanu'u (1992) provide a most informative overview of the trial court proceedings.

11. For details of McEachern's biography and political connections, see R. T. Anderson (2011, 606–608).

12. *Delgamuukw v. British Columbia*, [1991] 79 D.L.R. (4th) 185.

13. Gordon Inglis et al. explain the system of names in Gitksan and Wet'suwet'en society that came about with missionization: "In the 1980s there was a dual naming system in operation: English names, which were used on an everyday basis as family names, and traditional name-titles, which are used to denote house membership and social standing along traditional lines. High-ranking names have remained, while some lesser ranking names have either fallen from use or have not been transferred" (1990, 285).

14. In contrast to many other indigenous rights cases, however, the case was not brought by the group as a whole for a collective land recognition; rather, every house brought a separate claim for its land.

15. Inglis et al. explain the relevance of Tsimshian feasts from an ethnographic perspective:

> Name-titles are still transferred through feasts with chiefs acting as witnesses; the extent to which other community members participated varied among the groups. The transfer of names was a serious matter, as the holdings of the corporate house group are embodied in particular titles. The most important ceremony in the 1980s was the memorial or settlement feast, when a title is publicly transferred. Such a ceremony follows the death of a chief, after the leading men and women of a house and clan have decided on the successor and have amassed enough money and goods to repay those from other clans who performed services for the deceased. Members of the deceased's father's clan play an important part in providing these services. Though different in detail in each of the communities, the memorial feast allows the heir and his house group to "settle" the debts incurred with members of other clans and publicly have the transfer of title witnessed and validated. (1990, 286)

16. All quoted materials in this chapter that are otherwise unattributed refer to text of the Supreme Court of Canada decision *Delgamuukw v. British Columbia*, [1997] 3 S.C.R. 1010. Those materials designated "trial court" refer to the previous decision before the Supreme Court of British Columbia, *Delgamuukw v. British Columbia*, [1991] 79 D.L.R. (4th) 185.

17. Both anthropologists have written ethnographic accounts of their experiences in the court proceedings (see Mills 1994; Daly 2005).

18. Appellate court judge Wallace expresses a different position in his concurring opinion: "An appellate court should find error on the part of the trial judge with respect to those aspects of the finding of facts which involve questions of credibility or weight to be given the evidence of a witness only if it is established that the trial judge made some 'palpable and overriding error' which affected his assessment of the material facts" (para. 41).

19. Since acknowledging existing aboriginal rights in section 35(1) of the Canadian constitution, the Canadian Supreme Court has taken the position that the Crown cannot extinguish aboriginal title without aboriginal consent.

20. This is a quote from *Stein v. The Ship "Kathy K,"* [1976] 2 S.C.R. 802, at 808.

21. Lamer also cites McLeod's finding that aboriginal oral history accounts are not merely "a repository of historical knowledge for a culture," but also express "the values and mores of [that] culture" (McLeod 1992, 1297).

22. *Black's Law Dictionary* defines "hearsay" as "testimony that is given by a witness who relates not what he or she knows personally, but what others have said, and that is therefore dependent on the credibility of someone other than the witness. Such testimony is generally inadmissible under the law of evidence" (Garner 2011, 352). The chief reasoning for this "hearsay rule" is "that out-of-court statements amounting to hearsay are not made under oath and are not subject to cross-examination" (Garner 2011, 352). There are, however, several exceptions to the hearsay rule under common law.

23. Marjorie Halpin and Margaret Seguin (1990, 276) elaborate on these material manifestations: "Crests are images and privileges (acquired by one's ancestors during encounters with supernatural beings) that are owned as property by a house and ceremonially displayed by its members. . . . Categories of artifacts most often specified for crest representations were: architectural features—totem poles, including house entrance poles, house posts, housefront paintings, beams, rafters, and ceremonial entrances; costume features—robes and headdresses; and feast dishes and ladles."

24. An affidavit is "a voluntary declaration of facts written down and sworn to by the declarant before an officer authorized to administer oaths. A great deal of evidence is submitted by affidavits" (Garner 2011, 22).

25. This rule exists not only in common law but also in continental law. It is, for example, codified in § 1006 I 1 of the German Civil Law Code (Bürgerliches Gesetzbuch): "Zugunsten des Besitzers einer beweglichen Sache wird vermutet, dass er Eigentümer der Sache sei" (The person who possesses an item of movable property is presumed to be its owner). In German civil law, however, this only applies to chattels.

26. British sovereignty over British Columbia was established by the Oregon Boundary Treaty of June 15, 1846. For additional information, see Commager (1927).

27. Lamer abbreviates "occupation at the time of the establishment of sovereignty by the Crown" to the phrase "pre-sovereignty occupation." I try to avoid this term because it only refers to the British or Canadian perspective regarding sovereignty. There was sovereignty in "pre-sovereignty" times, but it was the sovereignty of aboriginal peoples. This view is in line with Marshall's usage in the Marshall trilogy.

Chapter 6

1. For a brief history of the inter-American human rights system, see García Ramírez (2011). For a concise overview of its rules, practice, and jurisprudence, see Cerna (2012).

2. While the United States never seriously considered ratifying the Convention, Canada has declared that it is in principle in favor of the treaty and even signed it, but never ratified it. The country has hesitated to join because of its domestic policy of not legally restricting abortion. Canada sees inconsistencies with article 4(1) of the Convention, which imposes the duty to safeguard human life from the moment of conception. Canada could ratify the Convention and attach a reservation against this provision, but has chosen not to do so, citing its general policy of not signing on to multilateral treaties unless it can do so unconditionally (i.e., without reservations). Although these states have not ratified the Convention, their national courts are still obligated in principle to take the case law of the Inter-American Court of Human Rights

into consideration. The United States Supreme Court is particularly reluctant to do this (see Abi-Mershed 2009).

3. According to article 61 of the American Convention, only states or the Commission have the right to present a case before the Court. Lawyers and human rights activists have proposed changing the system so that individuals themselves would be enabled to address the court directly, as is possible in the European human rights system (García Ramírez 2011, xxi).

4. For a history of the beginnings and evolution of the case referral system, see Burgorgue-Larsen and Úbeda de Torres (2011, 30–40, paras. 2.05–2.19).

5. Contentious jurisdiction means that the Court can generally entertain all cases against a member state without the need for the member state to agree to the jurisdiction on a case-by-case basis. In its case law the Court has restricted the optional element in the clause of contentious jurisdiction in article 62(1). The Court has decided in three cases—*Hilaire v. Trinidad and Tobago* (2001), *Benjamin v. Trinidad and Tobago* (2001), and *Constantine v. Trinidad and Tobago* (2001)—that a member state must accept the contentious jurisdiction of the Court in all cases concerning the Convention, reservations notwithstanding. This is an opinion it had already expressed in its second Advisory Opinion, "The Effects of Reservations on the Entry into Force of the American Convention on Human Rights" (Arts. 74 and 75) (1982). Most prominently, the Court decided in *Ivcher Bronstein v. Peru* (1999) that a member state that has accepted the contentious jurisdiction of the Court cannot withdraw that acceptance without denouncing the Convention altogether. This strict view is still dominant despite some criticism in the literature (Rey Caro 2005). For a comprehensive overview of the question of contentious jurisdiction of the Court, see Burgorgue-Larsen and Úbeda de Torres (2011, 7–21, paras. 1.01–1.29). For a detailed description of the Inter-American system of human rights with special regard to indigenous rights, see Anaya (2004a, 258–271).

6. For background information on the conflict between the Yanomami and Brazil, see Albert (1992).

7. All quoted materials in this chapter that are otherwise unattributed refer to text of the judgment of the Inter-American Court of Human Rights on costs and reparations: *Aloeboetoe v. Suriname* (1993), Series C No. 15.

8. "General principles of law" are one of the sources for deciding a case in international law, as codified in Article 38(1)c of the Statute of the International Court of Justice.

9. I believe the Court's argumentation in regard to the treaty between the Dutch and the Saramakas is not convincing. Article 53 of the Vienna Convention on the Law of Treaties (the "Vienna Convention") states: "A treaty is void if, at the time of its conclusion, it conflicts with a peremptory norm of general international law." The prohibition against slavery was not yet a norm of *jus cogens* in 1792. Although the provisions concerned with the extradition of slaves could not be invoked today, that does not automatically render the treaty in all its aspects "null and void." One could argue, however, that with regard to the rule of *rebus sic stantibus*, codified in article 62 of the Vienna Convention, there has been a fundamental change of circumstances. Nevertheless, such an argument would not make the treaty void as such, but only provide grounds for the parties to terminate it.

10. Elizabeth Povinelli (2002) has described this as the "invisible asterisk" of indigenous rights and has made it an integral part of her critique of the "cunning of recognition." The "invisible asterisk" means that the multicultural society recognizes indigenous alterity, but only so long as the indigenous practices and traditions thus recognized are not "deemed legally and publicly abhorrent" by the majority society (Povinelli 2002, 266). We will come back to these topics in the Chapter 10.

11. The Court also ordered Nicaragua to reopen the school and a medical facility on Saramaka territory (para. 96). Although this could be seen as a form of collective reparations to the community, the Court framed this measure as directed to the victims' children individually: "The compensation fixed for the victims' heirs includes an amount that will enable the minor children to continue their education until they reach a certain age. Nevertheless, these goals will not be met merely by granting compensatory damages; it is also essential that the children be offered a school where they can receive adequate education and basic medical attention. At the present time, this is not available in several of the Saramaka villages" (para. 96).

12. Some have accused the Court of paternalism because it stipulated that the monetary payments to the victims' relatives be placed in a trust fund (Russell 2015).

13. The U.S. jurisprudence generally found that the U.S. Constitution has no effect in Indian country but tried to extend basic civil rights to Indian reservations by passing the Indian Civil Rights Act in 1968. Concerning sexual discrimination in awarding tribal citizenship according to the Indian Civil Rights Act, the Supreme Court decided in *Santa Clara Pueblo v. Martinez* (1978) that it considers itself to have no jurisdiction over the case because of the tribe's sovereign immunity. Many Indian tribal courts in the United States now apply civil liberties in their proceedings, but those derived not from the U.S. Bill of Rights but from international human rights law. They therefore see themselves as bound by international civil and political human rights (Carpenter and Riley 2013). This solution is possible because the civil rights contained in the U.S. Constitution are considered national law, binding in the United States and benefiting U.S. citizens but generally not extending to foreign sovereigns. As such it would be improper for a U.S. court to impose the same restrictions on sovereign Indian nations. As an international court, the Inter-American Court of Human Rights would have had a much more difficult time enforcing human rights against a sovereign member state not for the benefit of a citizen but for the benefit of another sovereign that it had just recognized and that it was not holding to the same universal human rights. The Court wished to avoid these kinds of questions.

Chapter 7

1. At the time of the judgment the autonomous region had another name: Región Autónoma del Atlántico Norte (RAAN). The autonomous region is an administrative institution whose organs encompass a regional council and a regional coordinator. It has the authority to manage several regional and municipal affairs inside its jurisdiction in the region along the northern Atlantic coast of Nicaragua.

2. Article 5 of the Nicaraguan Constitution states that:

> (1) Freedom, justice, respect for the dignity of the human person, political, social, and ethnic pluralism, recognition of the various forms of property, free international cooperation and respect for free self-determination are principles of the Nicaraguan nation. . . .
>
> (2) The State recognizes the existence of the indigenous peoples, who have the rights, duties and guarantees set forth in the Constitution, and especially those of maintaining and developing their identity and culture, having their own forms of social organization and managing their local affairs, as well as maintaining communal forms of ownership of their lands, and also the use and enjoyment of those lands, in accordance with the law. An autonomous regime is established in the . . . Constitution for the communities of the Atlantic Coast.

(3) The various forms of property: public, private, associative, cooperative, and communitarian, must be guaranteed and promoted with no discrimination, to produce wealth, and all of them while functioning freely must carry out a social function.

Article 89 states:

(1) The Communities of the Atlantic Coast are an inseparable part of the Nicaraguan people, and as such they have the same rights and the same obligations.

(2) The Communities of the Atlantic Coast have the right to maintain and develop their cultural identity within national unity; to have their own forms of social organization and to manage their local affairs according to their traditions.

(3) The State recognizes the communal forms of land ownership of the Community of the Atlantic Coast. It also recognizes the use and enjoyment of the waters and forests on their communal lands.

The English translation is taken from Mayagna (Sumo) Awas Tingni Community v. Nicaragua ["Awas Tingni v. Nicaragua"], Judgment of August 31, 2001, IACtHR, Series C No. 79 (2001), paras. 116–117.

3. Law No. 28 established that "the Regions inhabited by the Communities of the Atlantic Coast enjoy, within the unity of the Nicaraguan State, an Autonomous Regime which guarantees effective exercise of their historical and other rights, set forth in the Constitution" (article 4); and that "rational use of the mining, forestry, fishing, and other natural resources of the Autonomous Regions will recognize the property rights to their communal lands, and must benefit their inhabitants in a just proportion through agreements between the Regional Government and the Central Government" (article 9). The English translation of Law No. 28, from October 30, 1987, which is published in *La Gaceta* (the official gazette of the Republic of Nicaragua), no. 238, is taken from the Awas Tingni judgment on the merits, para. 119.

4. The *amparo* is a customary legal remedy against an unconstitutional act of public law in Latin America; see Burgoa 1992. The *amparo* is codified in articles 45 and 188 of the Constitution of Nicaragua. The procedural aspects are codified in Law No. 49 (Amparo Law).

5. For a comprehensive summary of the legal proceedings and the case background, see Anaya and Grossman (2002, 3–8); and Amiott (2002, 880–898). The relevant documents of the case, including the court decision and the court transcript, have been published in the 2002 special issue of the *Arizona Journal for of International and Comparative Law* 2002, 19 (1).

6. A reprint of the report can be found in the 2002 special issue of the *Arizona Journal of International and Comparative Law* 19 (1): 17–100.

7. Nicaragua has been a state party to the American Convention since 1979 and also recognized the contentious jurisdiction of the Inter-American Court in 1991. According to article 62(3) of the Convention, the Court had jurisdiction to consider the merits of the case (para. 5).

8. According to article 22 of the Court's Rules of Procedure, the Commission has its own legal representatives in the proceedings. In the case of Awas Tingni (and other cases), the legal representative was James Anaya. The Commission usually appoints its legal representatives in consultation with the plaintiffs. In *Awas Tingni* the lawyers had already represented the community in the proceedings before the Commission.

9. How exceptional such a proceeding was at the time can be illustrated by the fact that, when the president of the Court first ordered the hearing for June 2000, the secretariat of the Court could not find enough money in its budget to hold it. The hearing had to be postponed until November 2000 (paras. 46, 62). The transcript of this hearing has been published, along with the judgment and other court documents, in the 2002 special issue of the *Arizona Journal of International and Comparative Law* 19 (1): 129–306.

10. Quoted materials in this chapter that are otherwise unattributed refer to Mayagna (Sumo) Awas Tingni Community v. Nicaragua ["Awas Tingni v. Nicaragua"], Judgment of August 31, 2001, IACtHR, Series C No. 79 (2001).

11. References to the public hearing in parentheses refer to the page numbers of the version reprinted in the 2002 special issue of the *Arizona Journal of International and Comparative Law* 19 (1): 129–306.

12. Macdonald was at the time associate director of the Program on Nonviolent Sanctions and Cultural Survival at the Weatherhead Center for International Affairs at Harvard University.

13. For an overview over the importance of mapping in indigenous rights cases, see Herlihy and Knapp (2003).

14. Macdonald was formally not an expert witness in the hearing; he was a regular witness who was only to speak about issues he had witnessed personally. As such he was not allowed to bring in other information outside of his personal experience (for example, research from the ethnographic literature) into his testimony. The community's representatives wanted to "upgrade" Macdonald to the status of "expert witness," but they failed to do so on a technicality (para. 54). Nevertheless, there is no doubt that his expertise as an anthropologist influenced how the Court perceived his testimony.

15. Several other witnesses, indigenous officials, lawyers, and a third anthropologist, Charles Hale, presented further testimony generally in line with what we have heard before. I have left these out here for the sake of brevity.

16. Only one judge, Montiel Argüello, dissented. His dissenting opinion, however, is not directed at issues of central relevance to our study. First, he dismisses the claim that article 25 of the Convention, the right to judicial protection, had been violated. Instead Argüello argues that Nicaragua had done enough to provide an effective legal process and that the courts had denied the Awas Tingni's actions against the logging concession to SOLCARSA according to established legal principles. With regard to article 21, Argüello contends that Nicaragua had recognized indigenous land rights and that, as the list of the relevant laws proved, a viable legal framework exists. It was the Awas Tingni community's fault that they had failed to invoke the legal instruments available for their land recognition.

17. As early as 1960 Claude Lévi-Strauss had already noted in *Tristes Tropiques* that "Rousseau is much decried these days; never has his work been so little known; and he has to face, above all, the absurd accusation that he glorified the state of nature for its own sake. (That may have been Diderot's error, but it was never Rousseau's.) What Rousseau said was the exact contrary" (1961, 389). The seminal study on the topic of the noble savage, which clarifies the common misconception about Rousseau's authorship, is Ellingson (2001).

18. Montaigne had met a group of Tupinambá in France after they had traveled on one of the ships of the French colonialist Nicolas Durand de Villegaignon (Bakewell 2010, 184). For an ethnographic account of the Tupinambá in the context of other groups on the Brazilian eastern coast, see Münzel (2006).

Chapter 8

1. There are certain differences between the common-law tradition, where subsurface minerals are in principal connected to the real estate property, and continental law traditions, where subsurface minerals are in principle excluded from private property title. In the continental tradition the state exerts much tighter control over subsurface minerals than in common law. In the German tradition, for instance, the long-standing legal institution of the *Bergregal*, which is derived from customary law in the Middle Ages, stated that all subsurface minerals belonged to the Crown. It was not until 1982 that the *Bundesberggesetz* liberalized this system considerably and brought it closer to other continental systems more influenced by the *Code Napoléon*. According to this system, most subsurface minerals (such as gold, coal, and oil) are excluded from real estate property but are not automatically the property of the state. The state, however, has an exclusive right to appropriate the subsurface minerals or to license their exploitation exclusively (Kremer and Neuhaus 2001). This model of tight state control over natural resources is typical of continental law and also prevalent in Latin America. The common-law system varies in that the property owner is in principle entitled to the exploitation of the minerals under the surface (in the British tradition there is an exception for gold and silver). In practice, however, the state in common-law systems reserves licensing rights for itself and collects taxes, charges, or fees from the property owner.

2. For a brief overview of the Saramakas, see the beginning of Chapter 6.

3. Quoted materials in this chapter that are otherwise unattributed refer to Saramaka People v. Suriname, Judgment of November 28, 2007, IACtHR, Series C No. 172 (2007).

Chapter 10

1. The idea of the cultural embeddedness of the individual is, of course, a basic assumption of anthropology that connects the discipline at least on some basic level to the multicultural project (Turner 1993). That is another reason why it is particularly productive to investigate the politics of recognition—and its outcomes in the form of legal texts—through anthropological eyes.

2. Povinelli (2002, 17) is aware of this problem and hence limits herself to an examination of what liberalism does instead of deciding for or against it in any abstract or general sense. I would argue, however, that the interest scholars have expressed in her critique of late liberalism is based precisely on the assumption that a more radical democracy is possible.

REFERENCES

Abi-Mershed, Elizabeth A. H. 2009. "The United States and the Inter-American Court of Human Rights." In *The Sword and the Scales: The United States and International Courts and Tribunals*, edited by Cesare P. R. Romano, 185–209. Cambridge: Cambridge University Press.

Ackerman, Bruce. 1997. "The Rise of World Constitutionalism." *Virginia Law Review* 83 (4): 771–797.

Albert, Bruce. 1992. "Indian Lands, Environmental Policy and Military Geopolitics in the Development of the Brazilian Amazon: The Case of the Yanomami." *Development and Change* 23:35–70.

Alfred, Gerald Robert. 1995. *Heeding the Voices of Our Ancestors: Kahnawake Mohawk Politics and the Rise of Native Nationalism*. Toronto: Oxford University Press.

Alfred, Taiaiake. 1999. *Peace, Power, Righteousness: An Indigenous Manifesto*. Oxford: Oxford University Press.

Altamirano-Jiménez, Isabel. 2014. *Indigenous Encounters with Neoliberalism: Place, Women, and the Environment in Canada and Mexico*. Vancouver: University of British Columbia Press.

Amiott, Jennifer A. 2002. "Environment, Equality, and Indigenous Peoples' Land Rights in the Inter-American Human Rights System: *Mayagna (Sumo) Indigenous Community of Awas Tingni v. Nicaragua*." *Environmental Law* 32 (4): 873–903.

Anaya, S. James. 2004a. *Indigenous Peoples in International Law*. 2nd ed. Oxford: Oxford University Press.

Anaya, S. James. 2004b. "International Human Rights and Indigenous Peoples: The Move Toward the Multicultural State." *Arizona Journal of International and Comparative Law* 21 (1): 13–61.

Anaya, S. James, and Claudio Grossman. 2002. "The Case of Awas Tingni v. Nicaragua: A New Step in the International Law of Indigenous Peoples." *Arizona Journal of International and Comparative Law* 19 (1): 1–15.

Anderson, Benedict. 1983. *Imagined Communities: Reflections on the Origin and Spread of Nationalism*. London: Verso.

Anderson, Robert T. 2011. "Aboriginal Title in the Canadian Legal System: The Story of *Delgamuukw v. British Columbia*." In *Indian Law Stories*, edited by Carole Goldberg, Kevin K. Washburn, and Philip P. Frickey, 591–619. New York: Thomson Reuters/Foundation Press.

Anderson, William L., ed. 1991. *Cherokee Removal: Before and After*. Athens: University of Georgia Press.

Anghie, Antony. 2005. *Imperialism, Sovereignty and the Making of International Law*. Cambridge Studies in International and Comparative Law. Cambridge: Cambridge University Press.

Asch, Michael. 2014. *On Being Here to Stay: Treaties and Aboriginal Rights in Canada*. Toronto: University of Toronto Press.

Bakewell, Sarah. 2010. *How to Live; or, A Life of Montaigne in One Question and Twenty Attempts at an Answer*. New York: Other Press.

Banner, Stuart. 2005. *How the Indians Lost Their Land: Law and Power on the Frontier*. Cambridge, Mass.: Belknap Press of Harvard University Press.

Barelli, Mauro. 2009. "The Role of Soft Law in the International Legal System: The Case of the United Nations Declaration on the Rights of Indigenous Peoples." *International and Comparative Law Quarterly* 58 (4): 957–983.

Barker, Joanne, ed. 2005. *Sovereignty Matters: Locations of Contestation and in Indigenous Struggles for Self-Determination*. Lincoln: University of Nebraska Press.

Barry, Brian. 2002. *Culture and Equality: An Egalitarian Critique of Multiculturalism*. Cambridge, Mass.: Harvard University Press.

Bass, Althea. 1996. *Cherokee Messenger*. Civilization of the American Indian Series, vol. 12. Norman: University of Oklahoma Press.

Bateman, Fiona, and Lionel Pilkington, eds. 2011. *Studies in Settler Colonialism: Politics, Identity and Culture*. New York: Palgrave Macmillan.

Beck, Ulrich. 2012. "Globale Ungleichheit und Menschenrechte: Eine kosmopolitische Perspektive." In *Gesellschaft innovativ*, edited by Gerald Beck and Cordula Kropp, 273–295. Wiesbaden: VS Verlag für Sozialwissenschaften.

Beier, J. Marshall, ed. 2009. *Indigenous Diplomacies*. New York: Palgrave Macmillan.

Benda-Beckmann, Franz von. 2002. "Who's Afraid of Legal Pluralism?" *Journal of Legal Pluralism and Unofficial Law* 47 (1):37–82.

Bens, Jonas. 2018. "When the Cherokee Became Indigenous: *Cherokee Nation v. Georgia* and Its Paradoxical Legalities." *Ethnohistory* 65 (2): 247–267.

Berman, Paul Schiff. 2012. *Global Legal Pluralism: A Jurisprudence of Law Beyond Borders*. Cambridge: Cambridge University Press.

Biolsi, Thomas. 2001. *Deadliest Enemies: Law and the Making of Race Relations on and off Rosebud Reservation*. Berkeley: University of California Press.

Borrows, John. 1997. "Frozen Rights in Canada: Constitutional Interpretation and the Trickster." *American Indian Law Review* 22 (1): 37–64.

Borrows, John, and Kevin Coyle, eds. 2017. *The Right Relationship: Reimagining the Implementation of Historical Treaties*. Toronto: University of Toronto Press.

Borrows, John, and Leonard I. Rotman. 1997. "The *Sui Generis* Nature of Aboriginal Rights: Does It Make a Difference." *Alberta Law Review* 36 (1): 9–45.

Bowen, John R. 2003. *Islam, Law, and Equality in Indonesia: An Anthropology of Public Reasoning*. New York: Cambridge University Press.

Brooks, Peter, and Paul Gewirtz, eds. 1998. *Law's Stories: Narrative and Rhetoric in the Law*. New Haven, Conn.: Yale University Press.

Bruyneel, Kevin. 2007. *The Third Space of Sovereignty: The Postcolonial Politics of U.S.–Indigenous Relations*. Minneapolis: University of Minnesota Press.

Brysk, Alison. 1996. "Turning Weakness into Strength: The Internationalization of Indian Rights." *Latin American Perspectives* 23 (2): 38–57.

Brysk, Alison. 2000. *From Tribal Village to Global Village: Indian Rights and International Relations in Latin America*. Stanford, Calif.: Stanford University Press.

Burgoa, Ignacio. 1992. *El juicio de amparo*. 29th ed. Mexico City: Editorial Porrúa.

Burgorgue-Larsen, Laurence, and Amaya Úbeda de Torres. 2011. *The Inter-American Court of Human Rights: Case Law and Commentary*. Oxford: Oxford University Press.

Calloway, Colin G. 2013. *Pen and Ink Witchcraft: Treaties and Treaty Making in American Indian History*. New York: Oxford University Press.

Canby, William C. 2009. *American Indian Law in a Nutshell*. 5th ed. West Nutshell Series. St. Paul, Minn.: West Academic.

Carlson, Leonard A., and Mark A. Roberts. 2006. "Indian Lands, 'Squatterism,' and Slavery: Economic Interests and the Passage of the Indian Removal Act of 1830." *Explorations in Economic History* 43 (3): 486–504.

Carpenter, Kristen A., and Angela R. Riley. 2013. "Tribal Rights, Human Rights." *Michigan State Law Review* 2013 (2): 293–306.

Cassese, Antonio. 1995. *Self-Determination of Peoples: A Legal Reappraisal*. New York: Cambridge University Press.

Cave, Alfred A. 2003. "Abuse of Power: Andrew Jackson and the Indian Removal Act of 1830." *Historian* 65 (6): 1330–1353.

Cerna, Christina. 2012. "The Inter-American Commission on Human Rights and the Inter-American Court of Human Rights." In *The Rules, Practice and Jurisprudence of International Courts and Tribunals*, edited by Chiara Gioretti, 365–392. Leiden: Martinus Nijhoff.

Césaire, Aimé. 2001. *Notebook of a Return to the Native Land, Wesleyan Poetry*. Trans. and ed. Clayton Eshleman and Annette Smith. Middletown, Conn.: Wesleyan University Press.

Cheyfitz, Eric, N. Bruce Duthu, and Shari M. Huhndorf, eds. 2011. "Sovereignty, Indigeneity, and the Law." Special issue, *Atlantic Quarterly* 110 (2).

Chroust, Anton-Hermann. 1960. "Did President Jackson Actually Threaten the Supreme Court of the United States with Nonenforcement of Its Injunction Against the State of Georgia?" *American Journal of Legal History* 4 (1): 76–78.

Clifford, James. 1986. *The Predicament of Culture: Twentieth-Century Ethnography, Literature, and Art*. Cambridge, Mass.: Harvard University Press.

Clifford, James. 2013. *Returns: Becoming Indigenous in the Twenty-First Century*. Cambridge, Mass.: Harvard University Press.

Clifford, James, and George E. Marcus, eds. 1986. *Writing Culture: The Poetics and Politics of Ethnography: A School of American Research Advanced Seminar*. Berkeley: University of California Press.

Clinton, Robert N. 1989. "The Proclamation of 1763: Colonial Prelude to Two Centuries of Federal-State Conflict over the Management of Indian Affairs." *Boston University Law Review* 69:329–385.

Clinton, Robert N. 1995 "The Dormant Indian Commerce Clause." *Connecticut Law Review* 27:1055–1249.

Cohen, Felix S. 1942. "The Spanish Origin of Indian Rights in the Law of the United States." *Georgetown Law Review* 31 (1): 1–21.

Cohen, Felix S. 1947. "Original Indian Title." *Minnesota Law Review* 32:28–59.

Cohen, Felix S. 1948. *How We Bought the United States*. Washington, D.C: U.S. Department of the Interior, United States Indian Service.

Collins, Richard B. 1989. "Indian Consent to American Government." *Arizona Law Review* 31:365–387.

Comaroff, Jean, and John Comaroff. 2006. *Law and Disorder in the Postcolony*. Chicago: University of Chicago Press.

Comaroff, Jean, and John Comaroff. 2007. "Law and Disorder in the Postcolony." *Social Anthropology* 15:133–152.

Commager, Henry. 1927. "England and Oregon Treaty of 1846." *Oregon Historical Quarterly* 28:18–38.

Corntassel, Jeff. 2018. *Everyday Acts of Resurgence: People, Places, Practices*. Olympia, Wash.: Daykeeper Press.

Corntassel, Jeff, and Richard C. Witmer. 2008. *Forced Federalism: Contemporary Challenges to Indigenous Nationhood*. Norman: University of Oklahoma Press.

Coulthard, Glen. 2014. *Red Skin, White Masks: Rejecting the Colonial Politics of Recognition*. Minneapolis: University of Minnesota Press.

Coutin, Susan Bibler. 2000. *Legalizing Moves: Salvadoran Immigrants' Struggle for U.S. Residency*. Ann Arbor: University of Michigan Press.

Culhane, Dara. 1998. *The Pleasure of the Crown: Anthropology, Law, and First Nations*. Burnaby: Talon Books.

Daes, Erica-Irene A. 2001. *Indigenous Peoples and Their Relationship to Land*. Geneva: United Nations Sub-Commission on the Promotion and Protection of Human Rights.

Daes, Erica-Irene A. 2005. "Indigenous Peoples' Rights to Land and Natural Resources." In *Minorities, Peoples, and Self-Determination: Essays in Honour of Patrick Thornberry*, edited by Nazila Ghanea-Hercock and Alexandra Xanthaki, 75–92. Leiden: Martinus Nijhoff.

Daly, Richard Heywood. 2005. *Our Box Was Full: An Ethnography for the Delgamuukw Plaintiffs*. Vancouver: UBC Press.

Davidov, Veronica. 2011. "From Colonial Primitivism to Ecoprimitivism: Constructing the Indigenous 'Savage' in South America." *Arcadia: International Journal of Literary Culture* 46 (2): 467–487.

Davis, Shelton H. 1988. *Land Rights and Indigenous People: The Role of the Inter-American Commission on Human Rights*. Cultural Survival Report. Cambridge, Mass.: Cultural Survival.

Debo, Angie. 1970. *A History of the Indians of the United States*. Civilization of the American Indian Series. Norman: University of Oklahoma Press.

Deloria, Philip J. 1999. *Playing Indian*. New Haven, Conn.: Yale University Press.

Dinwoodie, David W. 1998. "Authorizing Voices: Going Public in an Indigenous Language." *Cultural Anthropology* 13 (2): 193–223.

Dinwoodie, David W. 2010. "Ethnic Community in Early Tsilhqut'in Contact History." *Ethnohistory* 57 (4): 651–678.

Dinwoodie, David W. 2013. "'He Said He Would Show [the Tobacco] to M. Ogden:' Voice and Historical Role in The Tsilhqu'tin Fur Trade." In *Transforming Ethnohistories: Narrative, Meaning, and Community*, edited by Sebastian Braun, 97–112. Norman: University of Oklahoma Press.

Dolin, Kieran. 2007. *A Critical Introduction to Law and Literature*. Cambridge: Cambridge University Press.

Domingo, Pilar. 2004. "Judicialization of Politics or Politicization of the Judiciary? Recent Trends in Latin America." *Democratization* 11:104–126.

Donahoe, Brian. 2012. "Naming, Claiming, Proving: The Burden of Proof Issue for Russia's Indigenous People." In *Law Against the State: Ethnographic Forays into Law's Transformations*, edited by Julia Eckert, Brian Donahoe, Christian Strümpell, and Zerrin Özlem Biner, 44–69. Cambridge: Cambridge University Press.

Du Gay, Paul, Jessica Evans, and Peter Redman, eds. 2001. *Identity: A Reader*. London: Sage.

Dworkin, Ronald. 1977. *Taking Rights Seriously*. Cambridge, Mass.: Harvard University Press.

Ellingson, Terry Jay. 2001. *The Myth of the Noble Savage*. Berkeley: University of California Press.

Engle, Karen. 2010. *The Elusive Promise of Indigenous Development: Rights, Culture, Strategy*. Durham, N.C.: Duke University Press.

Englund, Harri. 2006. *Prisoners of Freedom: Human Rights and the African Poor*. Berkeley: University of California Press.

Eriksen, Thomas Hylland. 2002. *Ethnicity and Nationalism: Anthropological Perspectives*. 2nd ed. London: Pluto.

Estin, Ann Laquer. 1984. "Lone Wolf v. Hitchcock: The Long Shadow." In *The Aggressions of Civilization: Federal Indian Policy Since the 1880s*, edited by Sandra L. Cadwalader and Vine Deloria Jr., 216–245. Philadelphia: Temple University Press.

Fabian, Johannes. 2002. *Time and the Other: How Anthropology Makes Its Object*. New York: Columbia University Press.

Fabricant, Nicole. 2013. "Good Living for Whom? Bolivia's Climate Justice Movement and the Limitations of Indigenous Cosmovisions." *Latin American and Caribbean Ethnic Studies* 8 (2): 159–178.

Fink-Eitel, Hinrich. 1994. *Die Philosophie und die Wilden: Über die Bedeutung des Fremden für die europäische Geistesgeschichte*. Hamburg: Junius.

Fogelson, Raymond D. 2004. "Cherokee in the East." In *Handbook of North American Indians*, vol. 14, *Southeast*, edited by Raymond D. Fogelson, 337–353. Washington, D.C.: Smithsonian Institution.

Fraser, Nancy. 1995. "From Redistribution to Recognition? Dilemmas of Justice in a 'Post-Socialist' Age." *New Left Review* 212 (July/August): 68–68.

Fraser, Nancy. 2000. "Rethinking Recognition." *New Left Review* 3 (May/June): 107–120.

French, Jan Hoffman. 2009. *Legalizing Identities: Becoming Black or Indian in Brazil's Northeast*. Chapel Hill: University of North Carolina Press.

García Ramírez, Sergio. 2011. "The Inter-American Human Rights Jurisdiction: A Long Journey." Foreword to *The Inter-American Court of Human Rights: Case-Law and Commentary*, by Laurence Burgorgue-Larsen and Amaya Úbeda de Torres, xvii–xxviii. Oxford: Oxford University Press.

Garner, Bryan A., ed. 2011. *Black's Law Dictionary*. 4th pocket ed. St. Paul, Minn.: Thomson Reuters.

Getches, David H., Charles F. Wilkinson, Robert A. Williams Jr., and Matthew L. M. Fletcher. 2011. *Cases and Materials on Federal Indian Law*. 6th ed. St. Paul, Minn.: West Academic.

Goodale, Mark. 2009. *Dilemmas of Modernity: Bolivian Encounters with Law and Liberalism*. Stanford: Stanford University Press.

Goodale, Mark. 2016. "Dark Matter: Toward a Political Economy of Indigenous Rights and Aspirational Politics." *Critique of Anthropology* 36 (4): 439–457.

Goodrich, Peter. 1995. *Oedipus Lex: Psychoanalysis, History, Law, Philosophy, Social Theory, and the Rule of Law*. Berkeley: University of California Press.

Goodrich, Peter. 1997. "Maladies of the Legal Soul: Psychoanalysis and Interpretation in Law." *Washington and Lee Law Review* 54 (3): 1035–1074.

Green, William Crawford. 2005. "Political-Question Doctrine." In *The Encyclopedia of Civil Liberties in America*, edited by David Schlutz and John R. Vile, 723–724. London: Routledge.

Griffiths, John. 1986. "What Is Legal Pluralism?" *Journal of Legal Pluralism and Unofficial Law* 24:1–55.

Grimm, Dieter. 1987. *Recht und Staat in der bürgerlichen Gesellschaft*. Frankfurt am Main: Suhrkamp.

Guevara Gil, J. Armando. 2009. *Diversidad y Complejidad Legal: Aproximaciones a la Antropología e Historia del Derecho*. Lima: Fondo Editorial de la Pontificia Universidad Católica del Perú.

Gutmann, Amy, and Charles Taylor. 1992. *Multiculturalism and "The Politics of Recognition": An Essay*. Princeton, N.J.: Princeton University Press.

Habermas, Jürgen. 2004. *Der gespaltene Westen*. Frankfurt am Main: Suhrkamp.

Hale, Charles R. 1994. *Resistance and Contradiction: Miskitu Indians and the Nicaraguan State, 1894–1987*. Stanford, Calif.: Stanford University Press.

Hale, Charles R. 2005. "Neoliberal Multiculturalism: The Remaking of Cultural Rights and Racial Dominance in Central America." *PoLAR: Political and Legal Anthropology Review* 28 (1): 10–28.

Hale, Charles R. 2006. "Activist Research v. Cultural Critique: Indigenous Land Rights and the Contradictions of Politically Engaged Anthropology." *Cultural Anthropology* 21 (1): 96–120.

Hall, Stuart, and Paul du Gay, eds. 1996. *Questions of Cultural Identity*. London: Sage.

Halpin, Marjorie M., and Margaret Seguin. 1990. "Tsimshian Peoples: Southern Tsimshian, Coast Tsimshian, Nishga, and Gitksan." In *Handbook of North American Indians*, vol. 7, *Northwest Coast*, edited by Wayne Suttles, 267–284. Washington, D.C.: Smithsonian Institution.

Hames, Raymond. 2007. "The Ecologically Noble Savage Debate." *Annual Review of Anthropology* 36:177–190.

Harjo, Suzan Shown, ed. 2014. *Nation to Nation: Treaties Between the United States and American Indian Nations*. Washington, D.C.: National Museum of the American Indian in association with Smithsonian Books.

Herlihy, Peter H., and Gregory Knapp. 2003. "Maps of, by, and for the Peoples of Latin America." *Human Organization* 62 (4): 303–314.

Hobsbawm, Eric. 1990. *Nations and Nationalism Since 1780*. Cambridge: Cambridge University Press.

Honneth, Axel. 1992. *Kampf um Anerkennung: Zur moralischen Grammatik sozialer Konflikte*. Frankfurt am Main: Suhrkamp.

Howard-Wagner, Deirdre, Maria Bargh, and Isabel Altamirano-Jiménez, eds. 2018. *The Neoliberal State, Recognition and Indigenous Rights: New Paternalism to New Imaginings*. Canberra: Australian National University Press.

Huhndorf, Roy M., and Shari M. Huhndorf. 2011. "Alaska Native Politics Since the Alaska Native Claims Settlement Act." *South Atlantic Quarterly* 110 (2): 385–401.

Huneeus, Alexandra, Javier Couso, and Rachel Sieder, eds. 2010. *Cultures of Legality: Judicialization and Political Activism in Latin America*. New York: Cambridge University Press.

ILO. 2009. *Indigenous and Tribal Peoples' Rights in Practice: A Guide to ILO Convention No. 169*. Geneva: ILO.

Imai, Shin. 1999. *Aboriginal Law Handbook*. 2nd ed. Scarborough, Ont.: Carswell.

Inglis, Gordon B., Douglas R. Hudson, Barbara R. Rigsby, and Bruce Rigsby. 1990. "Tsimshian of British Columbia Since 1900." In *Handbook of North American Indians*, vol. 7, *Northwest Coast*, edited by Wayne Suttles, 285–293. Washington, D.C.: Smithsonian Institution.

Isaac, Thomas. 1991. "The Constitution Act, 1982 and the Constitutionalization of Aboriginal Self-Government in Canada: Cree-Naskapi (of Quebec) Act." *Canadian Native Law Reporter* 1:1–21.

Jordan, Glenn, and Chris Weedon. 1995. *Cultural Politics: Class, Gender, Race, and the Postmodern World*. Oxford: Blackwell.

Kades, Eric. 2000. "The Dark Side of Efficiency: *Johnson v. M'Intosh* and the Expropriation of American Indian Lands." *University of Pennsylvania Law Review* 148 (4): 1065–1190.

Kauanui, J. Kēhaulani. 2008. *Hawaiian Blood: Colonialism and the Politics of Sovereignty and Indigeneity*. Durham: Duke University Press.

Kelsen, Hans. 1944. "The Principle of Sovereign Equality of States as a Basis for International Organization." *Yale Law Journal* 53 (2): 207–220.

Kennedy, Ellen Conroy, ed. 1975. *The Negritude Poets: An Anthology of Translations from the French*. New York: Viking Press.

Krech, Shepard. 1999. *The Ecological Indian: Myth and History*. New York: W. W. Norton.

Kremer, Eduard, and Peter Neuhaus. 2001. *Bergrecht*. Stuttgart: Kohlhammer.

Kristeva, Julia. 1986. *The Kristeva Reader*. New York: Columbia University Press.

Kuper, Adam. 1988. *The Invention of Primitive Society: Transformations of an Illusion*. London: Routledge.

Kuper, Adam. 2003. "The Return of the Native." *Current Anthropology* 44 (3): 389–402.

Kymlicka, Will. 1995. *The Rights of Minority Cultures*. Oxford: Oxford University Press.

Kymlicka, Will. 2007. *Multicultural Odysseys: Navigating the New International Politics of Diversity*. Oxford: Oxford University Press.

Kymlicka, Will. 2010. "The Rise and Fall of Multiculturalism? New Debates on Inclusion and Accommodation in Diverse Societies." *International Social Science Journal* 61:97–112.

Laclau, Ernesto. 1994. *The Making of Political Identities*. London: Verso.

Laclau, Ernesto, and Chantal Mouffe. 1985. *Hegemony and Socialist Strategy: Towards a Radical Democratic Politics*. London: Verso.

Larana, Enrique, Hank Johnston, and Joseph R. Gusfield. 1994. *New Social Movements: From Ideology to Identity*. Philadelphia: Temple University Press.

Lazarus-Black, Mindie. 1994. *Legitimate Acts and Illegal Encounters: Law and Society in Antigua and Barbuda*. Washington, D.C.: Smithsonian Institution Press.

Lévi-Strauss, Claude. 1961. *Tristes Tropiques*. New York: Criterion.

Lobban, Michael. 2004. "Introduction: The Tools and Tasks of the Legal Historian." In *Law and History*, Current Legal Issues, vol. 6, ed. Andrew Lewish and Michael Lobban, 1–32. Oxford: Oxford University Press.

Locke, John. (1764) 1772. *Two Treatises of Government*. 6th ed. Reprint, London: J. Whiston et al.

Lorde, Audre. 2003. "The Master's Tools Will Never Dismantle the Master's House." In *Feminist Postcolonial Theory: A Reader*, edited by Reina Lewis and Sara Mills, 25–28. Edinburgh: Edinburgh University Press.

Madariaga Cuneo, Isabel. 2005. "The Rights of Indigenous Peoples and the Inter-American Human Rights System." *Arizona Journal of International and Comparative Law* 22 (1): 53–64.

Margheritis, A., and A. W. Pereira. 2007. "The Neoliberal Turn in Latin America: The Cycle of Ideas and the Search for an Alternative." *Latin American Perspectives* 34:25–48.

Martínez Cobo, José R. 1987. *Study of the Problem of Discrimination Against Indigenous Populations*. Vol. 5, *Conclusions, Proposals and Recommendations*. New York: United Nations Human Rights Council.

Maurer, Bill. 1997. *Recharting the Caribbean: Land, Law, and Citizenship in the British Virgin Island*. Ann Arbor: University of Michigan Press.

McKay, William R. 2005. "Marshall Part 3: Are Aboriginal Rights Really Sui Generis?" *Windsor Review of Legal and Social Issues* 20:81–93.

McLeod, Clay. 1992. "The Oral Histories of Canada's Northern People, Anglo-Canadian Evidence Law, and Canada's Fiduciary Duty to First Nations: Breaking Down the Barriers of the Past." *Alberta Law Review* 30 (4): 1276–1290.

Merry, Sally Engle. 2006. *Human Rights and Gender Violence: Translating International Law Into Local Justice*. Chicago: University of Chicago Press.

Mertz, Elizabeth. 2007. "Semiotic Anthropology." *Annual Review of Anthropology* 36:337–353.

Messick, Brinkley. 1992. *The Calligraphic State: Textual Domination and History in a Muslim Society*. Berkeley: University of California Press.

Mikdashi, Maya. 2013. "What is Settler Colonialism?" *American Indian Culture and Research Journal* 37 (2): 23–34.

Mills, Antonia. 1994. *Eagle Down Is Our Law: Witsuwit'en Law, Feasts, and Land Claims*. Vancouver: UBC Press.

Miranda, Lillian Aponte. 2012. "The Role of International Law in Intrastate Natural Resource Allocation: Sovereignty, Human Rights, and Peoples-Based Development." *Vanderbilt Journal of Transnational Law* 45:785–840.

Monet, Don, and Skanu'u. 1992. *Colonialism on Trial: Indigenous Land Rights and the Gitksan and Wet'suwet'en Sovereignty Case*. Philadelphia: New Society Publishers.

Montaigne, Michel de. 2005. *The Complete Works*. Vol. 1. London: Everyman.

Mowbray, Alastair. 2005. "The Creativity of the European Court of Human Rights." *Human Rights Law Review* 5 (1): 57–79.

Münzel, Mark. 2006. *Brasilien: Alte Bücher, Neue Welt*. Stuttgart: Robert Bosch.

Negrón-Muntaner, Frances, ed. 2017. *Sovereign Acts: Contesting Colonialism Across Indigenous Nations and Latinx America*. Tuscon: University of Arizona Press.

Nesper, Larry. 2002. *The Walleye War: The Struggle for Ojibwe Spearfishing and Treaty Rights*. Lincoln: University of Nebraska Press.

Newcomb, Steven T. 2008. *Pagans in the Promised Land: Decoding the Doctrine of Christian Discovery*. Golden, Colo.: Fulcrum.

Newton, Nell Jessup, and Robert Anderson. 2012. *Cohen's Handbook of Federal Indian Law*. New Providence, N.J.: LexisNexis.

Niezen, Ronald. 2003. *The Origins of Indigenism: Human Rights and the Politics of Identity*. Berkeley: University of California Press.

Norgren, Jill. 2004. *The Cherokee Cases: Two Landmark Federal Decisions in the Fight for Sovereignty*. Norman: University of Oklahoma Press.

Nuijten, Monique. 2010. "Legal Responses to Cultural Diversity: Multi-Ethnicity, the State, and the Law in Latin America." In *Cultural Diversity and the Law: State Responses from Around the World*, edited by Marie-Claire Foblets, Jean-François Gaudreault-Desbiens, and Alison Dundes Renteln, 235–254. Brussels: Emile Bruylant.

Nussbaum, Martha Craven. 1997. "Capabilities and Human Rights." *Fordham Law Review* 66:273.

Odello, Marco. 2012. "Indigenous Peoples' Rights and Cultural Identity in the Inter-American Context." *International Journal of Human Rights* 16:25–50.

Olivares Alanís, Efrén C. 2013. "Indigenous Peoples' Rights and the Extractive Industry: Jurisprudence from the Inter-American System of Human Rights." *Goettingen Journal of International Law* 5 (1): 187–214.

Ortner, S. 2006. *Anthropology and Social Theory. Culture, Power and the Acting Subject.* Durham, N.C.: Duke University Press.

Pagden, Anthony. 1995. *Lords of All the World: Ideologies of Empire in Spain, Britain and France c. 1500–c. 1800.* New Haven, Conn.: Yale University Press.

Parekh, Bhikhu. 2004. "Redistribution or Recognition? A Misguided Debate." In *Ethnicity, Nationalism, and Minority Rights*, edited by Stephen May, Tariq Modood, and Judith Squires, 199–213. Cambridge: Cambridge University Press.

Pasqualucci, Jo M. 2006. "The Evolution of International Indigenous Rights in the Inter-American Human Rights System." *Human Rights Law Review* 6 (2): 281–322.

Pentney, William. 1988. "The Rights of the Aboriginal Peoples of Canada in the Constitution Act, 1982, Part II–Section 35: The Substantive Guarantee." *University of British Columbia Law Review* 22:207–278.

Perdue, Theda. 1989. "The Conflict Within: The Cherokee Power Structure and Removal." *Georgia Historical Quarterly* 73:467–491.

Perdue, Theda, and Michael D. Green, eds. 1995. *The Cherokee Removal: A Brief History with Documents.* Bedford Series in History and Culture. Boston: Bedford/St. Martin's.

Peters, Richard, ed. 1831. *The Case of the Cherokee Nation Against the State of Georgia: Argued and Determined at the Supreme Court of the United States, January Term 1831.* Philadelphia: John Grigg.

Povinelli, Elizabeth. 2002. *The Cunning of Recognition: Indigenous Alterities and the Making of Australian Multiculturalism.* Durham, N.C.: Duke University Press.

Pratt, Mary Louise. 1991. "Arts of the Contact Zone." *Profession* 91:33–40.

Price, Richard, and Sally Price. 1991. *Two Evenings in Saramaka.* Chicago: University of Chicago Press.

Prucha, Francis Paul. 1962. *American Indian Policy in the Formative Years: The Indian Trade and Intercourse Acts, 1780–1834.* Cambridge: Harvard University Press.

Prucha, Francis Paul. 1994. *American Indian Treaties: The History of a Political Anomaly.* Berkeley: University of California Press.

Prucha, Francis Paul. 1995. *The Great Father: The United States Government and the American Indians.* Lincoln: University of Nebraska Press.

Rawls, John. 1999. *The Law of Peoples.* Cambridge, Mass.: Harvard University Press.

Remini, Robert V. 2001. *Andrew Jackson and His Indian Wars.* New York: Viking.

Rey Caro, E. 2005. "La competencia de la Corte interamericana de derechos humanos: Reflexiones para una futura reforma." In *Soberanía des Estado y derecho internacional: homenaje al profesor Juan Antonio Carrillo Salcedo*, edited by A. Salinas de Frías and M. Vargas Gómez-Urrutia, 1201–1214. Seville: Universidad de Sevilla.

Riles, Annelise. 2001. *The Network Inside Out.* Ann Arbor: University of Michigan Press.

Robertson, Lindsay G. 1997. "John Marshall as Colonial Historian: Reconsidering the Origins of the Discovery Doctrine." *Journal of Law and Politics* 13:759–777.

Robertson, Lindsay G. 2005. *Conquest by Law: How the Discovery of America Dispossessed Indigenous Peoples of Their Lands.* Oxford: Oxford University Press.

Robertson, Lindsay G. 2011. "The Judicial Conquest of Native America: The Story of *Johnson v. M'Intosh*." In *Indian Law Stories*, edited by Carole Goldberg, Kevin K. Washburn, and Philip P. Frickey, 29–59. New York: Thomson Reuters/Foundation Press.

Rogin, Michael Paul. 1975. *Fathers and Children: Andrew Jackson and the Subjugation of the American Indian.* New York: Knopf.

Rostkowski, Joelle. 1995. "Deskaheh's Shadow: Indians on the International Scene." *European Review of Native American Studies* 9 (2): 1–4.

Russell, Steve. 2015. "The South Does Rights Thing: Why US & Canada Fear Human Rights Court." *Indian Country Today*, May 26.

Said, Edward W. 1978. *Orientalism*. New York: Pantheon Books.

Sanders, Douglas. 1983. "The Re-Emergence of Indigenous Questions in International Law." *Canadian Human Rights Yearbook* 1:3–30.

Sanders, Douglas. 1987. "Aboriginal Rights in Canada: An Overview." *Law and Anthropology (Internationales Jahrbuch fur Rechtsanthropologie)* 2:177–185.

Satz, Ronald N. 1975. *American Indian Policy in the Jacksonian Era*. Lincoln: University of Nebraska Press.

Senghor, Léopold Sédar. 1948. *Anthologie de la nouvelle poésie nègre et malgache de langue française*. Colonies et empire: Collection internationale de documentation coloniale. Cinquième série, Art et littérature. Paris: Presses Universitaires de France.

Shapiro, Ian, and Will Kymlicka, eds. 1997. *Ethnicity and Group Rights*. Nomos 39. New York: New York University Press.

Shapiro, Martin. 1994. "Juridicalization of Politics in the United States." *International Political Science Review / Revue internationale de science politique* 15:101–112.

Shelton, Dinah. 2013. "The Inter-American Human Rights Law of Indigenous Peoples." *University of Hawaii Law Review* 35:937–1013.

Sieder, Rachel, Line Schjolden, and Alan Angell. 2005. *The Judicialization of Politics in Latin America*. New York: Palgrave Macmillan.

Silverstein, Michael 2005. "Languages/Cultures are Dead! Long Live the Linguistic-Cultural." In *Unwrapping the Sacred Bundle: Reflections on the Disciplining of Anthropology*, edited by Daniel A. Segal and Sylvia J. Yanagisako, 99–125. Durham: Duke University Press.

Simpson, Audra. 2014. *Mohawk Interruptus: Political Life Across the Borders of Settler States*. Durham: Duke University Press.

Simpson, Leanne Betasamosake. 2017. *As We Have Always Done*. Minneapolis: University of Minnesota Press.

Slattery, Brian. 1982. "The Constitutional Guarantee of Aboriginal and Treaty Rights." *Queen's Law Journal* 8 (1–2): 232–273.

Slattery, Brian. 2007. "A Taxonomy of Aboriginal Rights." In *Let Right Be Done: Aboriginal Title, the Calder Case, and the Future of Indigenous Rights*. Vancouver: UBC Press.

Smith, Anthony D. 1996. *The Ethnic Origins of Nations*. Malden: Blackwell.

Speed, Shannon. 2008. *Rights in Rebellion: Indigenous Struggle and Human Rights in Chiapas*. Stanford: Stanford University Press.

Spivak, Gayatri Chakravorty. 1984/85. "Criticism, Feminism and the Institution: An Interview with Gayatri Chakravorty Spivak." By Elizabeth Gross. *Thesis Eleven*, nos. 10/11: 175–187.

Spivak, Gayatri Chakravorty. 1985. "Strategies of Vigilance: An Interview with Gayatri Chakravorty Spivak." By Angela McRobbie. *Block* 10:5–9.

Stern, Steve J. 1993. *Peru's Indian Peoples and the Challenge of Spanish Conquest: Huamanga to 1640*. Madison: University of Wisconsin Press.

Strickland, Rennard. 2011. "The Tribal Struggle for Indian Sovereignty: The Story of the *Cherokee Cases*." In *Indian Law Stories*, edited by Carole Goldberg, Kevin K. Washburn, and Philip P. Frickey, 61–80. New York: Thomson Reuters/Foundation Press.

Strum, Philippa. 1974. *The Supreme Court and "Political Questions": A Study in Judicial Evasion.* University: University of Alabama Press.
Swepston, Lee. 1990. "A New Step in the International Law on Indigenous and Tribal Peoples: ILO Convention No. 169 of 1989." *Oklahoma City University Law Review* 15 (3): 677–714.
Tamanaha, Brian Z. 2008. "Understanding Legal Pluralism: Past to Present, Local to Global." *Sydney Law Review* 30:375.
Tate, Winifred. 2007. *Counting the Dead: The Culture and Politics of Human Rights Activism in Colombia.* Berkeley: University of California Press.
Tate, Chester Neal, and Torbjörn Vallinder. 1995. *The Global Expansion of Judicial Power.* New York: New York University Press.
Thornberry, Patrick. 2002. *Indigenous Peoples and Human Rights.* Melland Schill Studies in International Law. Manchester: Manchester University Press; New York: Juris.
Tramontana, Enzamaria. 2010. "The Contribution of the Inter-American Human Rights Bodies to Evolving International Law on Indigenous Rights over Lands and Natural Resources." *International Journal on Minority and Group Rights* 17 (2): 241–263.
Tully, James. 2000. "Struggles over Recognition and Distribution." *Constellations: An International Journal of Critical and Democratic Theory* 7 (4): 469–482.
Turner, Terence. 1993. "Anthropology and Multiculturalism: What Is Anthropology That Multiculturalists Should Be Mindful of It?" *Cultural Anthropology* 8 (4): 411–429.
Tyler, S. Lyman. 1973. *A History of Indian Policy.* Washington, D.C.: United States, Department of the Interior, Bureau of Indian Affairs.
Veracini, Lorezno. 2010. *Settler Colonialism: A Theoretical Overview.* New York: Palgrave Macmillan.
Wagner, Roy. 1981. *The Invention of Culture.* Chicago: University of Chicago Press.
Washburn, Wilcomb E. 1975. *The Indian in America.* New American Nation Series. New York: Harper & Row.
Washington, George. 1889. *The Writings of George Washington.* Vol. 2. New York: G. P. Putnam's Sons.
Watson, Blake A. 2010. "The Impact of the American Doctrine of Discovery on Native Land Rights in Australia, Canada, and New Zealand." *Seattle Universtiy Law Review* 34:507.
White, G. Edward. 1988. *The Marshall Court and Cultural Change, 1815–35.* History of the Supreme Court of the United States, vols. 3–4. New York: Macmillan.
White, Richard. 1992. *The Middle Ground: Indians, Empires, and Republics in the Great Lakes Region, 1650–1815.* New York: Cambridge University Press.
White Face, Charmaine. 2013. *Indigenous Nations' Rights in the Balance: An Analysis of the Declaration on the Rights of Indigenous Peoples.* St. Paul, Minn.: Living Justice Press.
Wilkins, David, and K. Tsianina Lomawaima, eds. 2002. *Uneven Ground: American Indian Sovereignty and Federal Law.* Norman: University of Oklahoma Press.
Wilkinson, Charles F. 1987. *American Indians, Time, and the Law: Native Societies in a Modern Constitutional Democracy.* New Haven, Conn.: Yale University Press.
Williams, Robert A. 1983. "The Medieval and Renaissance Origins of the Status of the American Indian in Western Legal Thought." *Southern California Law Review* 57:1.
Williams, Robert A. 1990. *The American Indian in Western Legal Thought: The Discourses of Conquest.* New York: Oxford University Press.
Williams, Robert A. 2012. *Savage Anxieties: The Invention of Western Civilization.* New York: Palgrave Macmillan.

Wilson, Richard A., ed. 1997. *Human Rights, Culture and Context: Anthropological Perspectives.* London: Pluto Press.

Wolfe, Patrick. 1999. *Settler Colonialism and the Transformation of Anthropology: The Politics and Poetics of an Ethnographic Event.* London: Cassel.

Wolfe, Patrick. 2006. "Settler Colonialism and the Elimination of the Native." *Journal of Genocide Research* 8 (4): 387–409.

Worcester, S. A. 1968. *New Echota Letters: Contributions of Samuel A. Worcester to the Cherokee Phoenix.* Edited by Jack Frederick Kilpatrick and Anna Gritts Kilpatrick. Dallas: Southern Methodist University Press.

Yupsanis, Athanasios. 2010. "ILO Convention No. 169 Concerning Indigenous and Tribal Peoples in Independent Countries 1989–2009: An Overview." *Nordic Journal of International Law* 79 (3): 433–456.

Zenker, Olaf. 2016. "Anthropology on Trial: Exploring the Laws of Anthropological Expertise." *International Journal of Law in Context* 12 (3): 293–311.

Zenker, Olaf, and Karsten Kumoll. 2013. *Beyond Writing Culture: Current Intersections of Epistemologies and Representational Practices.* Oxford: Berghahn.

Cases Cited

Court of King's Bench (Great Britain)

Campbell v. Hall, 98 ER 1045 (1774).

United States Supreme Court

Cherokee Nation v. Georgia, 30 U.S. 1 (1831).

Draper v. United States, 164 U.S. 240 (1896).

Johnson v. McIntosh, 21 U.S. 543 (1823).

Lone Wolf v. Hitchcock, 187 U.S. 553 (1903).

Marbury v. Madison, 5 U.S. 137 (1803).

United States v. McBratney, 104 U.S. 621 (1881).

Santa Clara Pueblo v. Martinez, 436 U.S. 49 (1978).

Tee Hit Ton Indians v. United States, 348 U.S. 272 (1955).

United States v. Santa Fe Pacific Railroad, 314 U.S. 339 (1941).

Worcester v. Georgia, 31 U.S. 515 (1832).

Inter-American Court of Human Rights

Aloeboetoe et al. v. Suriname (Merits), IACtHR Series C No. 11 (1991).

Aloeboetoe et al. v. Suriname (Reparations and Costs), IACtHR Series C No. 15 (1993).

Benjamin v. Trinidad and Tobago (Preliminary Objections), IACtHR Series C No. 81 (2001).

Constantine v. Trinidad and Tobago (Preliminary Objections), IACtHR Series C No. 82 (2001).

Effects of Reservations on the Entry into Force of the American Convention on Human Rights (Arts. 74 and 75) (Advisory Opinion), IACtHR Series A No. 2 (1982).

Hilaire v. Trinidad and Tobago (Preliminary Objections), IACtHR Series C No. 80 (2001).

Indigenous Community Sawhoyamaxa v. Paraguay (Merits, Reparations and Costs), IACtHR Series C No. 146 (2006).

Indigenous Community Yakye Axa v. Paraguay (Merits, Reparations and Costs). Series C No. 125 (2005).

Ivcher Bronstein v. Peru (Judgment on Competence), Series C No. 54 (1999).
Mayagna (Sumo) Awas Tingni Community v. Nicaragua (Merits, Reparations and Costs), Series C No. 79 (2001).
Moiwana Community v. Suriname (Interpretation of the Judgment of Merits, Reparations and Costs), Series C No. 145 (2006).
Saramaka People v. Suriname (Preliminary Objections, Merits, Reparations, and Costs), Series C No. 172 (2007).

Inter-American Commission of Human Rights

Ache v. Paraguay, Case No. 1802, OAS Doc. OEA/Ser.L./V/II.43 (1978)
Guhaibo v. Colombia, Case No. 1690, OAS Doc. OEA/Ser.L./V/II.30, doc. 45, rev. 1 (1973)
Yanomami v. Brazil, Case No. 7651, Res. 12/85 OEA/Ser.L./V/II.66. (1987)

Judicial Committee of the Privy Council (Canada)

St. Catherine's Milling and Lumber Co. v. The Queen, [1888] 14 App. Cas. 46.

Canadian Supreme Court

Calder v. Attorney General of British Columbia, [1973] S.C.R. 313.
Canadian Pacific Ltd. v. Paul, [1988] 2 S.C.R. 654.
Delkamuukw v. British Columbia, [1997] 3 S.C.R. 1010.
Guerin v. The Queen, [1984] 2 S.C.R. 335.
R. v. Van der Peet, [1996] 2 S.C.R. 507.
Simon v. The Queen, [1985] 2 S.C.R. 287.
Sparrow v. R., [1990] 1 S.C.R. 1075.
Stein v. The Ship "Kathy K," [1976] 2 S.C.R. 802.

Supreme Court of British Columbia

Delgamuukw v. British Columbia, [1991] 79 D.L.R. (4th) 185.

High Court of Australia

Mabo v. Queensland (No. 2), [1992] HCA 23.

South African Constitutional Court

Alexkor Ltd. and the Government of South Africa v. Richtersveld Community and Others, *CCT/1903* (2003).

INDEX

ACKNOWLEDGMENTS

Writing a book, like any journey, has a beginning, a middle, and an end. This particular journey began when I was a graduate student in the Department for the Anthropology of the Americas at Rheinische Friedrich-Wilhelms-Universität in Bonn in 2012. My colleagues in the department were an enormous inspiration. Particularly Karoline Noack gave me all the support I could wish for. My thanks go also to Nikolai Grube, Eriko Yamasaki, Jennifer Lübke, Frauke Sachse, Christine Winter de Velarde, and Markus Reindl. With Patrik Kutzer and Carlos Pallan I had the great pleasure of sharing an office and witnessed how they analyzed the use of signs in Turkish protest movements and 3-D models of Maya steles filled with hieroglyphs respectively. They are a tribute to the enormous range of excellent scholarship that this small department is capable of generating. I would like to thank especially Michael Kraus, with whom I had many bowls of soup and cups of coffee at home and abroad; Antje Gunsenheimer, with whom I discussed indigeneity and land rights in the Americas, not least at a wonderful breakfast place in Minneapolis; Timo Duile, with whom I was able to discuss the post-Marxist political theorists over Christmas in Borneo; and Christian Mader, who showed me the physical and mental strains of archaeological fieldwork in Peru while listening to Johnny Cash.

Marie-Claire Foblets, the director of the Department of Law and Anthropology at the Max Planck Institute for Social Anthropology in Halle/Saale, Germany, was kind enough to invite me to spend two months as a visiting scholar in Halle, which brought me in contact with a number of wonderful colleagues whose input I cannot value highly enough. I would like to thank especially Brian Donahoe, Kalindi Kokal, Anette Mehlhorn, Martin Ramstedt, Mareike Riedel, Katrin Seidel, and Larissa Vetters. It was also there that I met Armando Guevara-Gil, whom I was later able to visit at the Pontificia Universidad Católica del Perú in Lima. He assured me that I was working on an interesting book at a time when I was not sure that I was. It was precisely the right nudge at the right time, the kind of thing that books probably never get finished without. I am very grateful.

Thanks to a long-established exchange fellowship between the University of Bonn and the University of Wisconsin-Madison, I was given the opportunity to spend some time in Madison in the Department of Anthropology. It is in large part thanks to Sabine Sielke from the Department of English, American, and Celtic Studies in Bonn (who supported me greatly in many ways, not least by reading through the whole first draft of this book) that I was able to go there. I wrote most of this book in Madison, and I have developed a great affection for this very special place. Not a day after my arrival I was rescued by Mike von Schneidemesser, who himself had received this scholarship in the 1960s and remained in Madison ever since. He made it a habit of helping visiting researchers like me find their way around and organizing a bed and a desk for them. He also invited me to the first Thanksgiving dinner of my life, for which I am eternally grateful.

I cannot thank Larry Nesper enough for welcoming me so warmly to the Anthropology Department. He drove me all the way to Indianapolis for my first ethnohistory conference, and his wonderful lectures on indigenous cultures in North America have inspired me enormously. Alexandra Huneeus welcomed me at the law school. Her work on the judicializations in Latin America were an important source of inspiration for me. Richard Monette let me listen in on his course on federal Indian law. The lessons and discussions there have shaped the ideas in this book probably more than any other course I took anywhere. I would also like to thank the organizers and participants of the Latin American Colloquium at the University of Wisconsin–Madison, who were kind enough to discuss an early draft of one of this book's chapters.

The journey of writing this book came to an end at the Freie Universität Berlin, where I was employed as a postdoctoral researcher. Olaf Zenker, the head of the research project I was working in, was very supportive and generous. Among other things, it went without saying with him that I would have the space and freedom to finish this book. One could not wish for a better and more conducive place for research than the Department of Social and Cultural Anthropology and the Collaborative Research Center "Affective Societies." Their respective directors, Hansjörg Dilger and Birgitt Röttger-Rössler, supported me in every way possible. With my colleagues I had numerous conversations about the ideas and arguments developed in this book and the process of publishing it. My thanks go to Marion Acker, Franziska Bedorf, Aletta Diefenbach, Marcos Freire de Andrade Neves, Ulrike Geiger, Edda

Heyken, Elisabeth Huber, Thomas John, Katharina Jörder, Antje Kahl, Omar Kasmani, Sirin Knecht, Ingrid Kummels, Hauke Lehmann, Matthias Lüthjohann, Katharina Metz, Rainer Mühlhoff, Friederike Oberkrome, Jean-Baptiste Pettier, Žiga Podgornik-Jakil, Hans Roth, Christian von Scheve, Theresa Schütz, Jan Slaby, Verena Straub, Laura Suna, Gerhard Thonhauser, Franz Templin, Nur Yasemin-Ural, Robert Walter-Jochum, and Jana Maria Weiß. Gabriel Scheidecker and Antje Kahl patiently tolerated me getting on their nerves as I was trying to get this book published. This kind of support often goes unappreciated, but not in this case. The help of my colleague Leonie Benker, who worked as a student assistant in the research project in which I was employed, was invaluable. With Tamar Blickstein I developed some new perspectives very late in the game that considerably shaped my thinking. Especially toward the very end, the moral support of Kerstin Schankweiler was key to finishing everything up.

The Rosa Luxemburg Foundation provided financial and institutional independence for most of the research project that was the basis for this book. I am very grateful for this privilege. The German Ancient America Foundation (Deutsche-Altamerika-Stiftung) and the German Academic Exchange Service (DAAD) awarded me travel grants to present my work at international conferences. The German Research Foundation (DFG) funded the postdoctoral position that allowed me to finish writing this book.

I am very grateful to Brian Donahoe, who has carefully and very skillfully edited the manuscript—a service that is invaluable to a nonnative English speaker like me. Brian's comments went well beyond proofreading and helped me say everything better and not so many times in the same—or only slightly different—words. The team at the University of Pennsylvania Press, particularly Peter Agree, have been very supportive in publishing this book and facilitating a very rewarding review process. Lily Palladino worked wonders as a production editor and Jennifer Shenk did a final copyediting in a manner so professional I have rarely, if ever, seen. Finally, thank you to all those who have read drafts of parts of this book, many named above as well as two anonymous reviewers. They have made this a better book.

FSC
www.fsc.org
MIX
Papier | Fördert
gute Waldnutzung
FSC® C083411

Kolibri 360 GmbH
Ferdinand-Jühlke-Straße 7
99095 Erfurt, Deutschland
produktsicherheit@kolibri360.de